Micro~Macramé Jewelry II

Artful Designs for the Adventurous Knotter

by

Joan R. Babcock

Graphics by Jeff Babcock

ISBN 978-0-9773052-3-0

Published by:
Joan Babcock Designs
16 Camerada Rd.
Santa Fe, NM, 87508-8766
www.joanbabcock.com
www.micro-macramejewelry.com

First Printing - November 2014

Other works by Joan Babcock:

Micro-Macramé Jewelry: Tips and Techniques for Knotting with Beads
Wired Micro-Macramé Jewelry: Enhancing Fiber Designs with Wire
Micro-Macramé and Cavandoli Knotting (DVD)

When you reach the end of your rope,
Tie a knot and hang on.

- American Proverb

Table of Contents

Introduction 4

Materials and Tools 5

Technical Tips and Techniques 6

Knot Diagrams 8

Projects

Project One - Bella Earrings 13

Project Two - Shambala Earrings 17

Project Three - Galaxy Earrings 22

Project Four - Sundial Earrings 26

Project Five - Big Zig Bracelet 30

Project Six - Crossing Paths Bracelet 38

Project Seven - Dragon Tail Bracelet 45

Project Eight - Harlequin Bracelet 50

Project Nine - Art Nouveau Bracelet 55

Project Ten - Merida Necklace 62

Project Eleven - Nile Necklace 67

Project Twelve - Moonflower Pendant 73

The Evolution of Micro-Macrame

In 2005, I wrote my first book, Micro-Macramé Jewelry: Tips & Techniques for Knotting with Beads. It was my desire to share the basic skills of macramé knotting with those who were eager to learn, while offering unique jewelry projects that would add to their enjoyment and understanding. Since then, micro-macramé has steadily grown in popularity and continues to gain new converts every day through the internet, books, DVDs, and online classes.

I'm happy to be a part of this and to know that thousands of novice knotters from all over the world have been introduced to the art of micro-macramé through my first book. I love hearing from those who have gotten hooked on knotting and continue to follow their muse, developing their skills through creating jewelry and exploring the limitless possibilities of this fascinating craft. It is for these kindred spirits and adventurous knotters everywhere that this latest book was written.

If you're a knotter who already has experience with micro-macramé but would like to try your hand at some sophisticated new designs, this book is for you. I designed these 12 new projects for those who are ready to go beyond the basics and delve into something a little more challenging. It's my hope that you'll pick up some fresh insights when making these designs, and that in making them you'll gain in your knowledge and enjoyment of micro-macramé knotting.

As I've continued to pursue my love for knotted jewelry through the years, I realize that there's always more to discover - new designs, fresh approaches and better solutions. I am glad to have the opportunity to share my latest ideas in these pages. I learn by doing, but also by appreciating the work of other artists who share my passion for knots and beads. I am amazed and inspired by the beauty and diversity of their creations. I look forward to seeing the beauty that is yet to come!

Happy Knotting,

Joan

Materials and Tools

1. 18 gauge Nylon Cord - I enjoy using nylon cord because of it's fine silky texture, broad range of colors, ease of knotting, and durability (see Fig.1). I designed all of the projects in this book using this type of cord, using SuperLon Bead/Macrame cord and C- Lon #18 interchangeably. Similar brands include Conso, Mastex, Tuffcord and Stringth #5. See each project's title page for a specific list of cord lengths. **Note -** Other types and widths of cord may not be suitable for every project.

2. Beads & Findings - You can substitute beads of your own choosing for the beads that I've used in a project, as long as they are the same size and have large enough holes for the cord(s). See each project's title page for a suggested list of beads & findings.

3. Knotting Board - You'll need a sturdy surface on which to pin your work. I recommend an 11" x 17" Macrame Project Board, like those manufactured by Pepperell Crafts (see Fig. 2). These boards are made of compressed fibers and come wrapped in plastic (the plastic should be left on to avoid the fibers shedding on your clothing). Another option is a cork board, $^3/_8$" thick or thicker. These are sold as frameless bulletin boards at chain craft stores. If you choose to use a foam macrame board, adhere it to a rigid material like foam core. Your board should not bend! I don't recommend using clipboards or soft foam pillows for these projects.

4. Pins - Use sturdy quilting or sewing pins that have a thin shank but do not bend easily (see Fig. 3a). The smaller size T-pins (1.25") are also fine, but not the larger size T-pins (1.75"). These are too thick for general use because they may damage the cord.

5. Scissors - These must be sharp and small enough to get into tight places. Dull scissors won't cut it!

6. Embroidery and Sewing Needles - You'll need a size #2 crewel embroidery needle for sewing the 18g nylon. These are about 2" long and have an eye that is large enough to accommodate the cord (see Fig. 3b). A standard sewing needle will also be needed for finishing work, such as linings and hems.

7. Sewing Thread - Nymo or similar. See "Working with Plies" in the next section for more information on making your own thread.

8. Clear Nail Polish - This is used to coat finishing knots and prevent them from coming undone. It can also be used to stiffen the ends of cord and prevent the cord from unraveling (see Fig. 3c).

9. Fray Check - This is used to stiffen the cord tips when needed to help with threading on beads. It can be found at most fabric stores (see Fig. 3d).

10. Chain nose pliers - These are used to attach findings but can also be helpful when sewing with an embroidery needle is required. It can sometimes be difficult to pull the needle and cord through a tight space. In this case grasp the needle with the pliers and pull (or yank!) it through.

11. Utility blade (optional) - This tool works great in situations where you have multiple cords descending from a bead and you want to cut off one of them flush with the bottom of the bead. Hold the cord taut and saw it off with the blade using the bottom of the bead as a guide. **Important! Before use, tape over the sharp corners, leaving only a $^1/_2$" area of the blade exposed for cutting** (see Fig. 4).

Figure 1

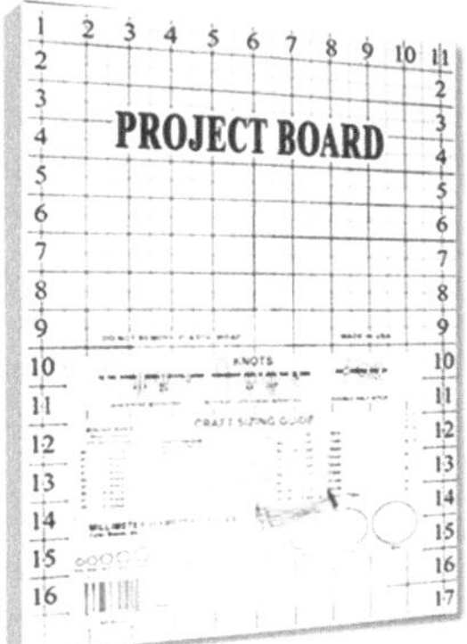

Figure 2

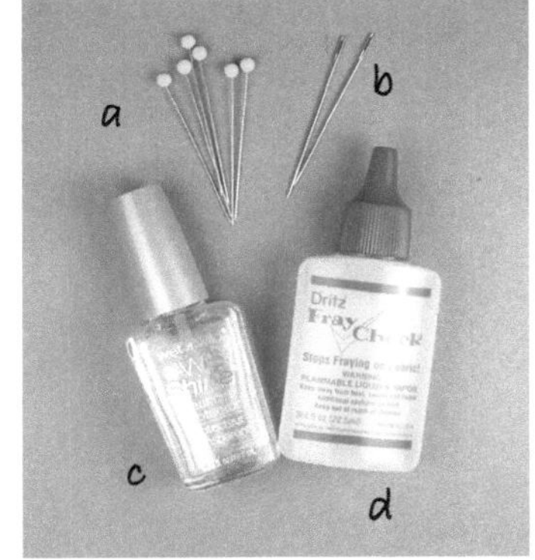

Figure 3

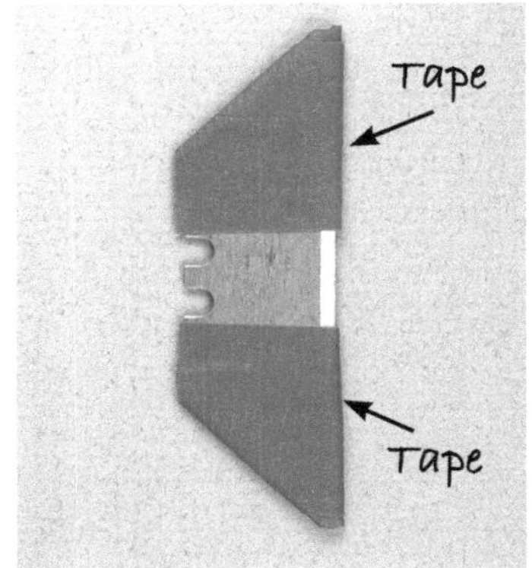

Figure 4

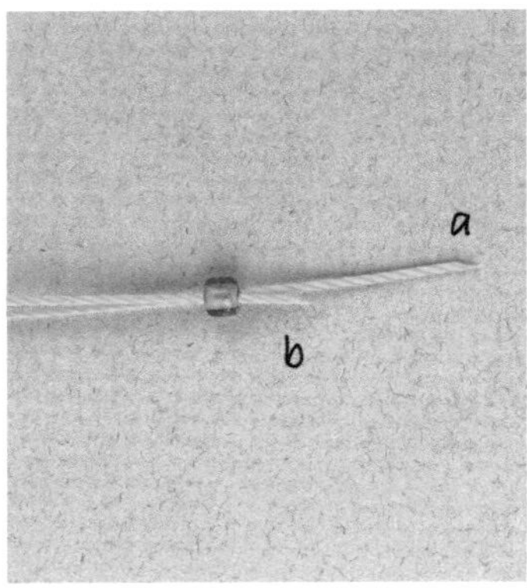

Figure 5

Figure 6

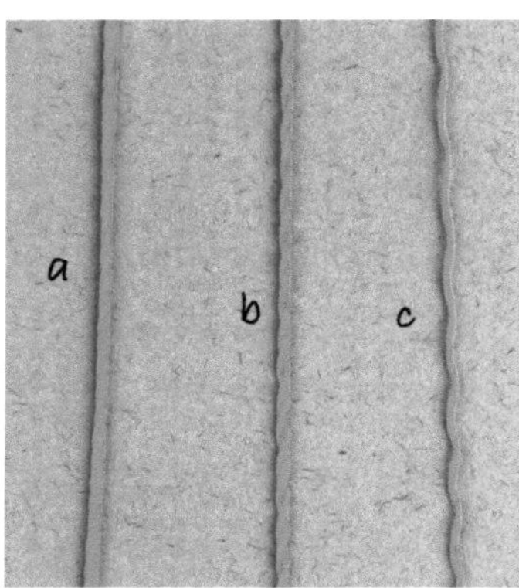

Figure 7

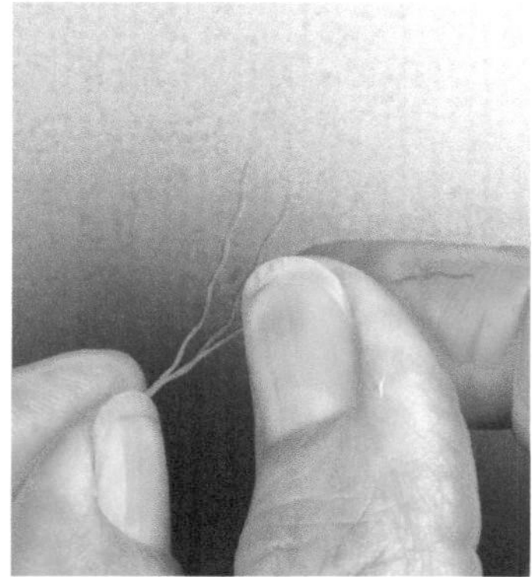
Figure 8

Knotting Tips and Techniques

1. Knotting Position - I prefer to work with my board resting in my lap and leaning against the table in front of me. Having the board in this slanted position gives you closer access and more control over your work. Another option is to attach your board to an easel. I don't recommend working flat on a tabletop as this lessens your control and increases arm and back strain.
2. Pinning your work - Pin your work to your knotting board at a comfortable level so that your arms can move freely. I find that a third of the way down from the top works for me. Reposition and repin the work as often as necessary to maintain the most comfortable knotting position.
In the project photos I have removed most of the pins so that you can see the progress of the work without obstructions. But I recommend that you keep your knotwork securely pinned down to the board! It will make the knotting process easier and produces a better looking result.

Tips For Threading Beads Onto Cord

18g Nylon cord is approximately .5 mm thick and can range between slightly stiff to soft. When you want to use seed beads and other small-holed beads it can present some challenges. Here are my tips:
1. To stiffen the end of your cord, dip it down into a bottle of Fray Check so that an inch or so is coated. Let it dry at least 10 - 15 minutes. It's not always necessary to use it, but if you're getting frustrated with beads that don't fit, it's worth the effort. **Note -** Clear nail polish can also be used to stiffen cord but it tends to make the cord a little bit thicker.
2. Cut off the tip of the cord at a sharp angle. You will have to repeat this if the cord starts to get dull and frayed (see Fig. 5a).
3. When threading a bead onto two or more cords, be sure to stagger the cord ends ½" or more and thread one cord through at a time (see Fig. 5b).
4. Reduce the cord thickness on fringes (see "Working With Plies" below).

Working With Plies

18g Nylon cords such as S-Lon, C-Lon, Conso, and Mastex have three threads, otherwise known as "plies" that are twisted together (see Fig. 6). I've found that in some circumstances reducing the number of plies from 3-ply (see Fig. 7a) to 2-ply (7b) or 1-ply (7c) is a good solution to too much bulk. Ply reduction is usually done at the finishing stage of a project and I use it often in this book. Here are a few instances where ply reduction might be used:
1. Sewing Thread - Separate the plies of a length of cord by holding the end between your thumb and finger and twisting to the right. Use the blunt end of a sewing needle to get between the threads if need be. Pull out one of the plies to use as a sewing thread (see Fig. 8). This is a good alternative to beading thread if you need an exact color to match your knotting cord. The thread will be wavy and slightly thicker than Nymo. Running it through beeswax will make it much easier to sew with.
2. Reducing Width - In some designs the left-over cords at the bottom of a piece will be used to make a beaded fringe. Eliminating one or two of the plies (this depends on the size of the beads) from the fringe cords before

adding beads will give it a more fluid look and feel. Untwist the cord all the way up to the top and separate the 1-ply segment from the 2-ply segment. Carefully cut off the unwanted segment flush with the knotwork (or bead). Another advantage is that you will be able to fit smaller beads onto your fringe strands.

3. Finishing Knots - When a finishing knot such as an Overhand Knot is called for, reducing the plies in the cord or cords will make a smaller and less noticeable knot.

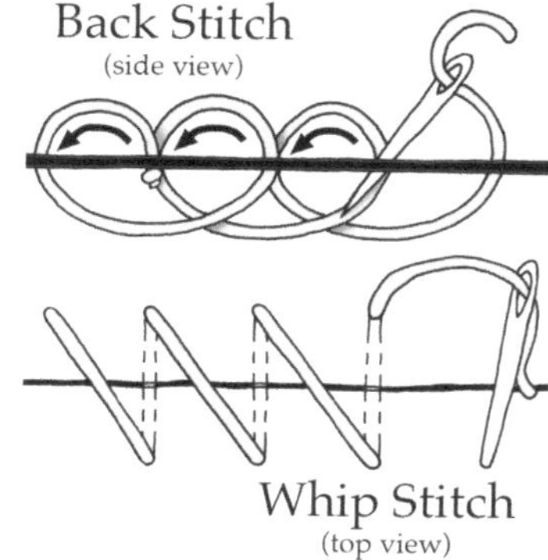

Figure 9

Sewing Tips

Many of the projects require some stitching at the finishing stage to make a hem or to attach a lining.

1. Use a sturdy sewing needle and Nymo (or similar) nylon thread or a 1-ply length of the 18g Nylon. Pull the thread through beeswax to prevent tangles (optional). Make an Overhand Knot at the end of the thread.

2. Hems - When sewing down a hem, use the backstitch method to secure the hem cords (see Fig. 9, top). Insure that the stitches won't be visible at the front of the piece by making small stitches in the "ditches" (or valleys) in between rows of knots (see Fig. 10). Check the front often to make sure all looks good.

3. Linings - When sewing an Ultrasuede lining onto the back of a piece it is not necessary to sew all the way through to the front of the knotwork. Pass the needle through the lining, then through a little bit of the cord on the back of the knotwork and pull the needle through. Continue on, making "whip stitches" around the entire lining (see Fig. 9, lower). To finish, make 2 or 3 additional passes over your final stitch and pass the needle under the lining about ¾" then back up and pull through. Cut off the thread flush with the top of the lining and it will disappear.

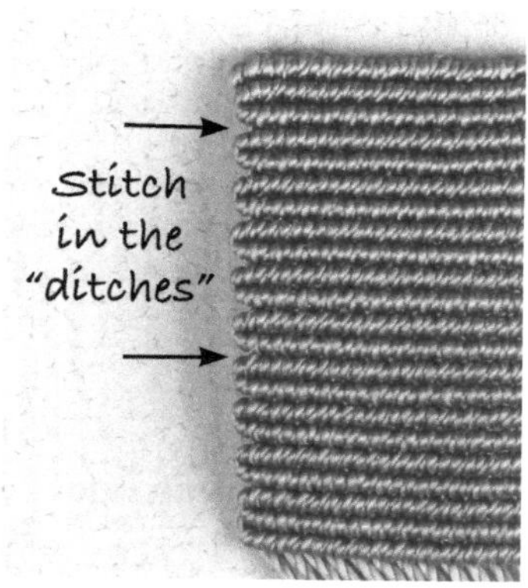

Figure 10

Tightening Overhand Knots

Here are a couple of ways to insure that an **OVK** is in the correct position and very tight. Practice this a few times with some spare cord to get the hang of it.

1. Form the **OVK** but keep it loose. Place a narrow pin in the board inside the **OVK** loop at the spot where you want it to tighten up (see Fig. 11). Slowly pull up the slack and tighten the knot around the pin. Before going on, make sure that the knot is exactly where you want it. It's easier to take out when it's still semi-loose!

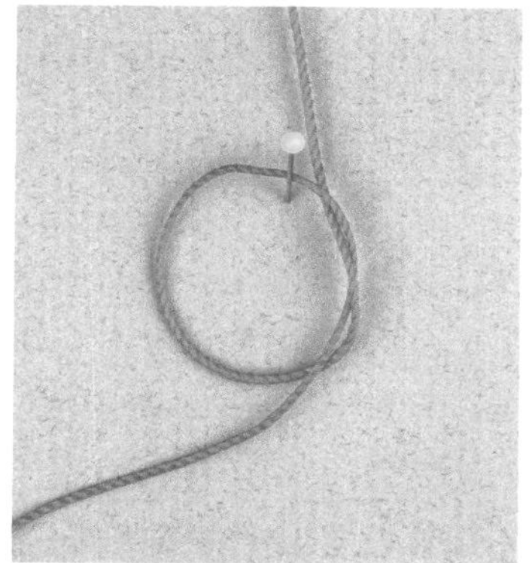

Figure 11

2. Before removing the pin, grasp the cord just below the knot with needle nose pliers (see Fig. 12). Remove the pin. Push upwards towards the knot with the pliers while pulling downwards on the cord. Finish with a dab of nail polish to keep it secure.

Shaping

If your knotwork is looking a bit lopsided (it happens!) or you need to adjust the angle of a **DHH** row, don't be afraid to manipulate it into shape. Knotwork is malleable and can be adjusted to a certain extent. Grasp it firmly with one hand and with the other hand pull down, out, or up in whichever direction it needs to go.

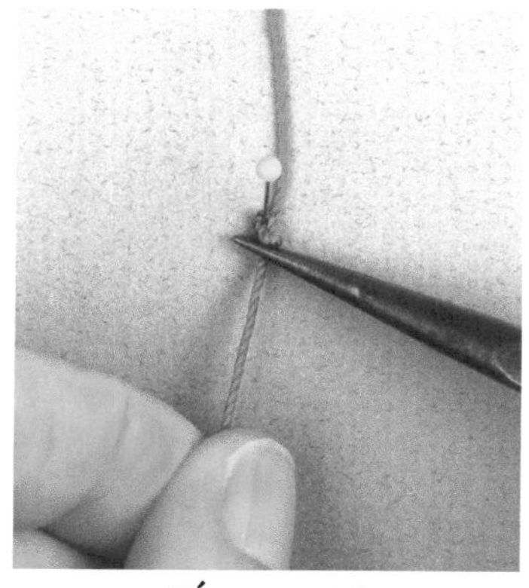

Figure 12

Knotting Terms and Abbreviations

KC - Knotting Cord : The active cord that wraps around another (anchor) cord.

AC - Anchor Cord : The passive cord which holds the Knotting Cord.

RC - Runner Cord : A cord that runs horizontally from row to row and can change it's function depending on the knot, acting as an **AC** (with horizontal **DHH**s) and also as a **KC** (with vertical **DHH**s).

Warp Cords : All working cords (except for the **RC** or **AC**).

MH - Mounting Hitch : A (horizontal) Lark's Head Knot, with the smooth side facing to the front and the bar to the back.

MTK - Mounting Knot : A **MH** with a **HH** added to each side to increase the width.

HH - Half Hitch : A single closed loop around an **AC.** Most macrame knots (except the **SQK**) are made up of **HH**s in various combinations.

DHH - Double Half Hitch : A knot comprised of 2 side by side **HH**s made with the **KC** around the **AC**. **DHH**s are usually used to make horizontal or diagonal rows of knots. The angle of the **AC** determines the angle of the row. The **DHH** can be made in a Right to Left or Left to Right direction depending on the pattern.

THH - Triple Half Hitch : A **DHH** with a third **HH** added on to increase the width.

VDHH - Vertical Double Half Hitch : This is the same basic knot as a horizontal **DHH**, however the **AC** is vertical rather than horizontal. The **VDHH** can be made in a Right to Left or Left to Right direction depending on the pattern.

AHHch - Alternating Half Hitch Chain : A series of **HHs** done with 2 cords, alternating back and forth from cord to cord.

LHKch - Lark's Head Knot Chain : A series of vertical **LHKs** made with 2 cords. The **KC** passes over the **AC**, then under, then over, then under, and so on. The order can be reversed to "under, over" when beads are added to produce a smoother look. The chain can face to the left or to the right depending on which cord acts as the **KC**.

SQK - Square Knot : The diagram shows a **SQK** which has two anchor or "filler" cords, however they can be made with only one or with several anchor cords.

FSQK - Flat Square Knot : A **SQK** made with the 2 knotting cords, omitting the 2 anchor cords. It is used to tie off cords at the back of a piece.

OVK - Overhand Knot : A knot used to tie off the end of a cord.

Mounting Hitch (MH) steps 1 & 2

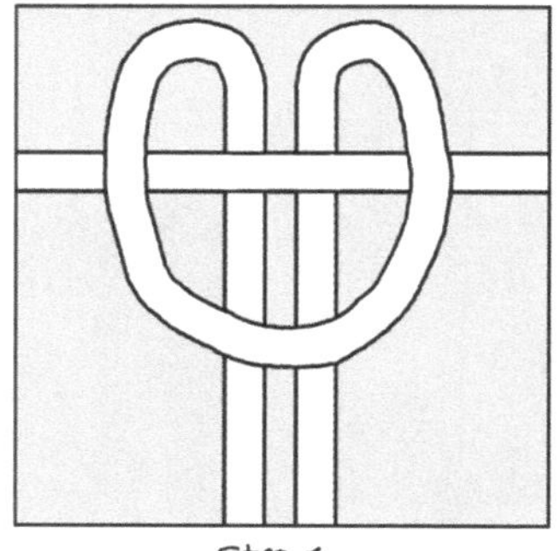
Step 1

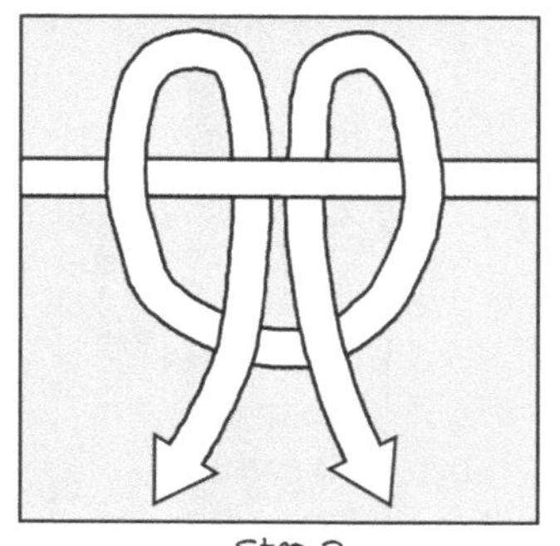
Step 2

Mounting Knot (MTK) steps 1 - 4

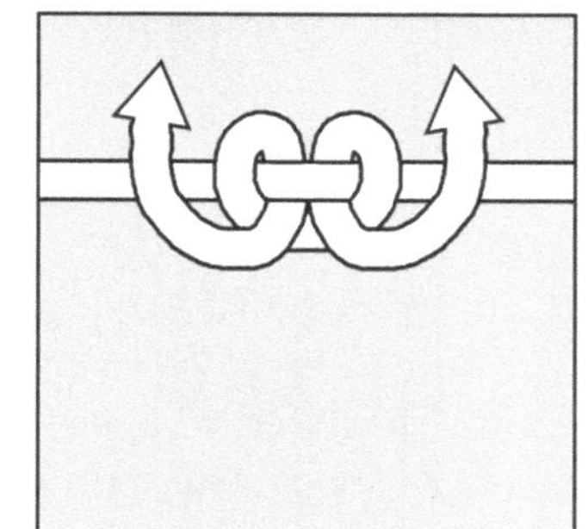
Step 3

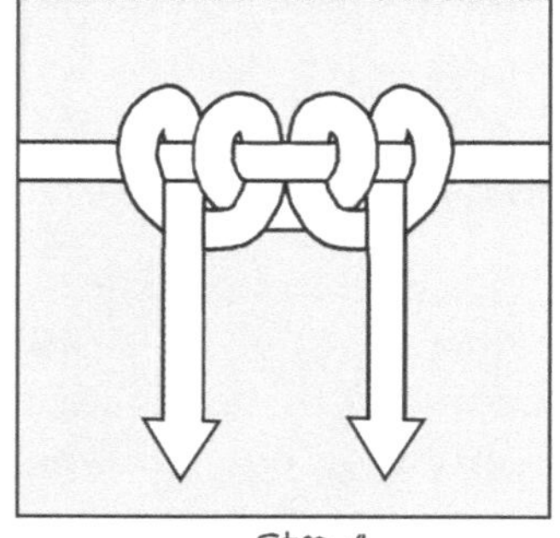
Step 4

Double Half Hitch (DHH)

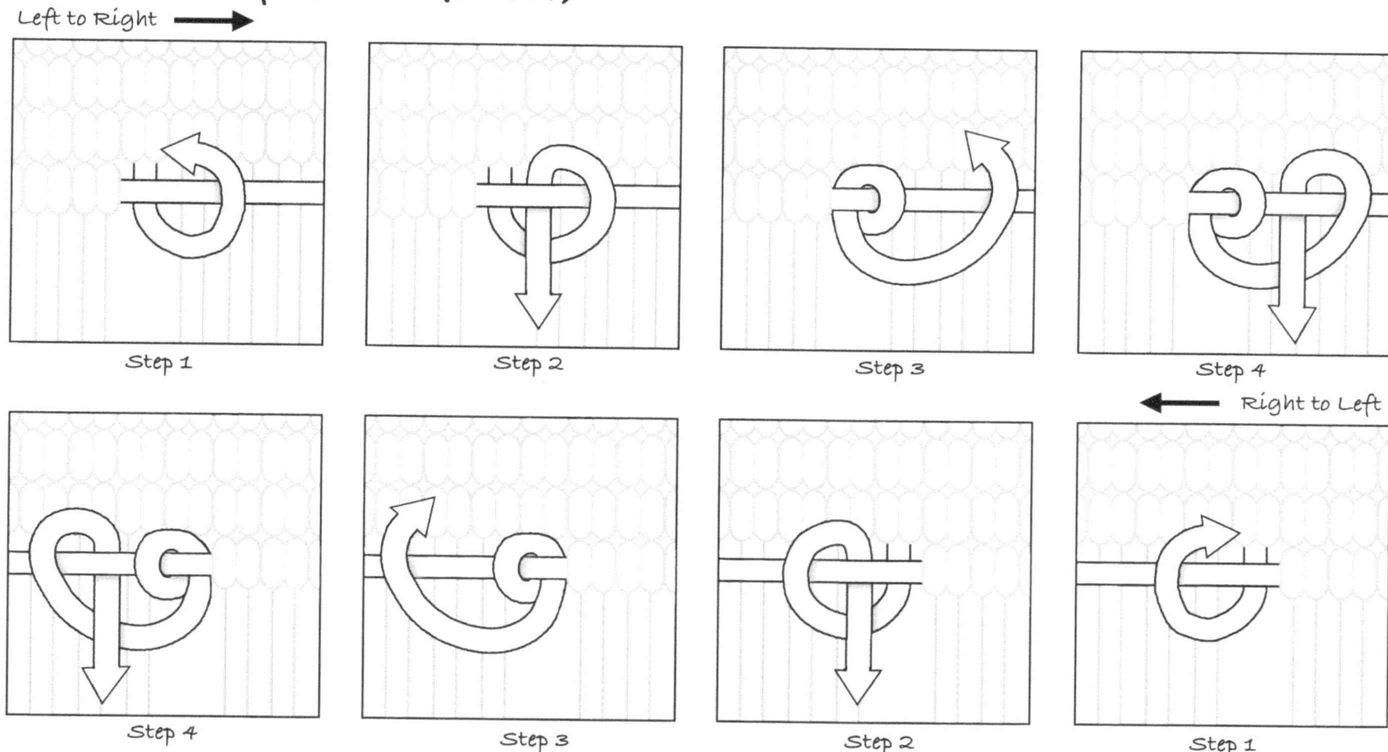

Vertical Double Half Hitch (VDHH)

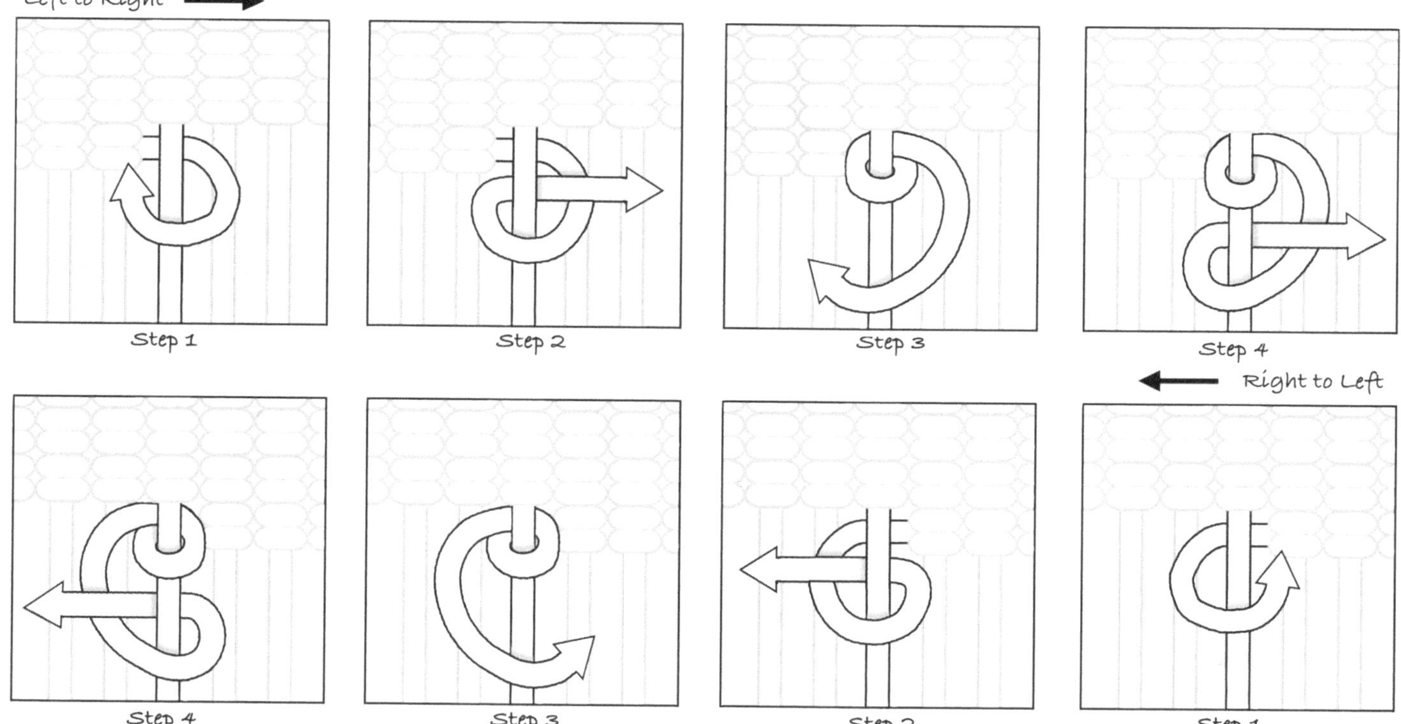

Alternating Half Hitch Chain (AHHch)

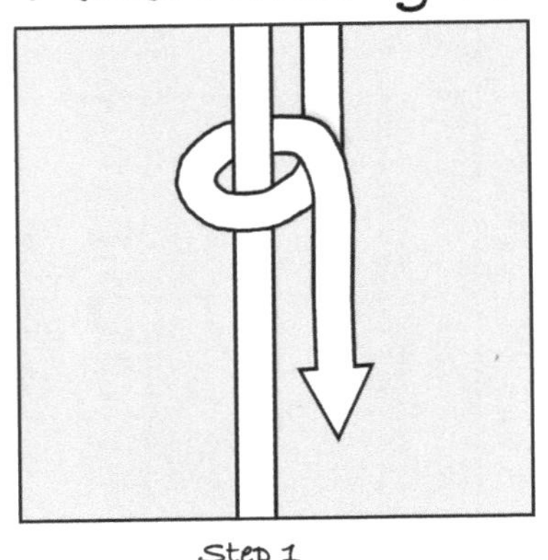
Step 1

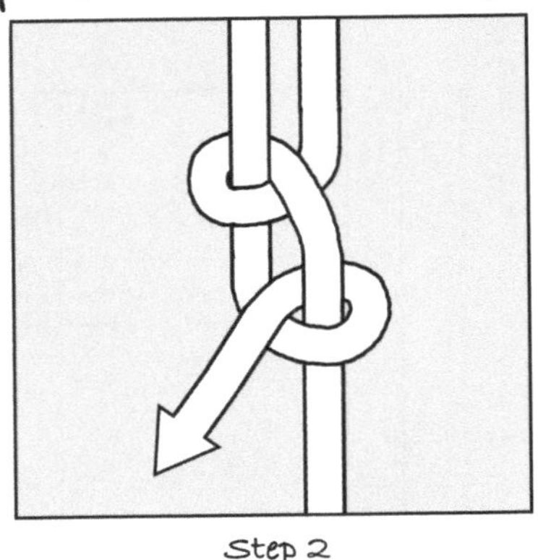
Step 2

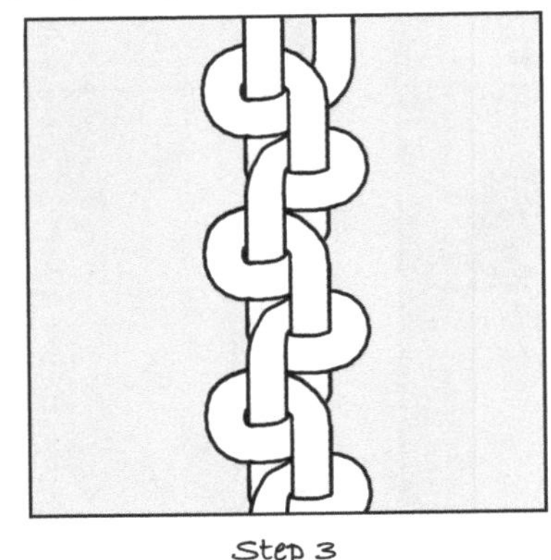
Step 3

Vertical Lark's Head Knot Chain (LHKch)

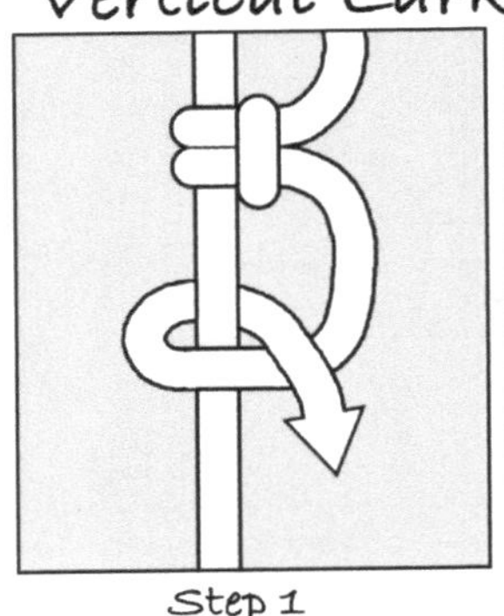
Step 1

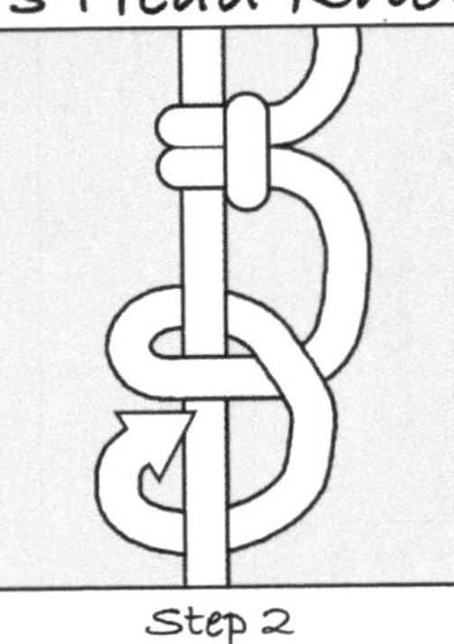
Step 2

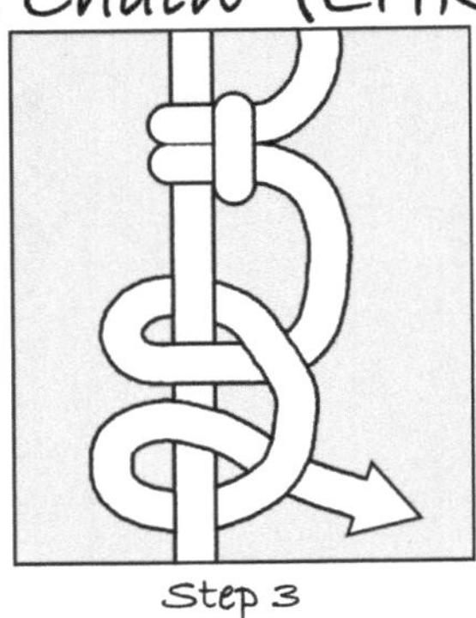
Step 3

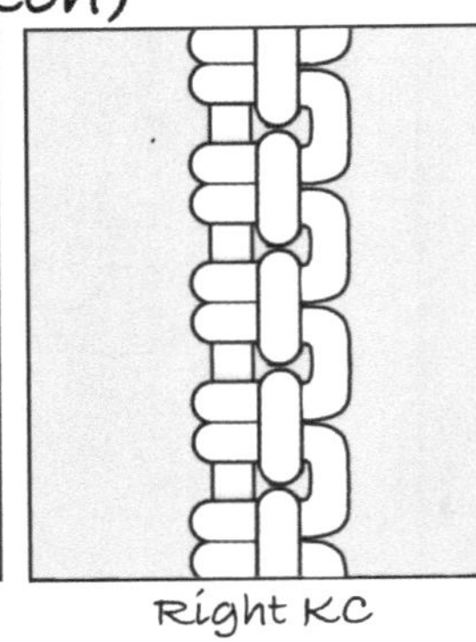
Right KC

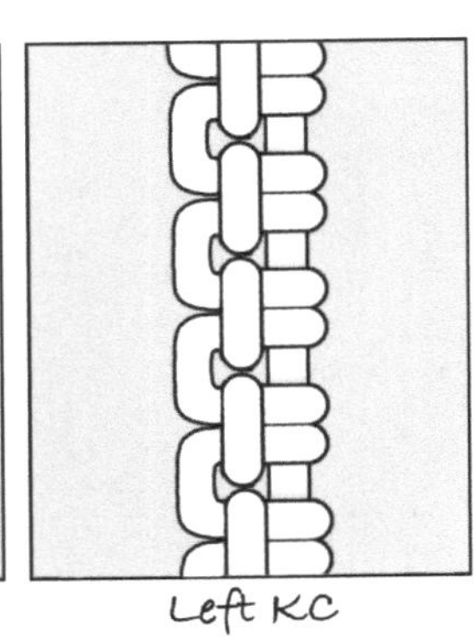
Left KC

Square Knot (SQK)

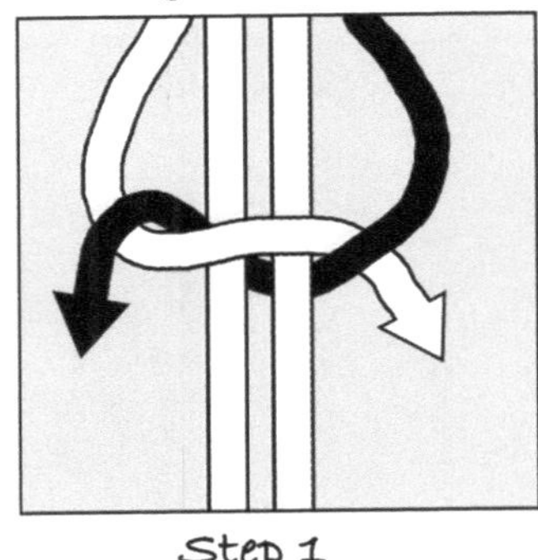
Step 1

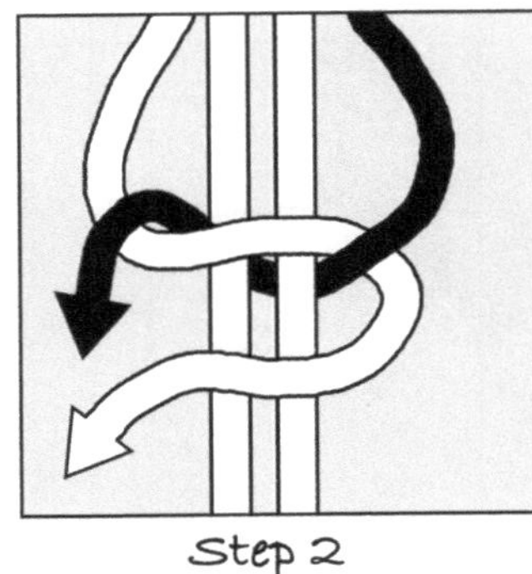
Step 2

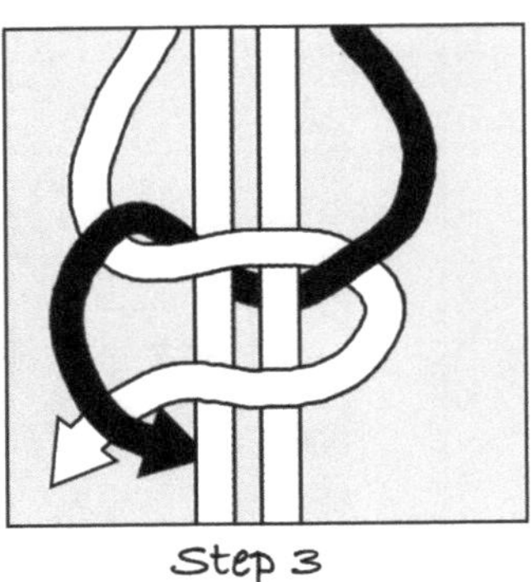
Step 3

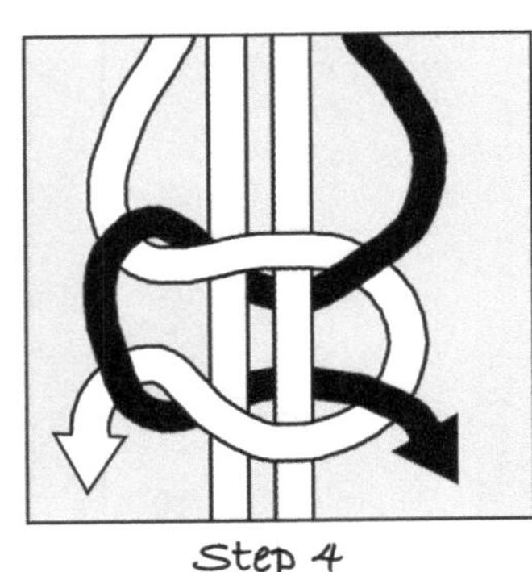
Step 4

Flat Square Knot (FSQK)

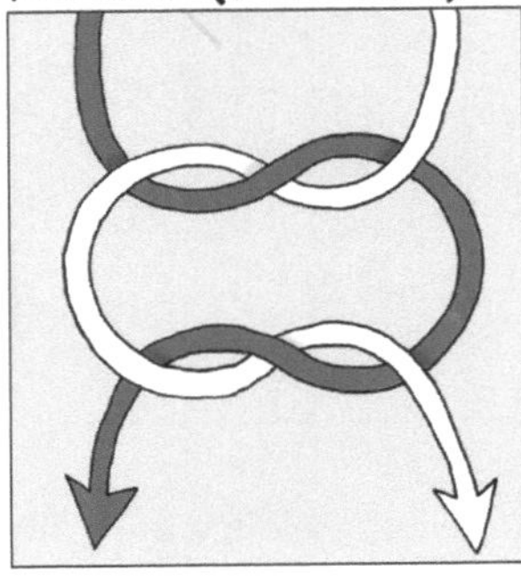

Overhand Knot (OVK)

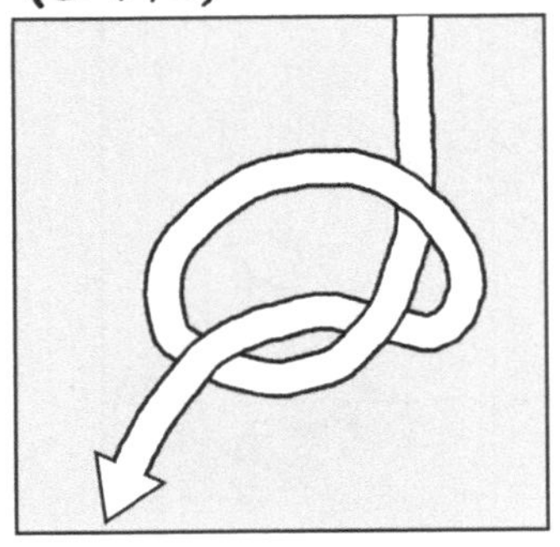

Lark's Head Knot (LHK)

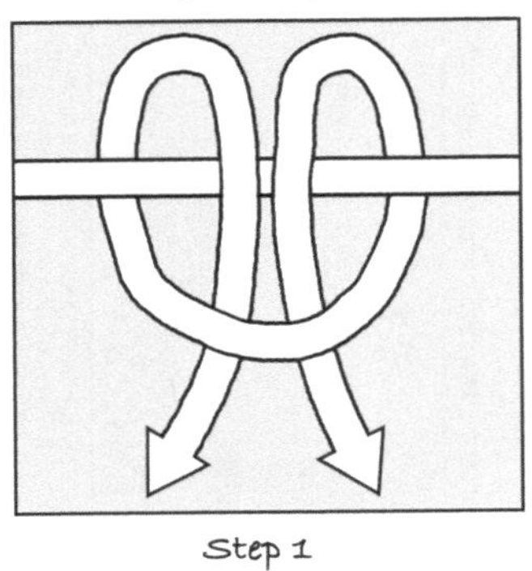
Step 1

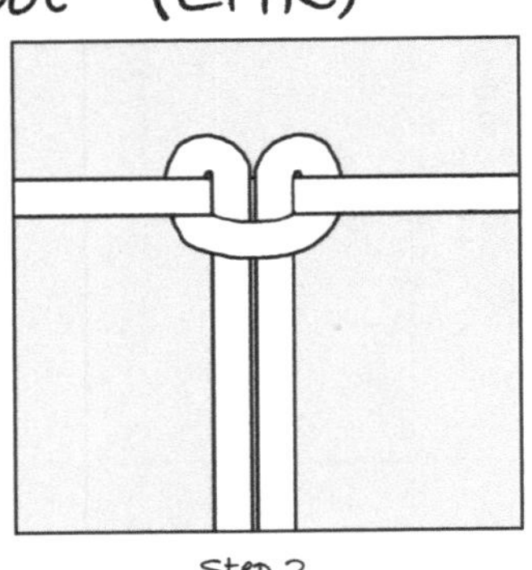
Step 2

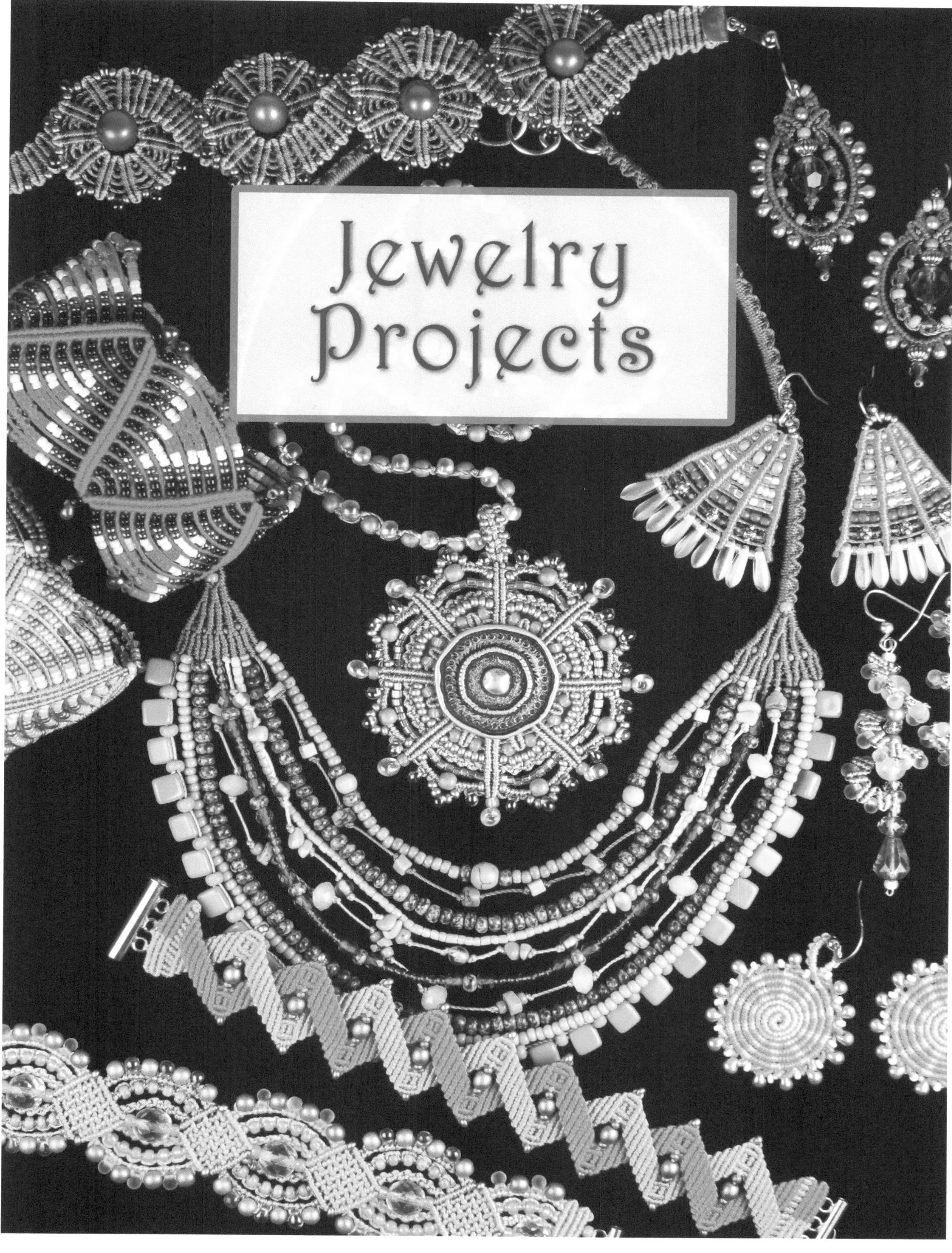
Jewelry Projects

Bella Earrings

The bell shape of these colorful earrings is fun and flattering and the dagger beads give a feathery look to the fringe.

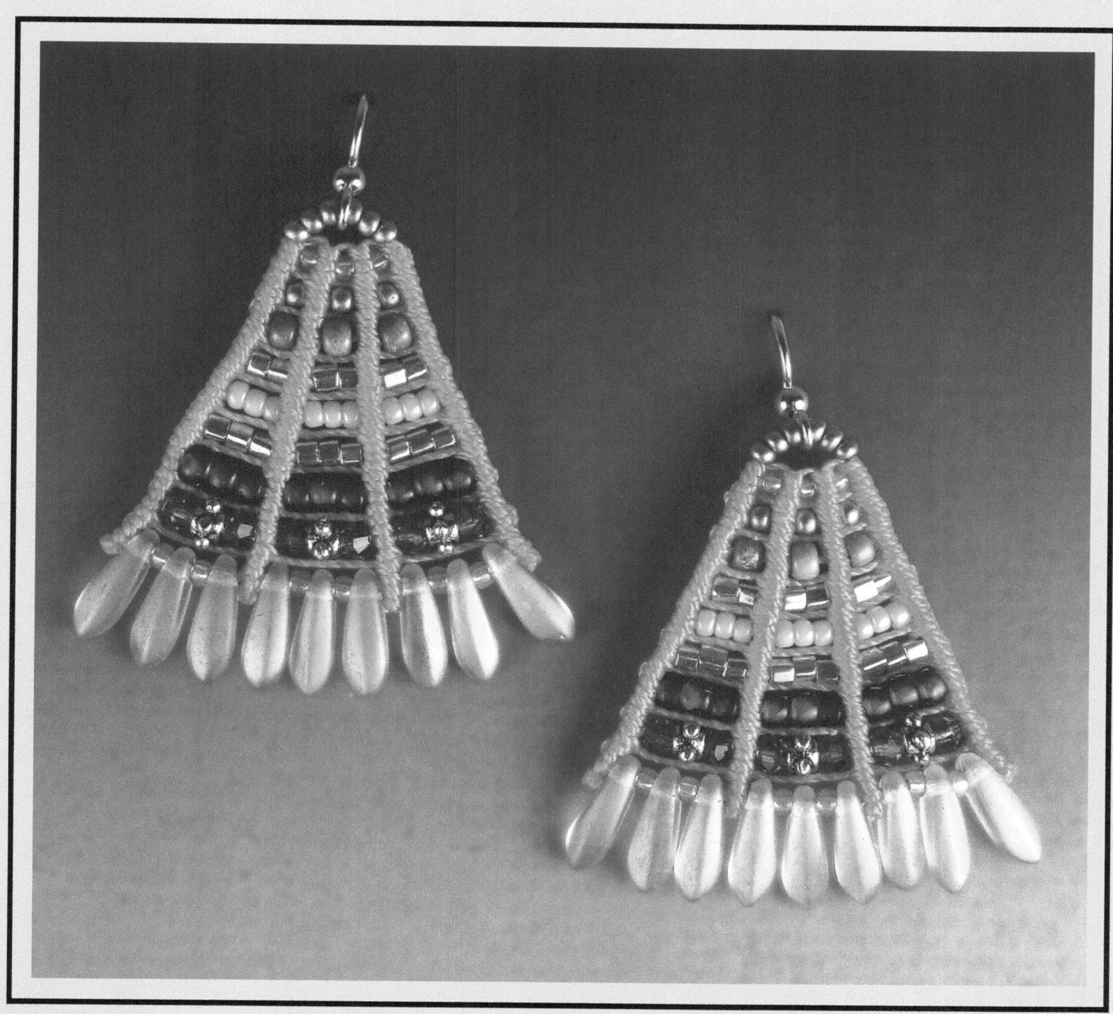

Materials

18g Nylon Cord: 8 @ 16" and 2 @ 55"
(2) Hook style earring wires

Beads: (some minor substitutions can be made as long as the shape of the earring is maintained)
(12) 11° metallic seed beads
(18) 11° seed beads (color A)
(18) 11° seed beads (color B)
(6) 10° seed beads
(30) 1.5mm cubes
(6) 8° seed beads (color A)
(18) 8° seed beads (color B)
(12) 3mm bicone crystals
(6) 3mm metal spacers
(18) 3x11mm dagger beads (spears)

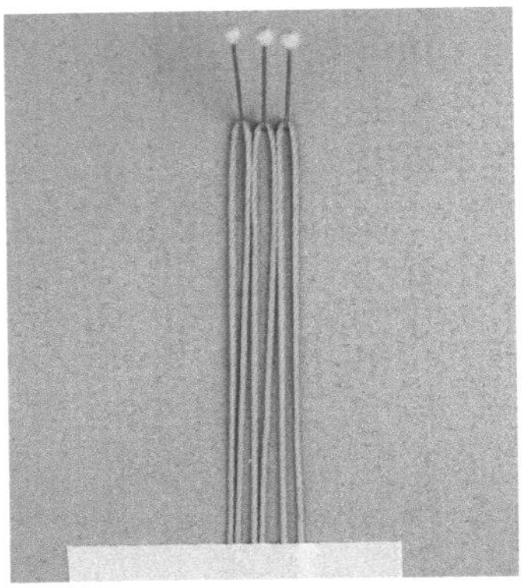
Figure 1

Part 1 - Beaded "A" Shape

1. Put 3 pins in the board, angled upwards and spaced ⅛" (4mm) apart. Take 3 of the 16" cords and fold them in half, draping each one over a pin. Place a piece of tape over the ends to hold them in place (see Fig. 1).

2. Thread (6) 11° metallic seed beads onto the remaining 16" cord and position them at the center of the cord. Tape this cord to the board so that the left half of it lines up just to the left of the six vertical cords, positioning the beads just above the pin line (see Fig. 2a).

3. Bring 4" of the 55" cord under the 2 left-most cords as in Fig. 2b and tape it down. The longer part of this cord should come out to the right and will act as the **KC** (Knotting Cord) (see Fig. 2c).

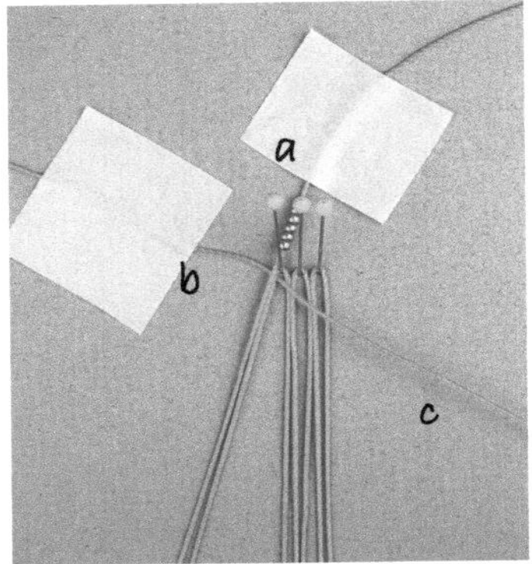

Figure 2

4. Make a **VDHH** (Vertical Double Half Hitch) around the 2 left-most cords, treating them as a single unit (see Fig. 3a).

5. Untape and bring the loose end of the 16" beaded cord downward to the right of the other vertical cords and tape it down. The beads should remain centered just above the pins (see Fig. 3b).

6. Row 1 - Thread a narrow 11° bead onto the **KC** and position it next to the **VDHH**. Bring the **KC** under the next 2 cords and make a **VDHH** around them (see Fig. 4). **Note -** untape cords when needed, but keep them taped down when not in use until Row 1 is complete.

7. Row 1, continued - Thread a narrow 11° bead onto the **KC** and position it next to the second **VDHH**. Bring the **KC** under the next 2 cords and make a **VDHH** around them. Thread a narrow 11° bead onto the **KC** and position it next to the third **VDHH**. Bring the **KC** under the last 2 cords and make a **VDHH** around them (see Fig. 5).

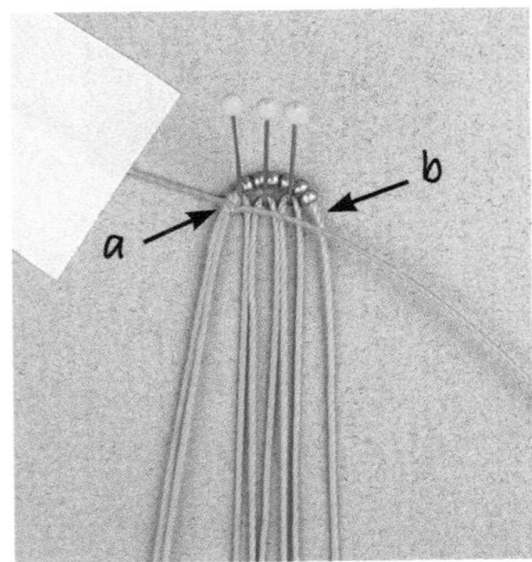

Figure 3

8. Unpin the knotwork and pull downward on each of the vertical cords to tighten them up. Repin the knotwork to the board.

9. Row 2 - Bring the **KC** back to the left and make 3 **VDHH**s, one around each cord pair, excluding the left-most cord pair (see Fig. 6a). Untape the 4" **KC** tail and bring it downward next to the leftmost cord pair. Make a **VDHH** around all 3 cords, treating them as a single unit (see Fig. 6b).

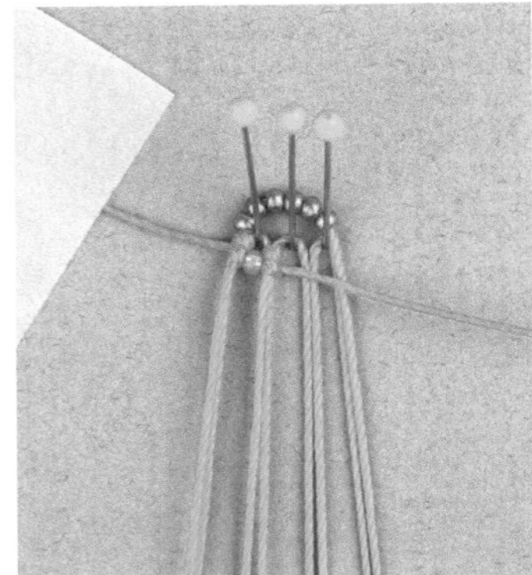
Figure 4

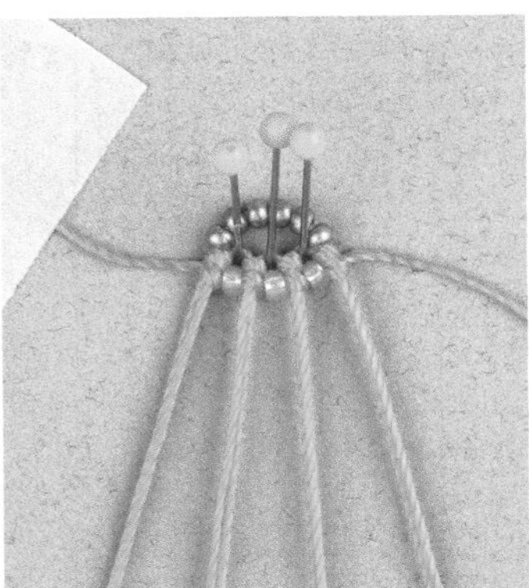
Figure 5

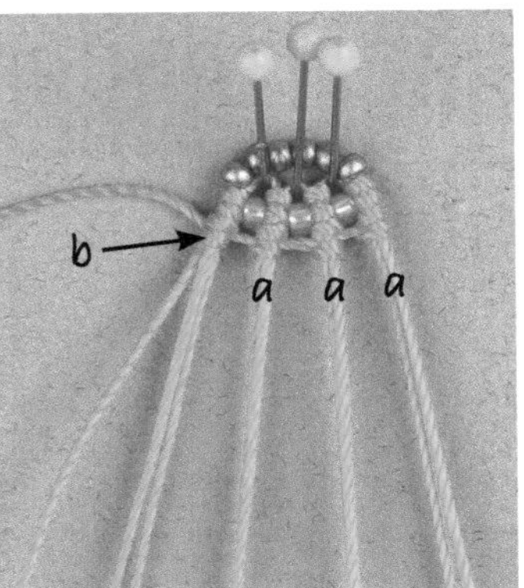

Figure 6

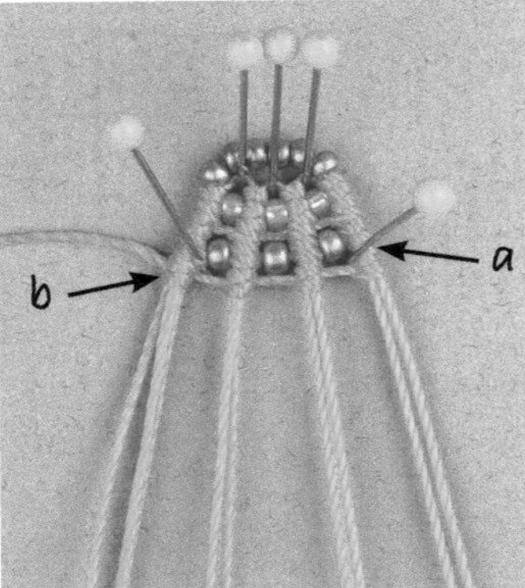

Figure 7

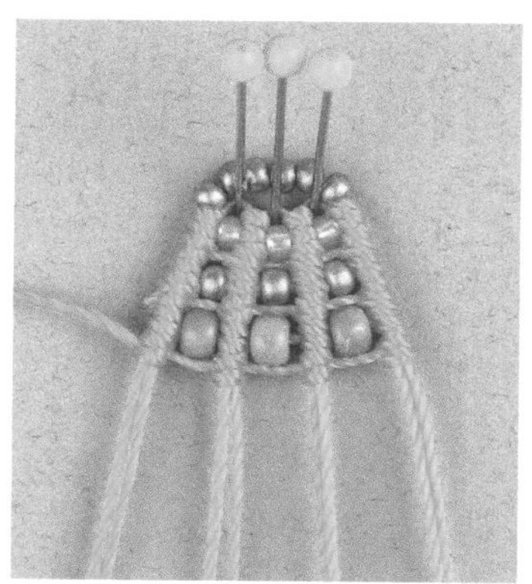

Figure 8

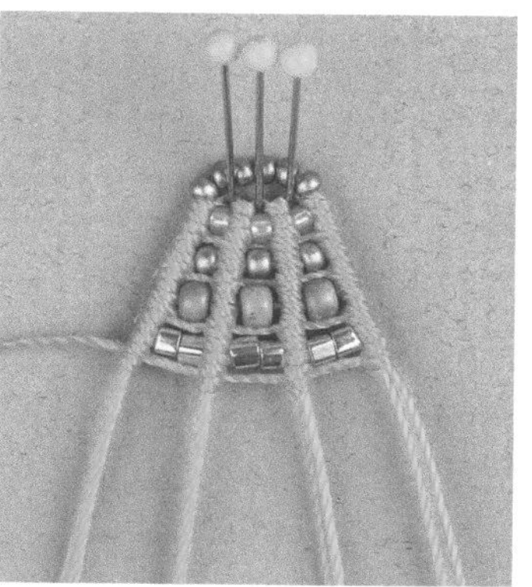

Figure 9

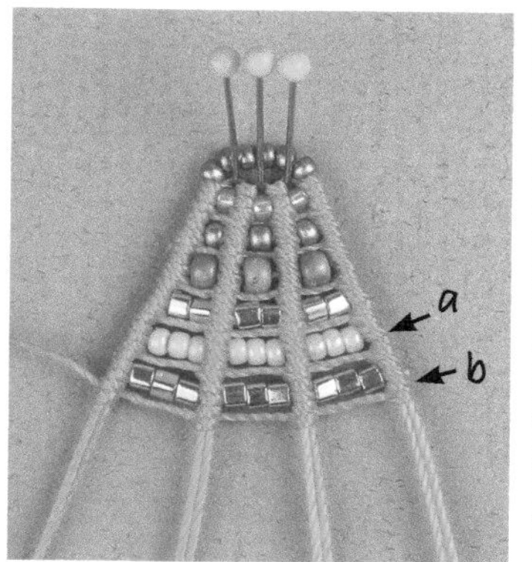

Figure 10

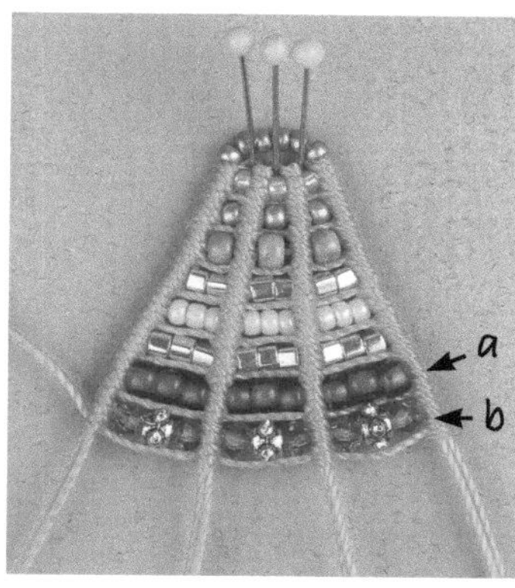

Figure 11

Note - Leave slightly more space between each **VDHH** as in the previous row. The outside edges of the earring will widen gradually, forming a 60° wedge, or "A" shape. As you progress use pins along the edges to hold the shape of the knotwork (see Fig. 7 for an example).

10. Row 3 - Bring the **KC** back towards the right and make a **VDHH** around the first 3-cord unit (this includes the 4" tail). Thread a 10° seed bead onto the **KC** and position it next to the **VDHH**. Bring the **KC** under the next 2 cords and make a **VDHH** around them. Complete the row in the same way (see Fig. 7a).

11. Row 4 - Bring the **KC** back to the left and make 4 **VDHH**s, leaving the 4" **KC** tail out of the last **VDHH** (see Fig. 7b).

12. Row 5 - Bring the **KC** back towards the right and make a **VDHH** around the first cord pair. Carefully cut off the remainder of the 4" **KC** at the back of the piece. Thread an 8° seed bead onto the **KC** and position it next to the **VDHH**. Bring the **KC** under the next 2 cords and make a **VDHH** around them. Complete the row in the same way (see Fig. 8).

13. Row 6 - Bring the **KC** back to the left and make 4 **VDHH**s, taking care to continue the "A" shape (see Fig. 8).

14. Rows 7 and 8 - Bring the **KC** to the right and make a **VDHH**. Thread (2) 1.5mm cube beads onto the **KC**. Make a **VDHH** around the next cord pair. Complete the row in the same way. Bring the **KC** to the left and make 4 **VDHH**s (see Fig. 9).

15. Rows 9 and 10 - Bring the **KC** to the right and make a **VDHH**. Thread (3) 11° seed beads onto the **KC**. Make a **VDHH** around the next cord pair. Complete the row in the same way. Bring the **KC** to the left and make 4 **VDHH**s (see Fig. 10a).

16. Rows 11 and 12 - Bring the **KC** to the right and make a **VDHH**. Thread (3) 1.5mm cube beads onto the **KC**. Make a **VDHH** around the next cord pair. Complete the row in the same way. Bring the **KC** to the left and make 4 **VDHH**s (see Fig. 10b).

17. Rows 13 and 14 - Bring the **KC** to the right and make a **VDHH**. Thread (3) 8° seed beads (these should be on the narrow side) onto the **KC**. Make a **VDHH** around the next cord pair. Complete the row in the same way. Bring the **KC** to the left and make 4 **VDHH**s (see Fig. 11a).

18. Rows 15 and 16 - Bring the **KC** to the right and make a **VDHH**. Thread (1) 3mm bicone, (1) 3mm spacer, and (1) 3mm bicone onto the **KC**. Make a **VDHH** around the next cord pair. Complete the row in the same way. Bring the **KC** to the left and make 4 **VDHH**s (see Fig. 11b).

Figure 12

Figure 13

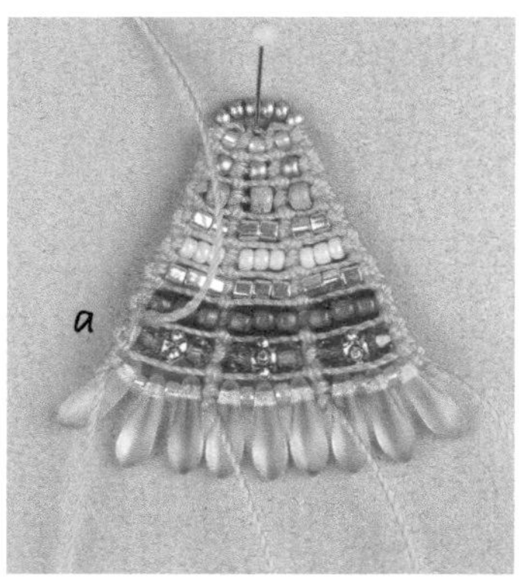

Figure 14

Figure 15

Part 2 - Bottom Fringe

19. Flip the piece to the back and pin down. Take each of the 4 cord pairs and pull one cord towards the back (see Fig. 12). Carefully cut off the back-facing cord from each pair, flush with the bottom of the last row. Flip the piece to the front and repin. There are now 4 vertical cords remaining.

20. Row 17 - Bring the **KC** to the right and make a **VDHH** around the first cord. Thread (1) spear bead, (1) 11°, (1) spear bead, (1) 11°, and (1) spear bead. Make a **VDHH** around the next cord. Complete the row in the same way (see Fig. 13).

21. Flip the piece to the back and pin down. Make an **OVK** (Overhand Knot) at the base of each of the 4 vertical columns of **VDHH**s (just below Row 16) (see Fig. 14). Pull the cords to the back away from the beads and apply a dab of clear nail polish to each **OVK**.

22. Thread the **KC** onto a narrow embroidery needle and sew it upwards under one or two knots along the back edge, making sure it doesn't show at the front. Make an **OVK** and apply nail polish (see Fig. 14a). Let dry, and cut off the excess cords below their **OVK**s.

23. Open the loop of the earring wire with pliers by sliding it sideways. Slip it through the top beads at the center point and then close it again (see Fig. 15).

24. Repeat Steps 1 - 23 to make the second earring.

Shambala Earrings

Materials

Cord and Thread:
18g. Nylon Cord: Outer chain color - 2 lengths @ 20" and 2 lengths @ 36"
Inner chain color - 2 lengths @ 20" and 2 lengths @ 30"

Other:
Fray Check (treat all cord ends and let them dry thoroughly)
Beads and Findings:
(2) earring wires
(26) 3.4mm drop/fringe beads
(26) 11° seed beads
(4) 4mm metallic spacer beads
(2) 4mm or 5mm crystal bicones
(2) 8mm round crystal bead
(18) 8° seed beads
(16) 3mm crystal bicones

Ornately beaded bands surrounding serene crystals bring all of the elements together into a balanced and harmonious design.

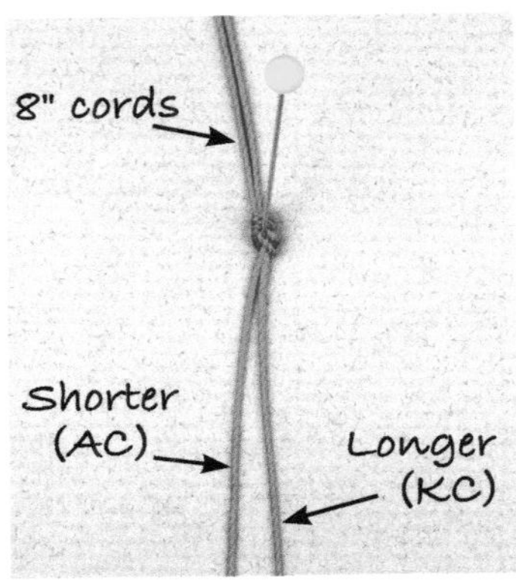

Figure 1

Part 1 - The Outer Chain

1. Bring (1) 20" cord and (1) 36" cord together so that the top ends are even. Approximately 8" from the top ends, tie them together with an **OVK** (Overhand Knot). Do not over-tighten the **OVK** because you will be removing it later.

2. Position the cords vertically on the board and pin through the **OVK**, with the 8" cords above the pin. Below the pin, the longer cord should be to the right and the shorter cord should be on the left (see Fig. 1).

3. Make two vertical **LHK**s using the right-hand (longer) cord as the **KC** (Knotting Cord) and the left-hand (shorter) cord as the **AC** (Anchor Cord) (see Fig. 3a). The **LHK**s are made like this: (1) Bring the **KC** under the **AC**, then (2) back over the **AC** and tighten. (3) Bring the **KC** over the **AC** then (4) back under the **AC** and tighten. This sequence will give a smooth texture to the chain when beads are placed between the **LHK**s (see Fig. 2, the picture shows the knot as it looks untightened).

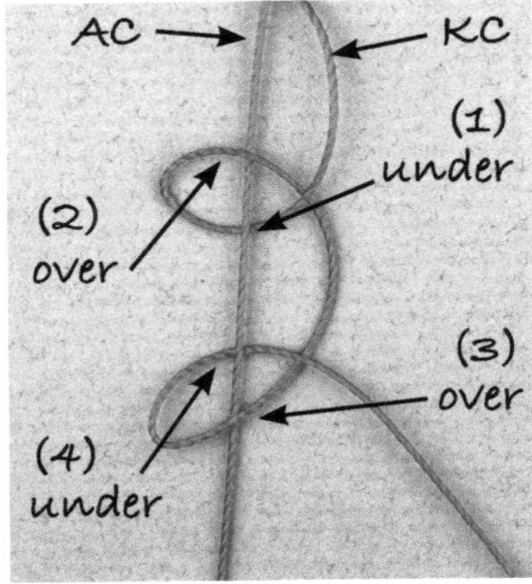

Figure 2

4. **Note -** all beads in this chain will be threaded onto the **KC**. Thread a drop bead onto the **KC** and push it up. Make a **LHK**. Thread an 11° seed bead onto the **KC** and push it up. Make a **LHK** (see Fig. 3b).

5. Repeat the previous step five more times, adding 5 more drop beads and 5 more seed beads to the chain (see Fig. 4).

6. Onto the **KC**, thread a spacer bead, followed by a 4 or 5mm bicone, followed by a seed bead (see Fig. 5).

7. Holding the beads 2 or 3" away from the chain, pass the **KC** back up through the bicone and the spacer bead, bypassing the seed bead (see Fig. 6). **Note -** this may be difficult if you haven't already treated the cord end with Fray Check and let it dry thoroughly. If not, do so now. Also, be sure to cut off the cord tip at a very sharp angle to make the cord easier to pass through the bicone bead. Pull up slowly and tighten the cord so that the beads are flush against the chain and the seed bead is centered (see Fig. 7a).

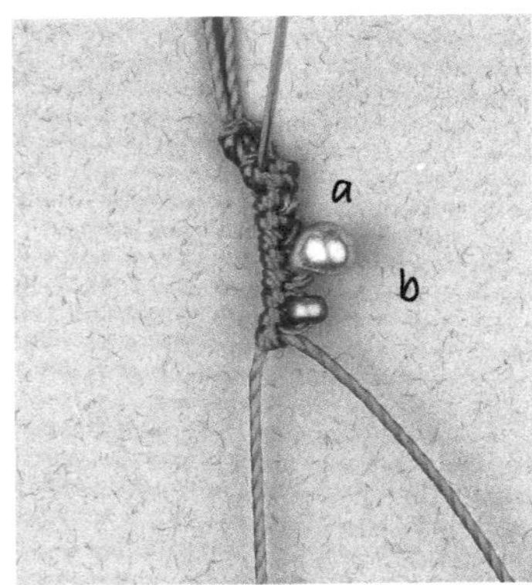

Figure 3

8. Make a **LHK**. Thread an 11° seed bead onto the **KC**. Make a **LHK.** Thread a drop bead onto the **KC**.

9. Repeat the previous step five more times, adding 5 more seed beads and 5 more drop beads to the chain (see Fig. 7b).

10. Make (2) more **LHK**s to complete the chain (see Fig. 7c).

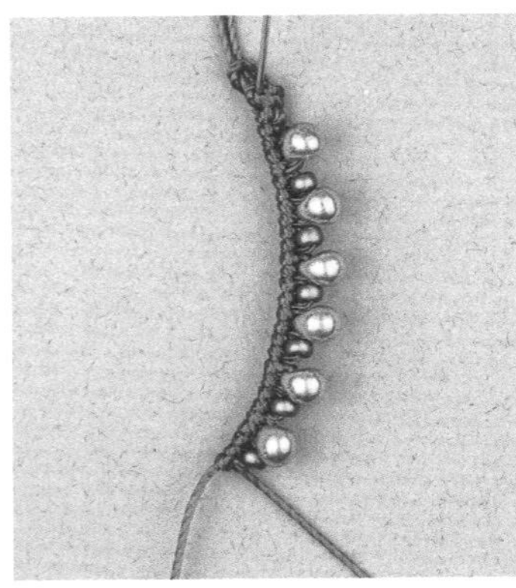
Figure 4

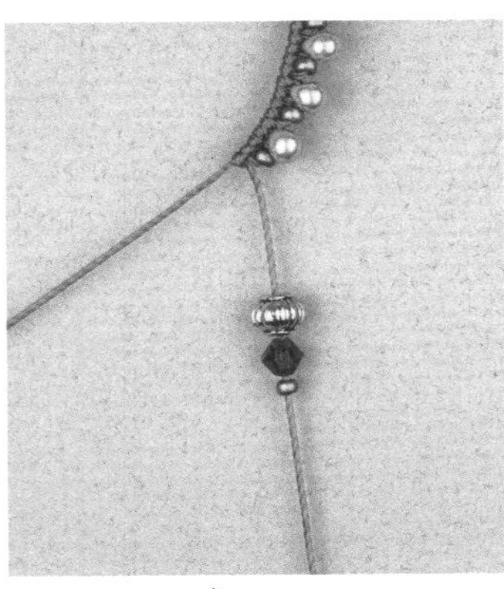
Figure 5

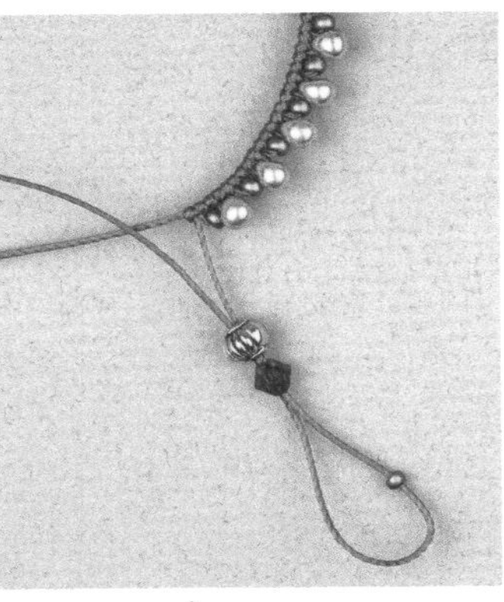
Figure 6

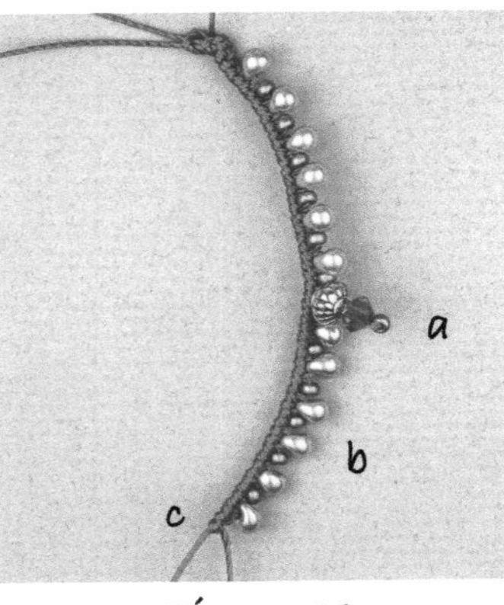

Figure 7

11. Repeat Steps 1 - 10 with the other two outer chain cords (this will be for the other earring). Remove the starting **OVK**s from the chains.

12. Make sure the knots are tight and neat. You may need to compress the knots on the chains together by pushing them towards the center while holding the **AC** ends firmly. Compare the two completed **LHK** chains to make sure that they are exactly the same length (see Fig. 8). Check for symmetry and that the centermost beads are in the correct position. Adjust if necessary.

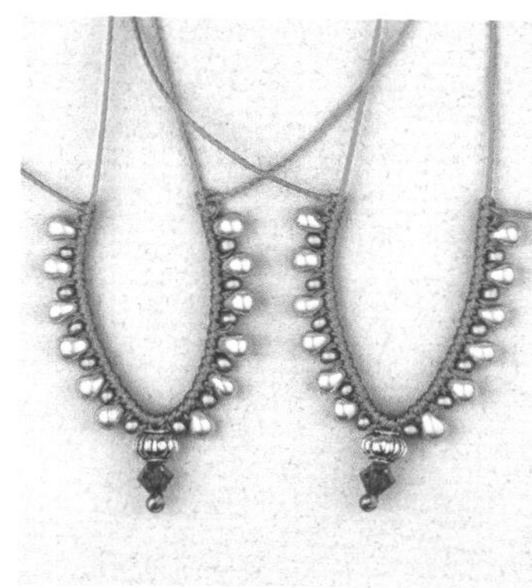

Figure 8

Part 2 - The Inner Chain

13. Bring (1) 20" cord and (1) 30" cord together so that the top ends are even. About 8" from the top ends, tie them together with an **OVK**. Do not over tighten the **OVK** because you will be removing it later (see Fig. 9 for completed chain, Steps 13 - 16).

14. Pin the cords vertically to the board through the **OVK**, with the 8" cords above the pin. The longer cord (**KC**) should be to the right of the shorter cord (**AC**).

15. With the **KC**, make a **LHK** around the **AC**. Thread a 3mm bicone onto the **AC**. Make a **LHK**. Thread an 8° seed bead onto the **AC.**

16. Repeat Step #15 five more times. Add (1) **LHK**, (1) bicone bead, and (1) **LHK** to complete the chain. There should be a total of (7) bicones and (6) 8° seed beads in the chain.

Figure 9

17. Repeat Steps 13 - 16 to make the inner chain for the other earring. Remove the starting **OVK**s from the chains.

18. Make sure the knots are tight and neat. You may need to compress the knots on the chains together slightly by pushing them towards the center while holding the **AC** ends firmly. Compare the two completed **LHK** chains to make sure that they are exactly the same length. Adjust if necessary.

Part 3 - Joining the Inner and Outer Chains

19. Pin the outer chain to the board so that the center beads are at the top and the two ends hang downward. Pin the inner chain so that it fits inside of the outer chain. The ends of the outer and inner chains should line up with the inner chain ends being be just slightly lower than the outer chain ends (see Fig. 10).

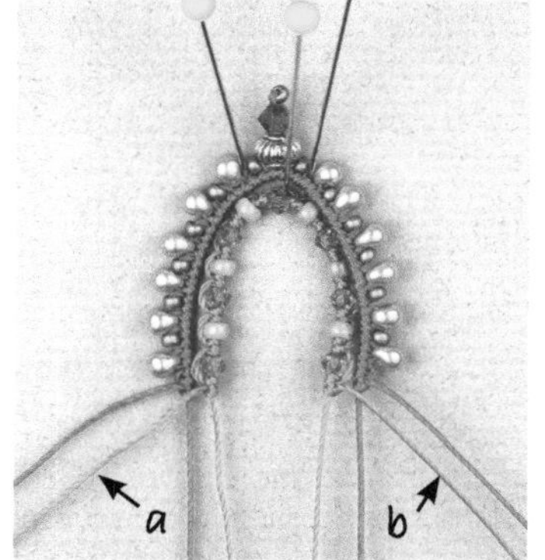

Figure 10

Note - Take your time to align the chains properly and pin them in place securely. I recommend that you use more pins than are in the photos.

20. Using the two **KC** ends of the inner chain as **AC**s (see Fig. 10a & b), bring them both outward horizontally and on each side, attach the two outer chain cords using **DHH**s (see Fig. 11, bottom).

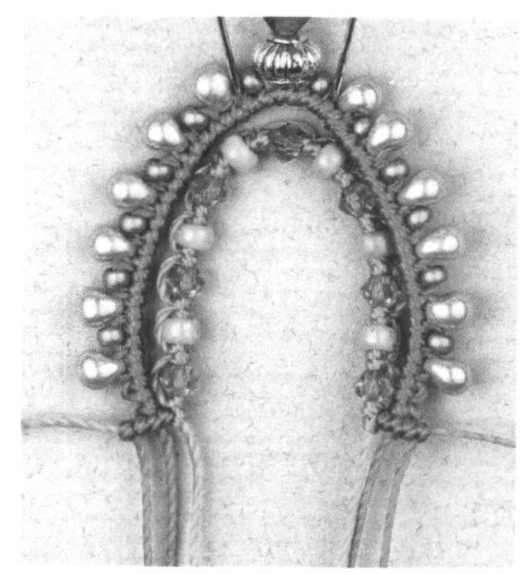

Figure 11

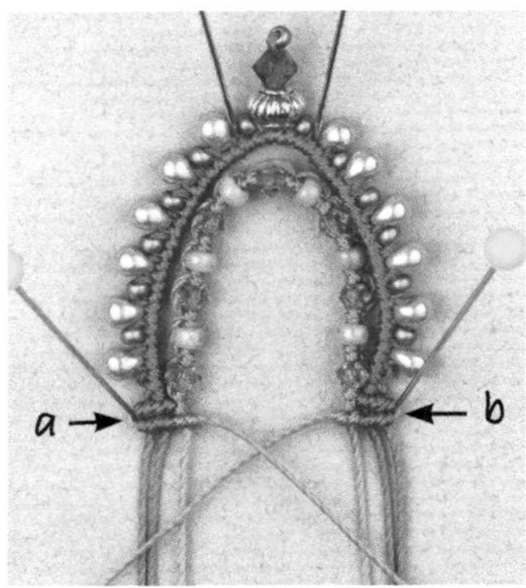

Figure 12

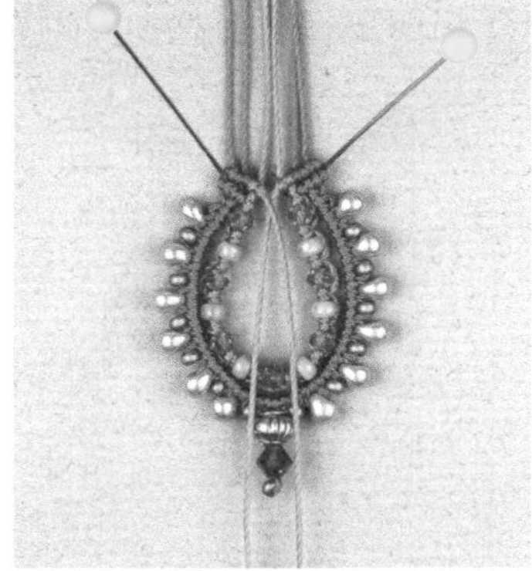
Figure 13

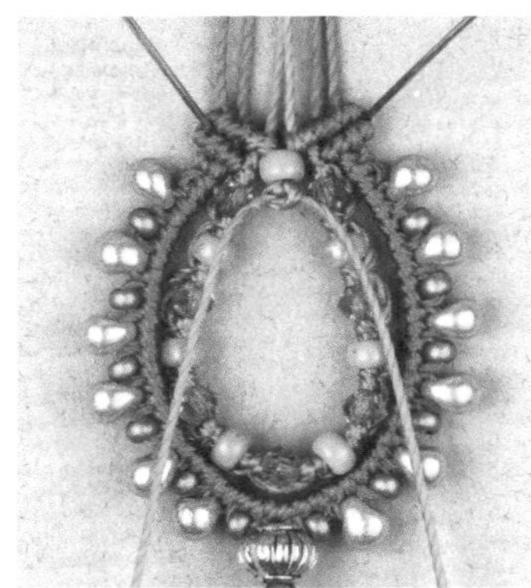
Figure 14

21. On each side, place a pin at the outer edge of the row, just below the **AC**. Bring the **AC** back towards the center (around the stabilizing pin) and make another row consisting of 3 **DHH**s, including the remaining inner chain cord (see Fig. 12a & b).

22. Unpin and flip the piece upside down so that the two **AC**s (from Step 21) meet at the center and hang downwards. Place pins in the valleys between the rows of **DHH**s to hold the earring in place (see Fig. 13).

23. Thread an 8° seed bead onto the two **AC**s and push it up. Make a **FSQK** (Flat Square Knot) below the bead to join the two **AC**s (see Fig. 14). The metal spacer should have a hole large enough to push up over the **FSQK**. If it doesn't; you can untie the **FSQK** and instead, join the two **AC**s together by wrapping beading thread tightly around them.

24. Thread a metal spacer bead onto the cords and push it up over the **FSQK** (or wrapped thread). Thread an 8mm crystal bead onto the cords (see Fig. 15).

25. Reduce each of the **AC**s to one ply. Cut off the 2-ply sections flush with the bottom of the 8mm bead. Thread a 3mm bicone bead onto the two 1-ply cords. Make an **OVK** below the bicone bead (see Fig. 16). Apply a dab of clear nail polish to the **OVK** and let dry. Cut off the cords below the **OVK**.

26. Unpin and flip the piece upside down so that the 6 remaining cords hang downward (see Fig. 17). **• I will refer to these cords as Cds #1 - 6 according to their sequence from left to right.**

27. Thread a drop bead (widest part facing the front) onto Cds #3 and 4 and push it up (see Fig. 17a).

28. On the left-hand side, take Cd #2 and using it as the **KC**, make two **LHK**s around Cd #1 (make the knots in a right to left direction) (see Fig. 18a).

29. On the right-hand side, take Cd #5 and using it as the **KC**, make two **LHK**s around Cd #6 (make the knots in a left to right direction) (see Fig. 18b).

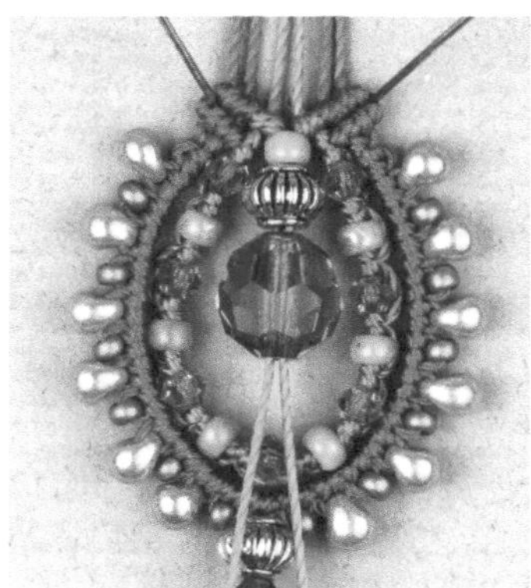
Figure 15

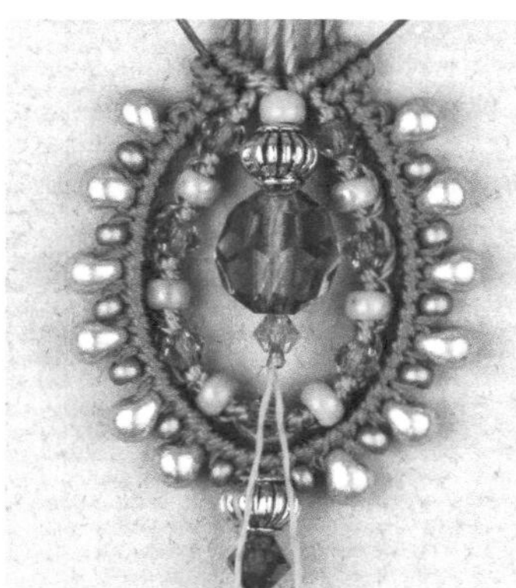
Figure 16

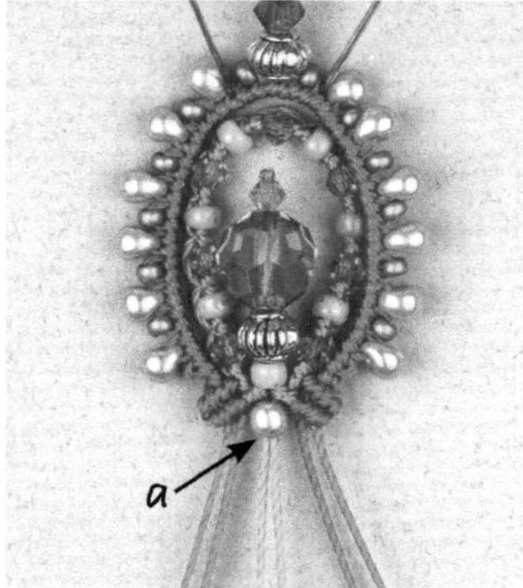

Figure 17

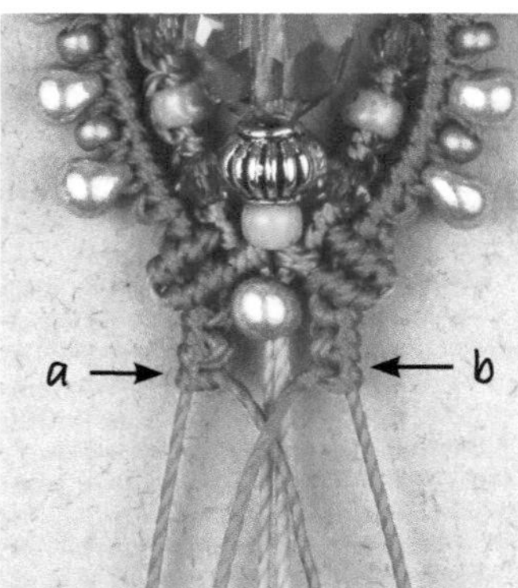

Figure 18

30. Turn the earring right-side up. On the left-hand side, sew Cd #3 (from back to front) through the small space in the "valley" between the **DHH** rows and in between the middle and outside **DHH**s (see Fig. 19a).

31. On the right-hand side, sew Cd #4 (from back to front) through the small space in the "valley" between the **DHH** rows and in between the middle and outside **DHH**s (see Fig. 19b).

32. On each side, move the needle towards the center and make a small stitch in the valley betwen the **DHH** rows, passing the cord through to the back (see Fig. 20a).

33. Flip the earring to the back and make tight **OVK**s in both cords that sit flush against the back of the earring (see Fig. 20b, back view). Apply a dab of clear nail polish to the **OVK**s and let dry. Cut off the cords next to the **OVK**s.

34. Continuing to work with the back of the earring facing you, sew Cd #2 and Cd #5 downward underneath the short cords to each side of the center drop bead (see Fig. 21a). Join Cd #2 and 5 together with a **FSQK** (see Fig. 21b). Apply a dab of clear nail polish to the **FSQK** and let dry. Cut off the cord ends next to the **FSQK**.

35. Flip the earring so that the front is facing you. Thread (1) 8° seed bead, (1) earring wire (with the tip facing backwards), and (1) 8° seed bead onto the left-hand cord (see Fig. 22a).

36. Pass the right-hand cord from right to left through the seed beads and the earring wire (see Fig. 22b). Pull outwards on the cords to bring the beads close against the **LHK**s (see Fig. 23a).

37. Flip the earring to the back and make a **FSQK** with the two cords, making sure it is centered on top of the earring wire (see Fig. 23b). Apply a dab of clear nail polish to the **FSQK** and let dry. Cut off the cord ends next to the **FSQK**.

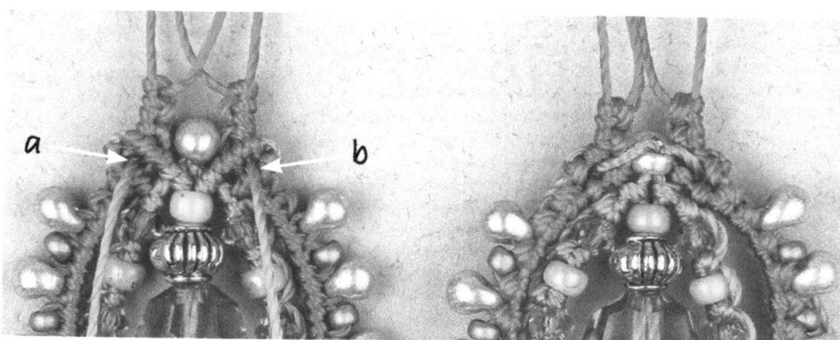

Front view Figure 19 Back view

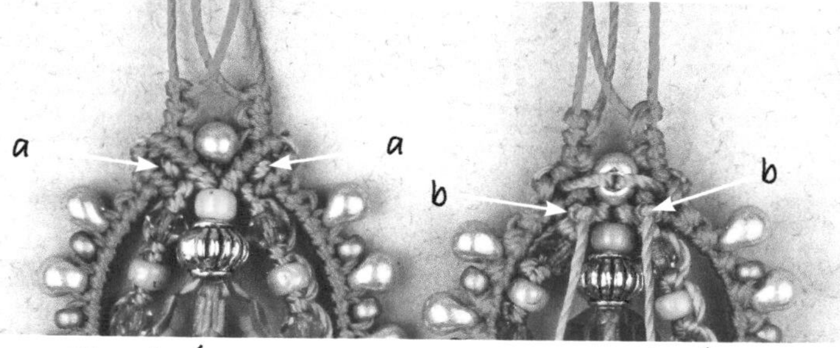

Front view Figure 20 Back view

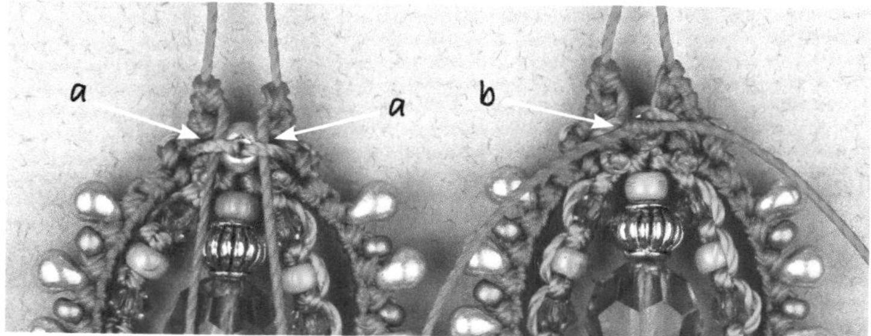

Back view Figure 21 Back view

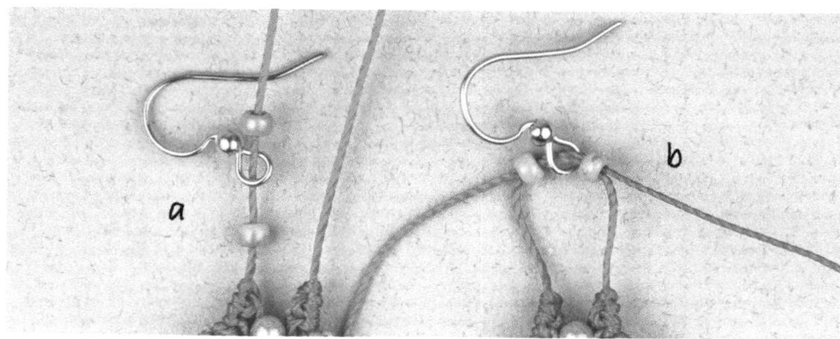

Front view Figure 22 Front view

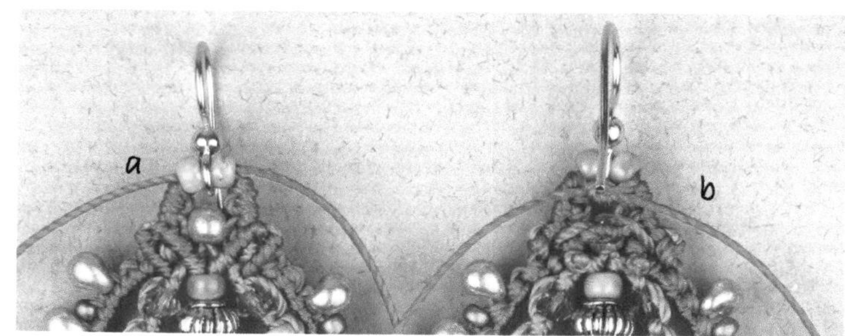

Front view Figure 23 Back view

Galaxy Earrings

Add some cosmic flair to your style with these celestial earrings. A wire structure within the knotted spiral insures that the earrings will keep their graceful shape.

Materials
- 24 g. wire (soft or half-hard) - 2 lengths @ 22"
- 18 g. Nylon Cord - 2 lengths @ 50"

Beads:
- (40) 3.4mm Japanese drop/fringe beads
- (2) 6x8 or 7x9mm fire polish (or crystal) teardrops
- (2) 6mm rondelles (or flat spacers)
- (4) 8° seed beads
- (4) 4mm round druks*
- (4) 6mm stone beads*
- (6) 3mm crystal rondelles*

* these beads were used for the interior strand in the sample, but you can substitute beads of your choice.

Other:
- Round nose pliers
- Flat or chain nose pliers (plastic tip or regular)

Part 1 - Earring #1 (Rightward Spiral)

1. Place a T-Pin (or sturdy quilting pin) in your board and angle it slightly upward. Take one length of wire and loop it around the T-Pin so that the wire to the right side of the pin is 8" long and the wire to the left side of the pin is 14" long (see Fig. 1). Tape down the wire on the right-hand side to stabilize it.

2. Position the left wire horizontally (this wire will act as the anchor wire for the knots). Fold a 50" length of cord in half and attach it to the left wire using a **MTK** (Mounting Knot) (see Fig. 2). Put a pin in the (top/back/center) **MTK** "bump" (see Fig. 3a) and another pin just below the wire at the left-hand edge of the **MTK** (see Fig. 3b). I will refer to the two cords as Cd (cord) #1 (left) and Cd #2 (right).

3. Wrap the wire closely around the left-hand pin bringing it horizontally to the right. Make a **DHH** (Double Half Hitch) around the wire with Cd #1 and then with Cd #2 (see Fig. 4).

4. Place a pin just below the wire at the right-hand edge of the row (see Fig. 5a). Wrap the wire closely around the pin and bring it to the left at a 45° angle (see Fig. 5b).

5. Make a **DHH** around the wire with Cd #2. Thread a drop bead onto Cd #1 and push it up. Attach Cd #1 to the wire with a **DHH** (see Fig. 6). Unpin and rotate the piece upward so that the anchor wire is horizontal. Repin in place (see Fig. 7).

6. Place a pin just below the wire at the left-hand edge of the row. Wrap the wire closely around the pin bringing it horizontally to the right. Make **DHH**s around the wire with Cds #1 and #2 (see Fig. 7).

7. Unpin and remove the top loop from the wire, straightening it lightly with pliers (it doesn't need to be perfectly straight, don't overwork the wire). Continue to add segments (as in Steps #4 - 6) rotating the piece and repinning after each segment so that the anchor wire is horizontal again (see Fig. 8a).

8. When you have finished 8 segments, the piece should form a circle (see Fig. 9).

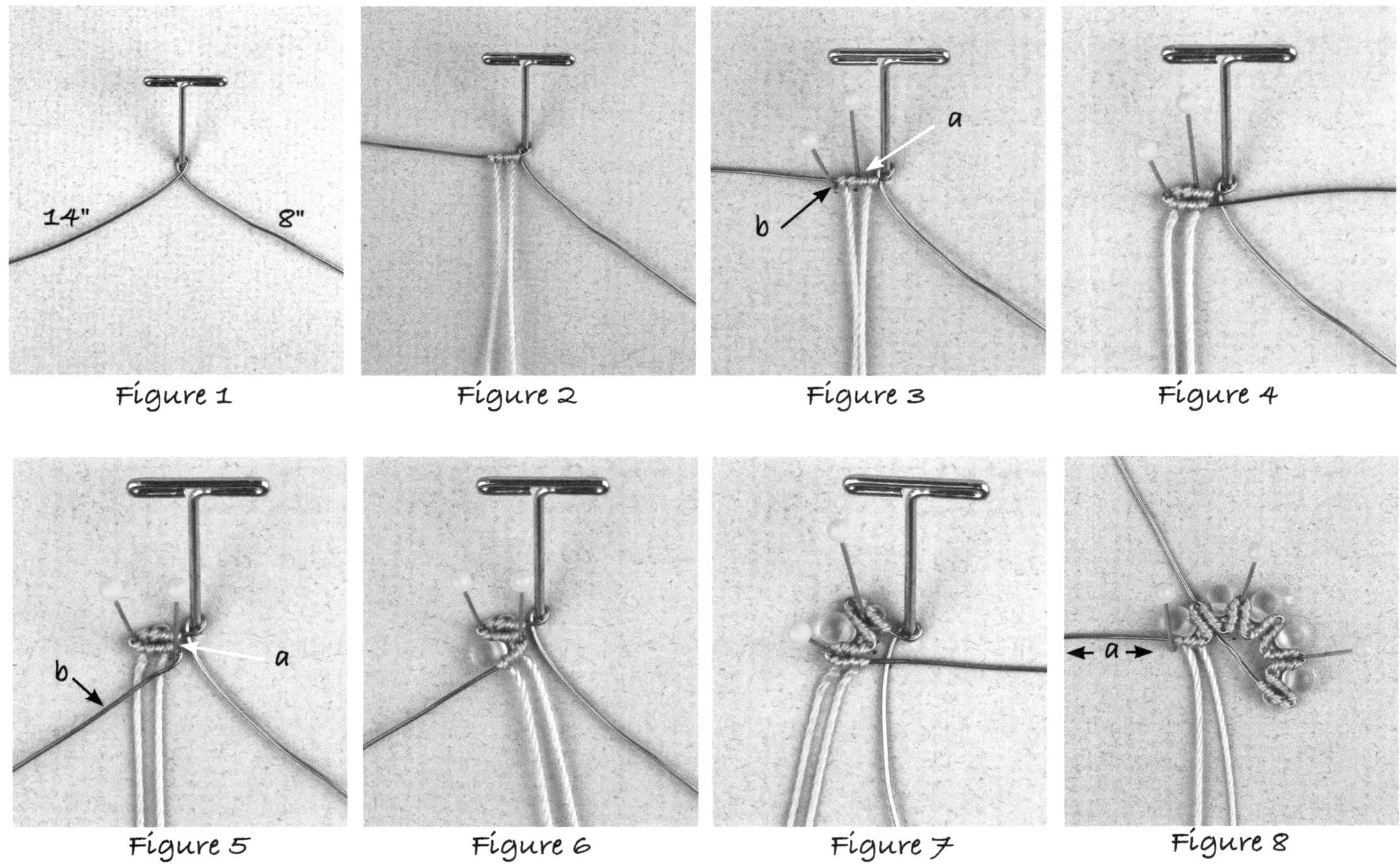

Figure 1 Figure 2 Figure 3 Figure 4

Figure 5 Figure 6 Figure 7 Figure 8

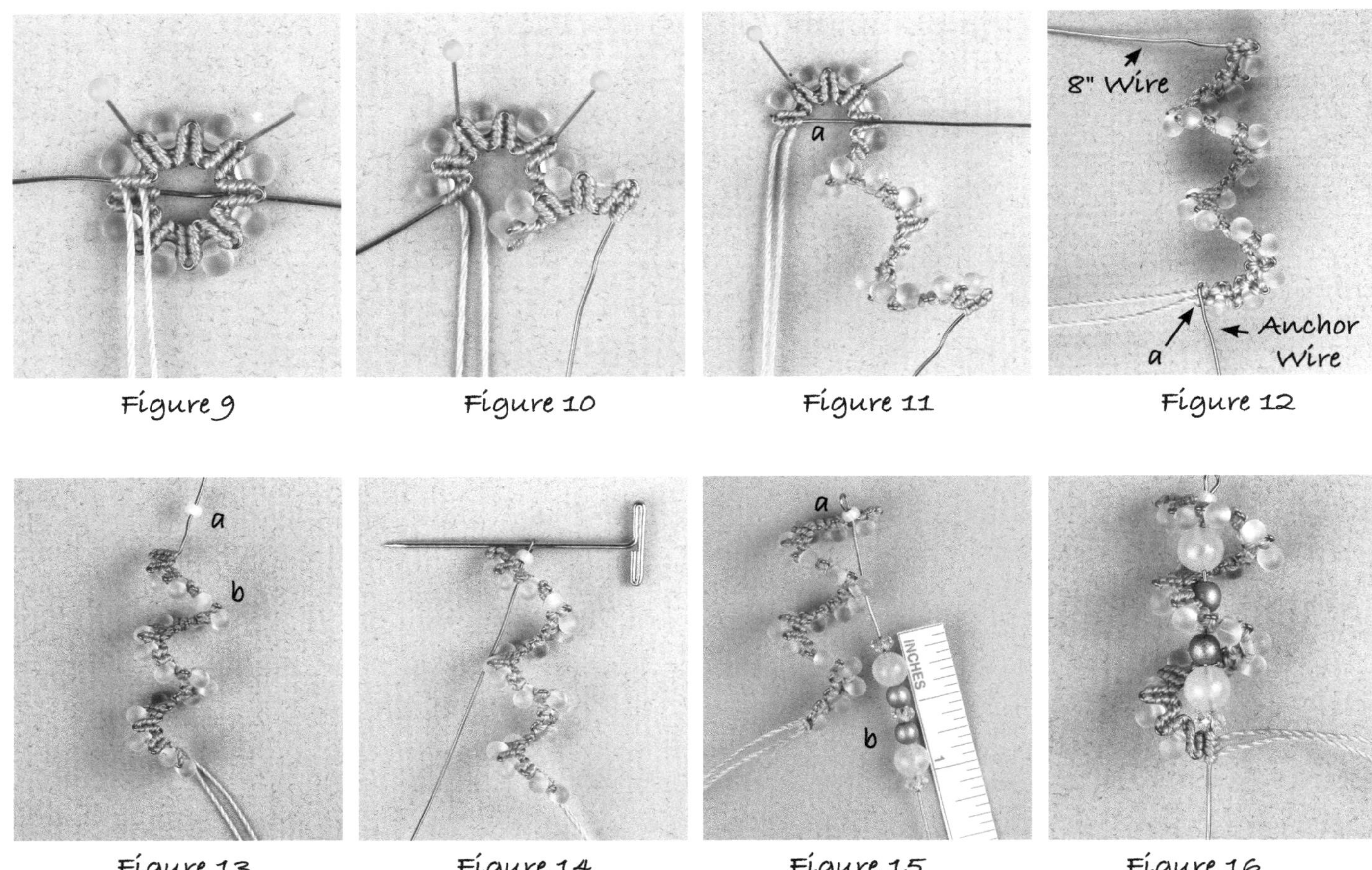

Figure 9 Figure 10 Figure 11 Figure 12

Figure 13 Figure 14 Figure 15 Figure 16

9. As you add more segments, open the circle up and form the piece into a long spiral, repositioning as needed to get the best angle to work with (see Fig. 10). Continue adding segments until you have used 19 beads. On the final row the anchor wire should face towards the inside (see Fig. 11a).

10. Remove the piece from the board and bend the anchor wire tightly over the back side of the final row (see Fig. 12a). Trim off the excess wire flush with the outside beaded edge. Flatten it into the cord with pliers so that the cut end does not stick out.

Note - Make sure that piece looks like Fig. 13 before preceding with the next steps. Sometimes the piece can get twisted into the wrong configuration when working on the previous steps. The knotwork on the top part of the spiral should twist downward towards the right (see Fig. 13b).

11. Bend the 8" wire upward. Thread an 8° bead onto the wire (see Fig. 13a) and push it down to the top edge of the knotting. Pass the end back down through the bead and begin pulling the wire through. When the loop of the wire is about an inch from the bead, insert a T-Pin and continue to tighten the wire around the T-Pin (see Fig. 14). This forms a small loop on which to attach the earring wire (see Fig. 15a).

12. Thread beads onto the wire (see Fig. 15b). These can be any beads of your choice (small beads between 3mm - 6mm work best). The length of the bead strand should be close to $1\frac{1}{8}$th" or 30mm.

13. Encircle the beaded strand with the knotted spiral. The bottom row should lie parallel with the hanging wire. Attach the two cords to the wire with **VDHH**s (see Fig. 16, bottom).

14. Thread a drop bead onto the top cord. Bring this cord downward and parallel with the wire. Make a **VDHH** around it with the lower cord (see Fig. 17).

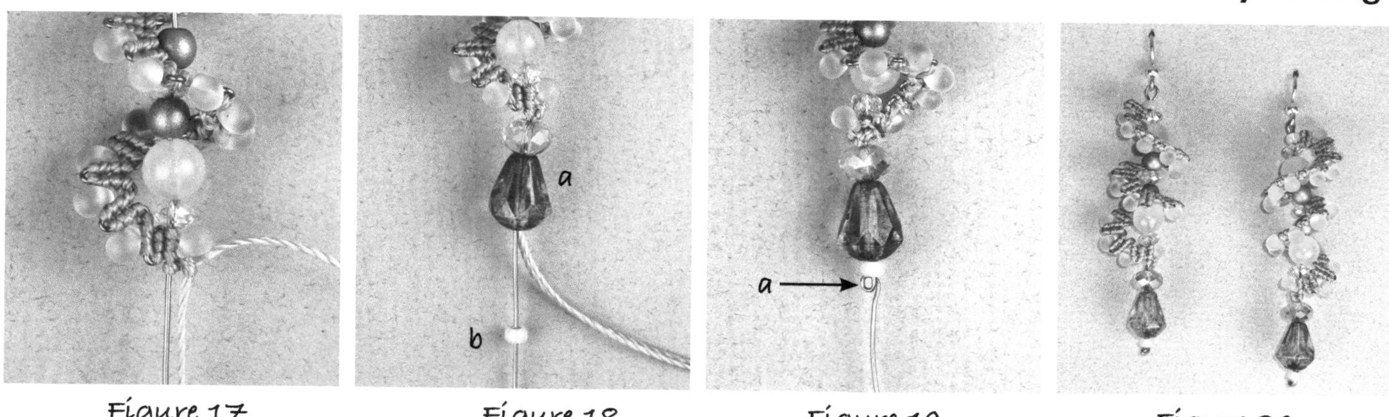

Figure 17 Figure 18 Figure 19 Figure 20

15. Thread a 4mm rondelle or spacer bead followed by a teardrop bead onto the two cords and the wire (see Fig. 18a). Thread a 8° seed bead onto the wire only (see Fig. 18b).

16. Cut off the two cords flush with the bottom of the teardrop bead. Using round or needle nose pliers, make a small tight loop just below the seed bead to hold the bead in place and to finish off the wire end (see Fig. 19a). Trim off the excess wire.

17. Add an ear wire to the top loop (see Fig. 20). See the following instructions for the second earring.

Part 2 - Earring #2 (Leftward Spiral)

18. To make an earring that is a mirror image of the first, the spiral should twist in the opposite (leftward) direction. Follow the directions for Earring #1 but substitute Right for Left and Left for Right in the directions. The pictures below show the progression of the earring. They correspond to Figures 2, 4, 7, 8, 9, 11, 13, and 17 in the Earring #1 directions.

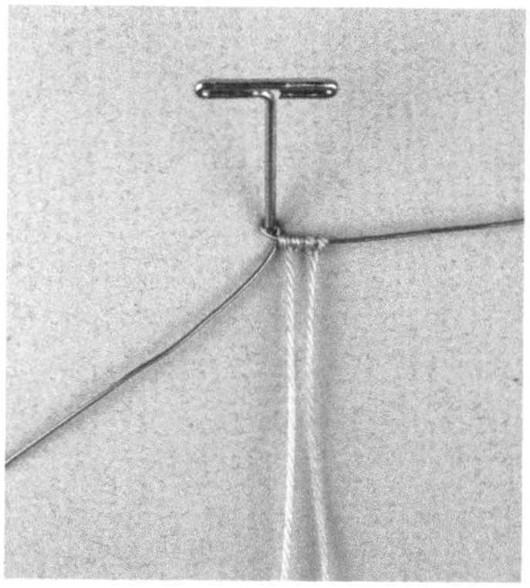

Figure 2 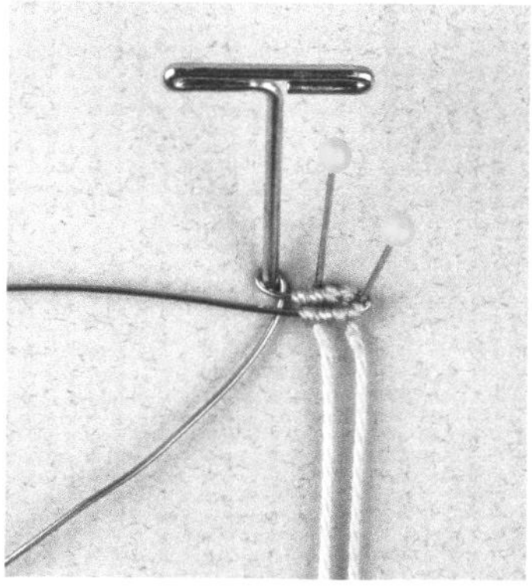 Figure 4 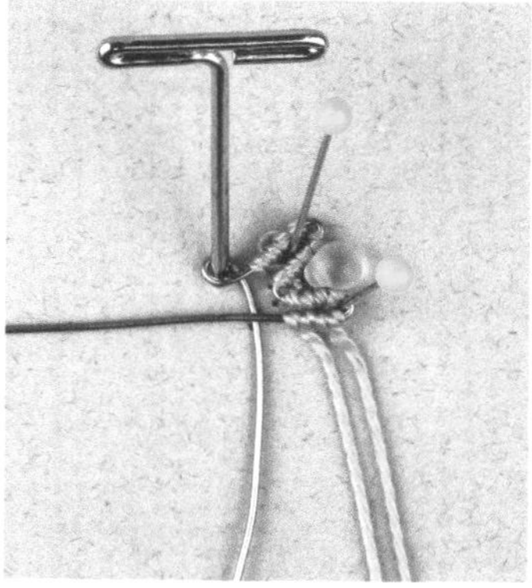 Figure 7 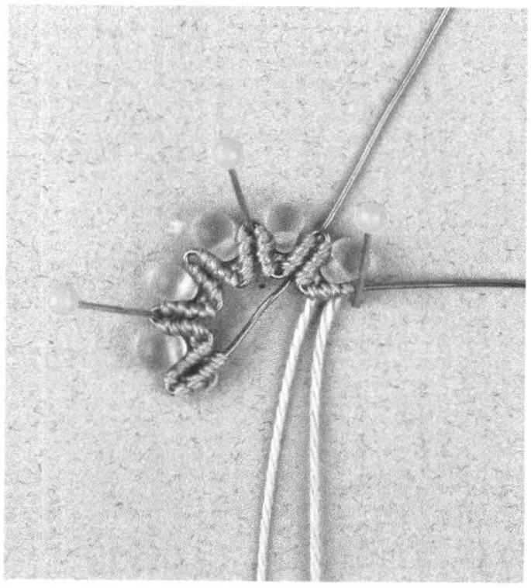 Figure 8

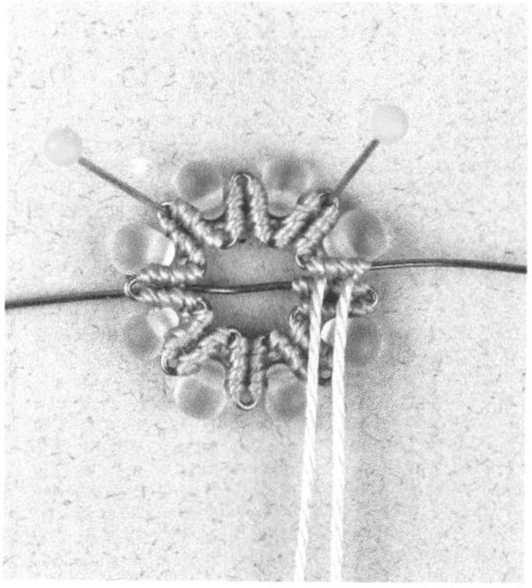

Figure 9 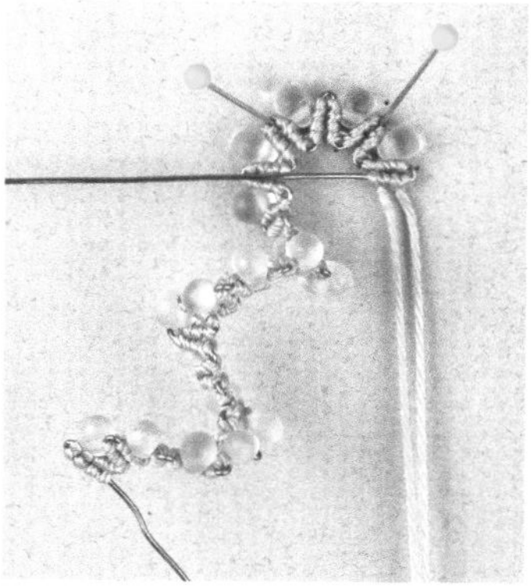 Figure 11 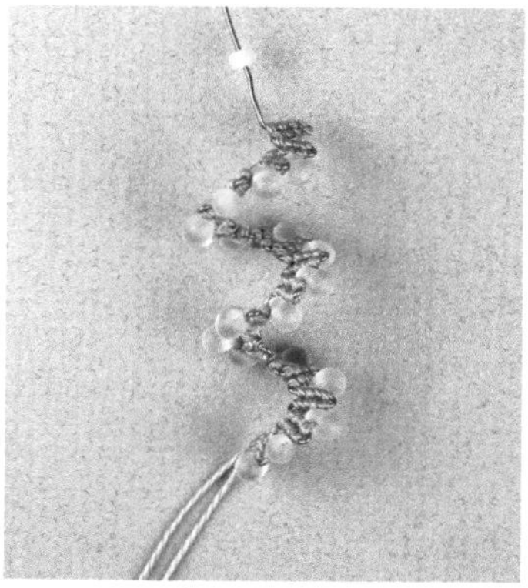 Figure 13  Figure 17

Sundial Earrings

The spiral is an ancient symbol believed to represent the sun, evolution, and the cycle of life. These earrings are a celebration of the sun and the spiral with rays of color emanating from the center outward to the beaded edges.

Materials

Cord:
18g.Nylon Cord :
Anchor Cords -
2 lengths @ 46"(Color-A)
Knotting Cords -
10 lengths @ 28"(Color-A),
20 lengths @ 28" (Color-B)

Beads and Findings:
(2) earring wires
(28) 3.4mm drop/fringe
(30) 10° seed beads

Part I - Knotting the Spiral (Rightward Direction)

1. Place two pins side by side in the board at knotting level. They should be spaced about 3 - 4" apart with the right-hand pin leaning outwards to the right at an angle (see Fig. 1a and b).

2. Fold one 46" **AC** (Anchor Cord) in half and loop it over the right-hand pin. Bring the two cords horizontally to the left and wrap them around the left-hand pin. Tape and pin the ends to hold them securely (see Fig. 1).

3. Fold one 28" (Color-A) cord in half and attach it to the lower **AC** with a **MH** (Mounting Hitch) (see Fig. 2a). Make an **OVK** (Overhand Knot) at the tip of the right-hand vertical cord (Fig. 2b). This is done to differentiate it from all of the other cords. **This knotted cord will be the first cord of each row (or round) in the spiral pattern. I will refer to it as the "starting cord".**

4. To the left of the first **MH**, attach four more 28" Color-A cords to **both** of the **AC**s, treating the two **AC** cords as a single unit (see Fig. 3). They will continue to function as a single unit for the rest of the spiral pattern.

5. Row 1 - Push all of the **MH**s closely together against the right-hand pin. Retighten and neaten them as much as possible. Release the **AC**s from the left-hand pin. Bring the **AC**s upward and around to the right forming a circle with the **MH**s so that the last **MH** meets up next to the first **MH**. Pin in place (see Fig. 4). The cords that radiate from the center will be called **KC**s (Knotting Cords).

6. Row 2 - Make a **DHH** around the **AC**s with the starting cord to secure the circle (see Fig. 5). Continue working in a right to left direction and make 9 more **DHH**s (Double Half Hitches), one with each of the **KC**s, until you get back around to the starting cord (see Fig. 6).

Important - Rotate and repin the piece frequently (after every two or three knots) to always maintain the easiest angle for knotting.

7. Row 3 - Make a **THH** (Triple Half Hitch) with the starting cord and continue making 9 more **THH**s around the circle (see Fig. 7).

8. Row 4 - In this row you will add the 10 Color-B cords in the following way: Make a **DHH** with the starting cord. Attach a Color-B cord to the **AC**s with a **MH** and push it next to the **DHH** (see Fig. 8). Make a **DHH** with the next Color-A cord and attach a Color-B cord next to it with a **MH**. Continue the same pattern until you have attached all 10 cords (see Fig. 9).

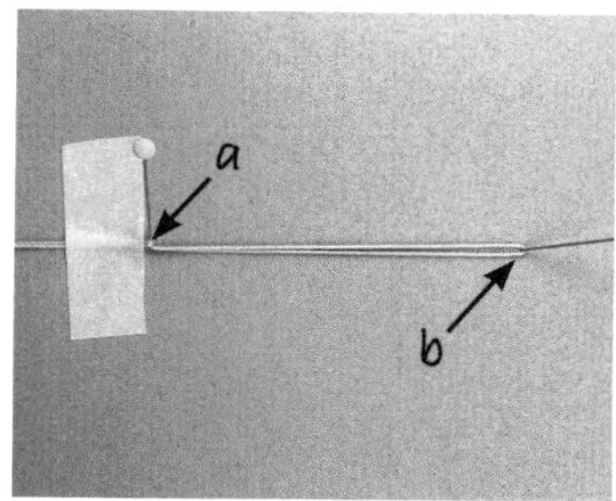

Figure 1

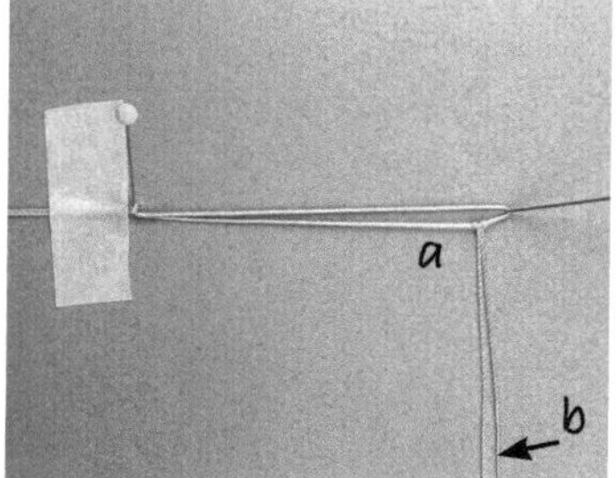

Figure 2

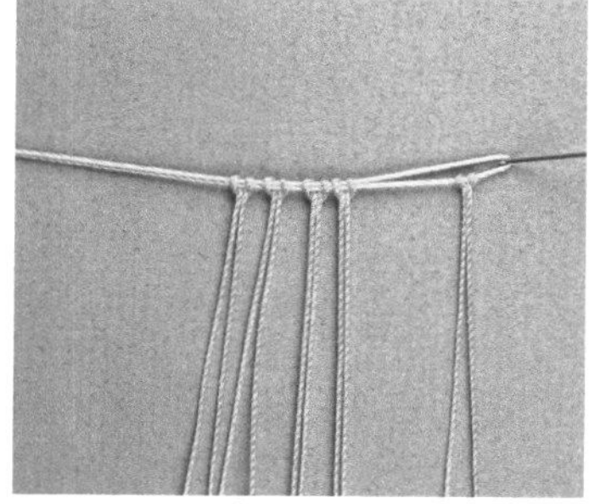
Figure 3

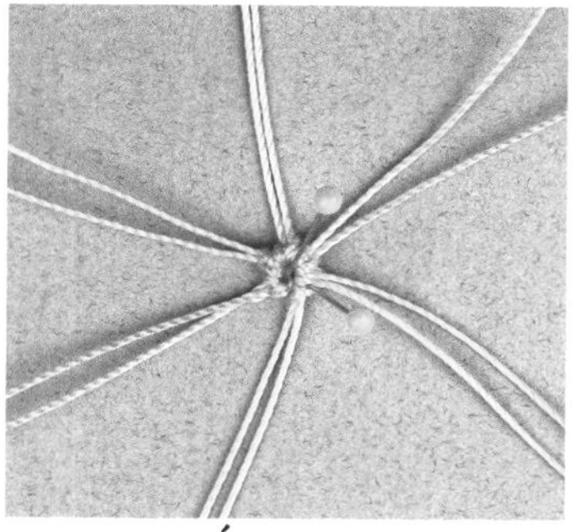
Figure 4

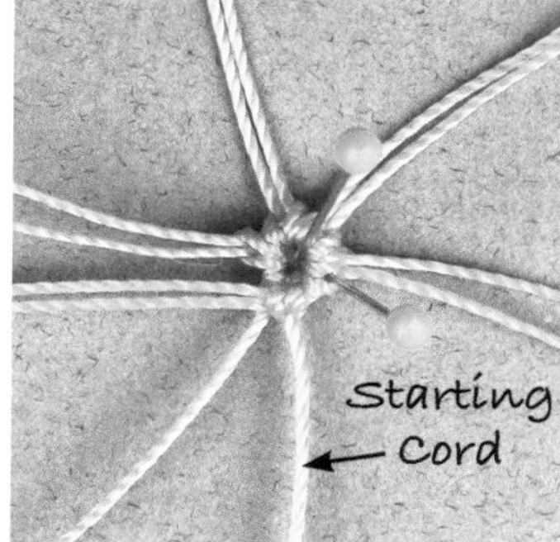

Figure 5

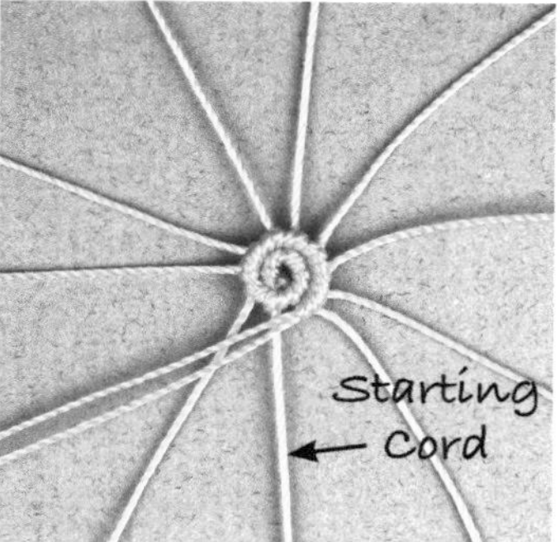

Figure 6

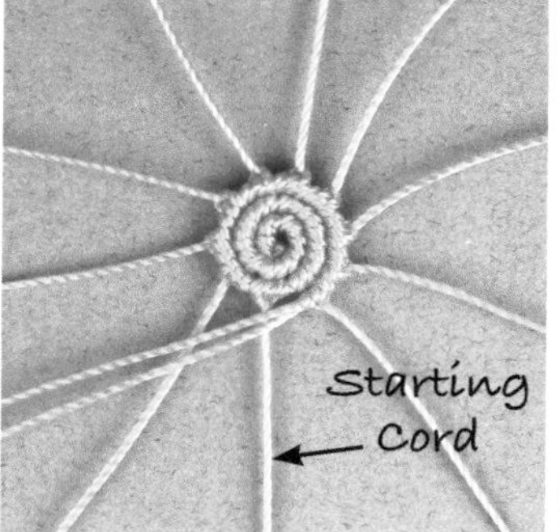

Figure 7

Figure 8

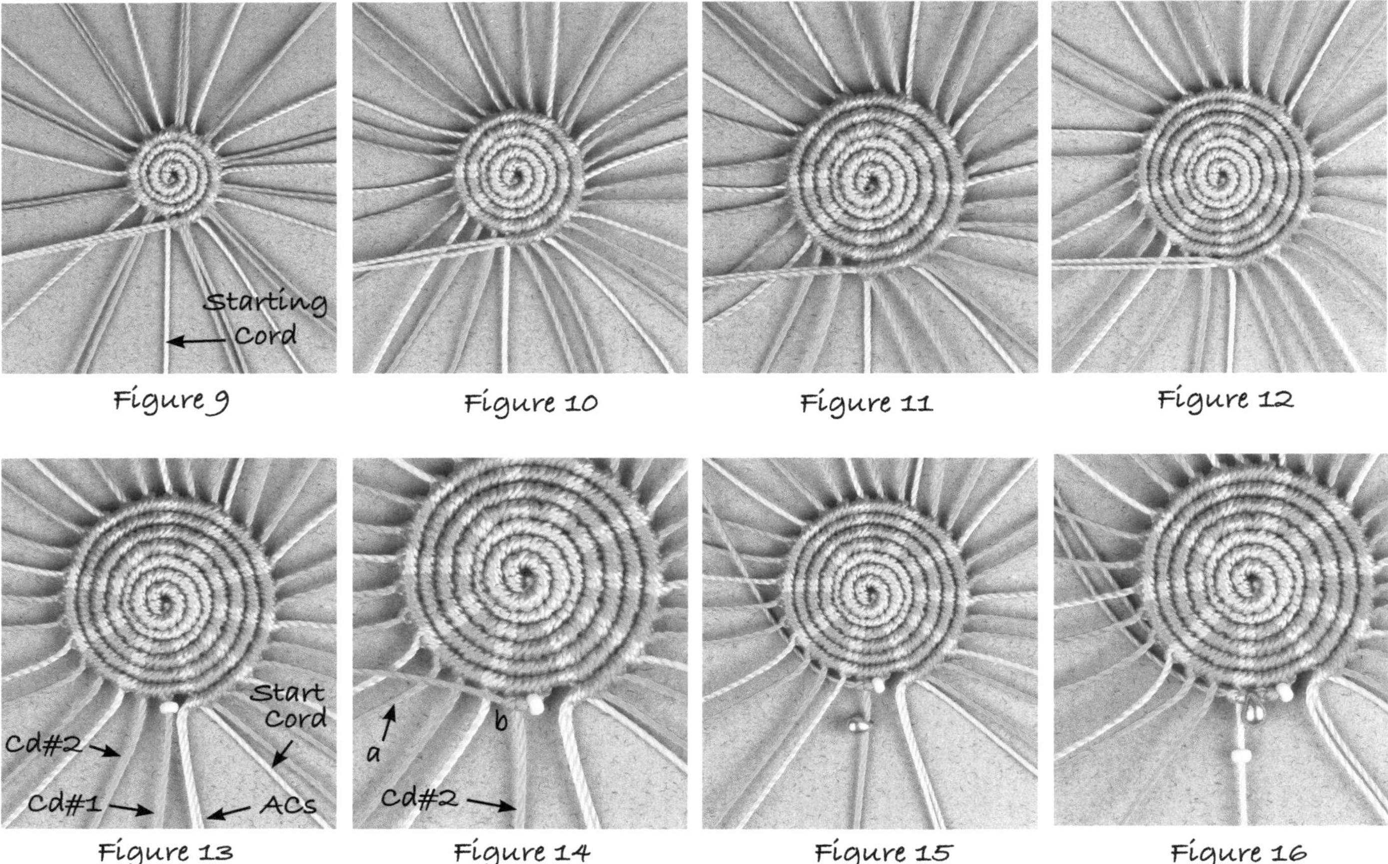

Figure 9 Figure 10 Figure 11 Figure 12

Figure 13 Figure 14 Figure 15 Figure 16

9. Row 5 - Make **DHH**s with all 30 cords (see Fig. 10).

10. Row 6 - The pattern for this row is 1 **DHH**, 2 **THH**s, repeat. (In other words, the Color-A cords will make **DHH**s and the Color-B cords will make **THH**s) (see Fig. 11).

11. Row 7 - Make a **DHH** with the starting cord. Make **THH**s with all other cords. Make one last **DHH** with the starting cord. This completes the spiral pattern (see Fig. 12).

Part 2 - Beaded Edge

12. Position the piece with the **AC**s at the bottom/center. Thread a 10° bead onto the first **KC** to the left of the **AC**s (it will be called Cd #1) and push it up (see Fig. 13). Bring Cd #1 horizontally to the left over Cd #2 and the other **KC**s (see Fig. 14a).

13. Make a tight **DHH** with Cd #2 around Cd #1, pulling Cd #1 as close as possible to the edge of the knotting (see Fig. 14b). Bring Cd #1 behind the remaining **KC**s and out of the way - it will no longer be used (see Fig. 15).

14. Thread a drop bead onto Cd #2 and push it up (see Fig. 15). Bring Cd #2 horizontally to the left over Cd #3.

15. Make a tight **DHH** with Cd #3 around Cd #2 pulling Cd #2 as close as possible to the edge of the knotting (see Fig. 16). Bring Cd #2 behind the remaining **KC**s and out of the way, it will no longer be used.

16. Continue working your way around the circle adding beads to the edge following the same pattern. The last bead added will be a 10° bead (see Fig. 17).

17. Tie the final two **KC**s and the two **AC**s together with a loose temporary **OVK** to separate them from the rest of the cords (see Fig. 18a).

18. Flip the piece to the back. Pull all of the rest of the **KC**s toward the center and cut each of them off close to the edge (see Fig. 18b).

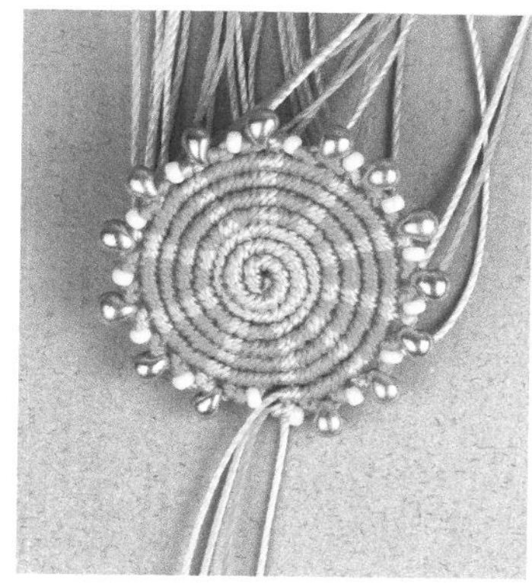

Figure 17

Part 3 - Top Loop

19. Position the piece with the **AC**s to the right and pin in place. Bring the two **KC**s behind the **AC**s and make a **DHH** with each one around the **AC**s (see Fig. 19). Bring both of the **KC**s to the back of the piece.

20. Reposition the piece with the two **AC**s at the bottom and pin in place. Using the leftmost cord as the **KC**, make a chain of (10) **LHK**s (Larks Head Knots). These should be made in a left to right direction (see Fig. 20).

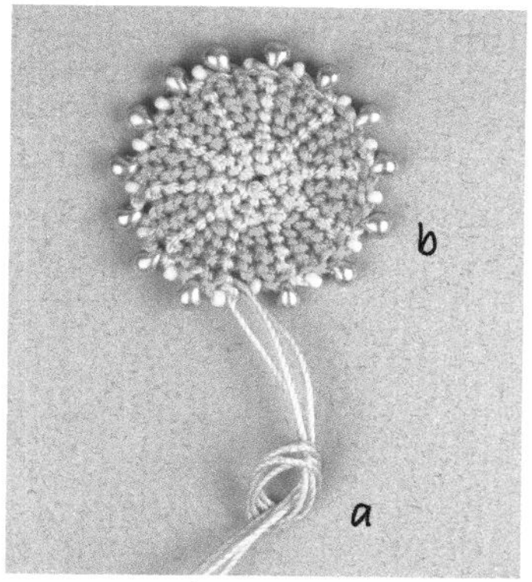

Figure 18

21. Unpin the piece from the board and hold it with the **LHK** chain at the top. Bring the **LHK** chain around to the left and form it into a loop (see Fig. 21). Sew the cords of the **LHK** chain (one at a time) from front to back through the space between the **DHH**s at the base of the chain and pull through.

22. Flip the piece to the back. Untwist each of the 4 cords (the 2 **AC**s and 2 **KC**s) and separate out one ply from each. Tie the 4 one-ply threads together with an **OVK** (see Fig. 22). Carefully cut off the remaining 2-ply segments of each cord (see Fig. 23).

23. Apply clear nail polish to the **OVK**. Let dry and cut off all the cords close below the **OVK** (not shown).

24. Attach an earring wire to the top loop (see front photo).

Part 4 - Knotting the Spiral (Leftward Direction)

25. The other earring is made with the spiral going in the opposite direction. Follow the directions in Parts 1 - 3 but substitute Left for Right and Right for Left in the directions.

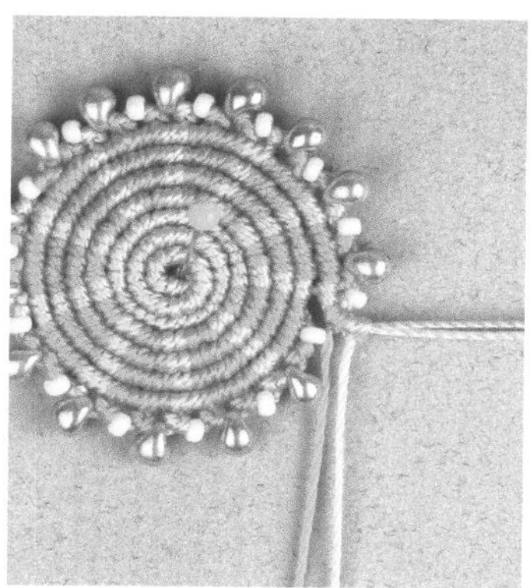

Figure 19

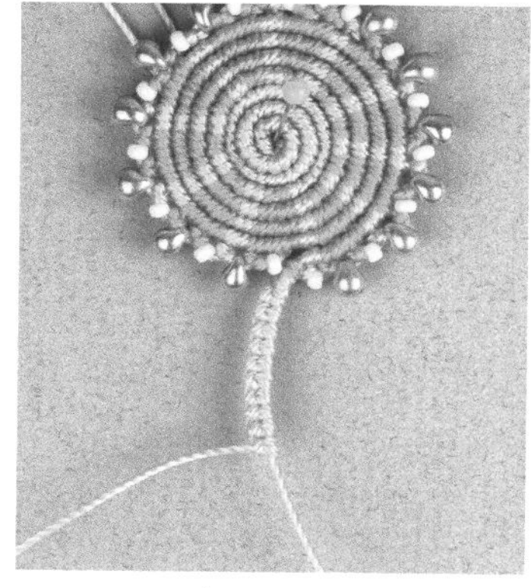

Figure 20

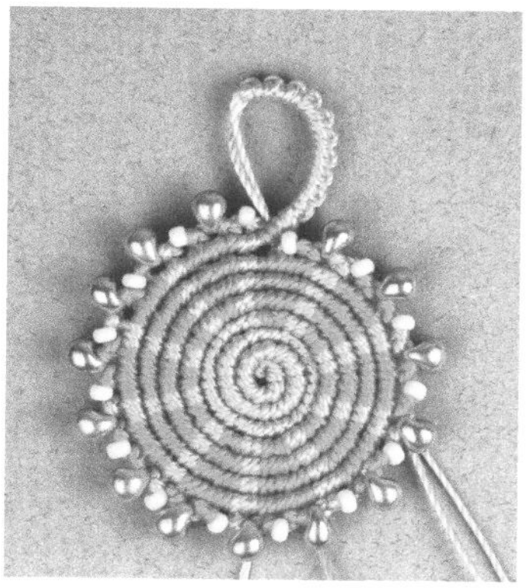

Figure 21

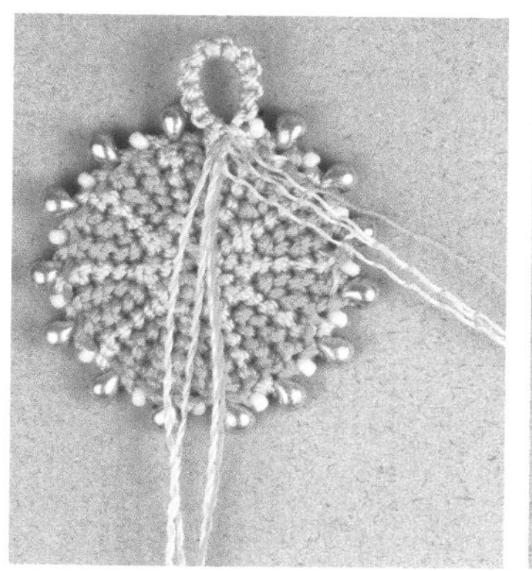

Figure 22

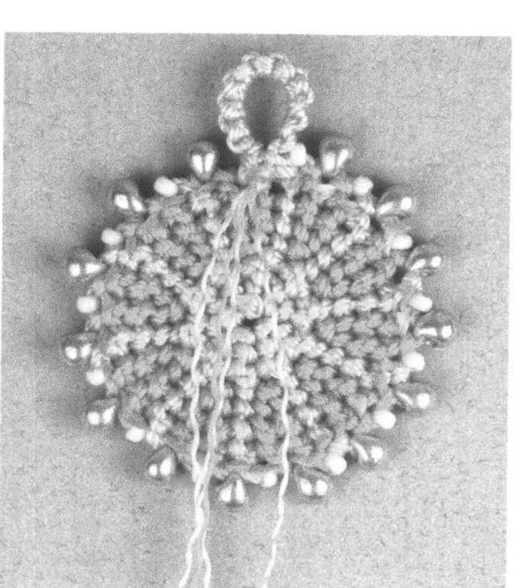

Figure 23

Big Zig Bracelet

A fresh version of the popular zig-zag style bracelet, The Big Zig features a wider width and a bold geometrical design. Choose your favorite colors and get knotting!

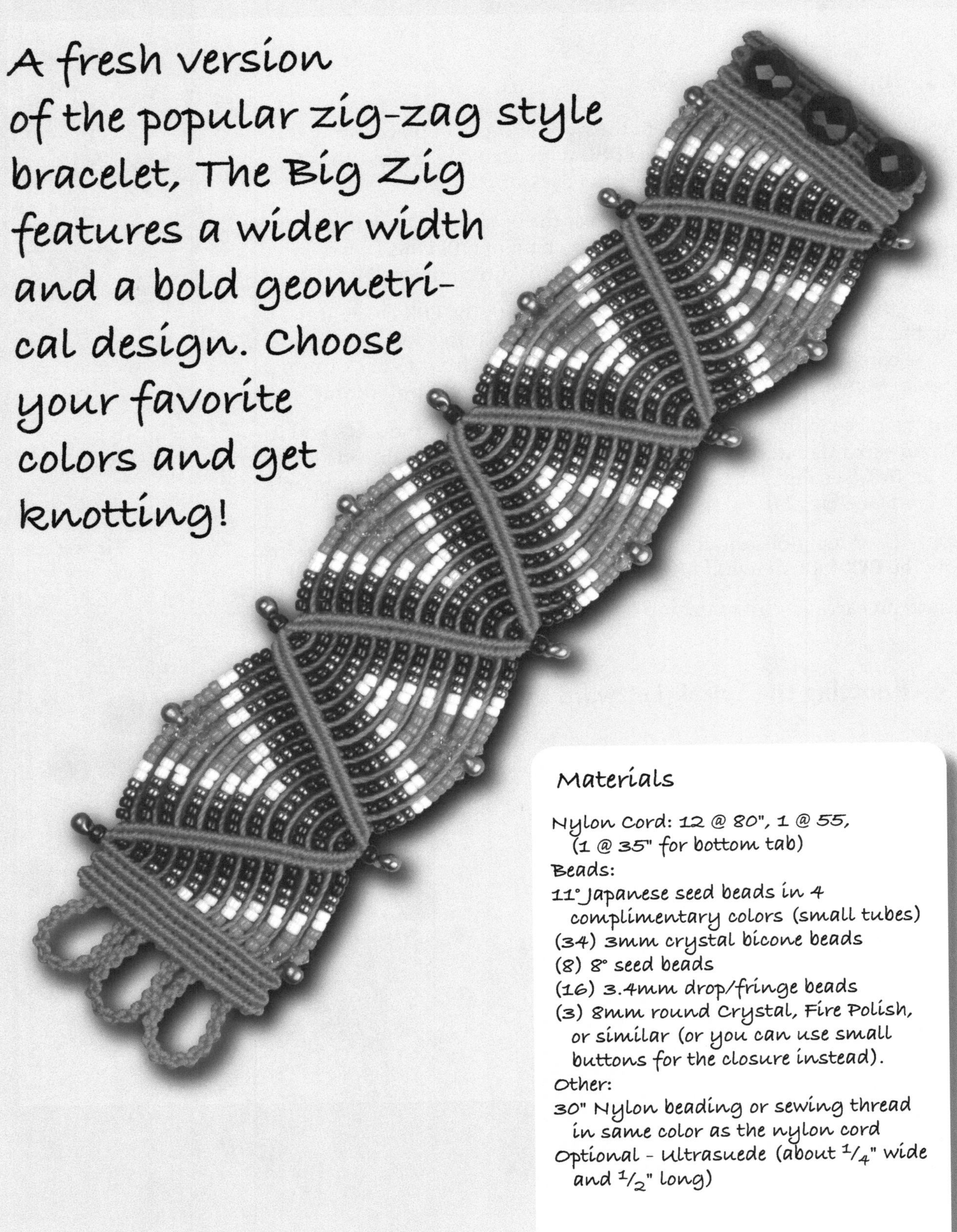

Materials

Nylon Cord: 12 @ 80", 1 @ 55, (1 @ 35" for bottom tab)

Beads:

11° Japanese seed beads in 4 complimentary colors (small tubes)

(34) 3mm crystal bicone beads

(8) 8° seed beads

(16) 3.4mm drop/fringe beads

(3) 8mm round Crystal, Fire Polish, or similar (or you can use small buttons for the closure instead).

Other:

30" Nylon beading or sewing thread in same color as the nylon cord

Optional - Ultrasuede (about 1/4" wide and 1/2" long)

Part 1 - The Top Tab

1. Place a pin in your board (about ⅓ down from the top) and angle it slightly upwards. Bring together 2 of the 80" cords so that they are parallel and the ends are even. Measure 38" from one end and at that point, wrap the cords together once around the pin, positioning the cords vertically on the board so that the 38" lengths are facing upward above the pin and the 42" lengths face downward below the pin. Tape the cords securely above the pin to keep them from slipping (see Fig. 1).

2. Make an **AHHch** (Alternating Half Hitch Chain) of 20 Half Hitches (see Fig. 2). Unpin and remove the chain from the board. Check the fit of the chain around the widest part of the 8mm bead (or button) that you are using for the closure. The fit should be very snug (especially if you are using round beads). You may have to add or delete **HH**s from the chains. Repeat (Steps #1 and 2) twice so that you have three identical chain segments which will be used to make the three loops on the top tab.

3. Place two pins in the board about 3 - 4" apart horizontally and angle them slightly upwards. Take the 55" cord and about 4" from the cord end, wrap it once around the left-hand pin. Bring the longer part of the cord to the right horizontally and wrap it once around the right-hand pin. Tape the cord down securely on the outsides of each pin so that the cord doesn't slip (pin too if necessary). This creates a temporary "bar" on which you will attach the other cords (see Fig. 3). This cord will act as the **AC** (Anchor Cord) for the top tab.

4. Pin the three **AHHch** loops to the board just above the **AC** "bar", positioning the hanging cords behind the bar. The ends of the chains should be even with the top of the bar.

5. Attach each of the chain's hanging cords to the bar using **DHH**s (Double Half Hitches) (see Fig. 4). Check the size of the loop around the bead once again to make sure it's correct and not too loose.

6. Fold the first of the five remaining 80" cords in half and attach it to the bar with a **MTK** (Mounting Knot). Position it between the left-hand pin and the first loop (see Fig. 5a).

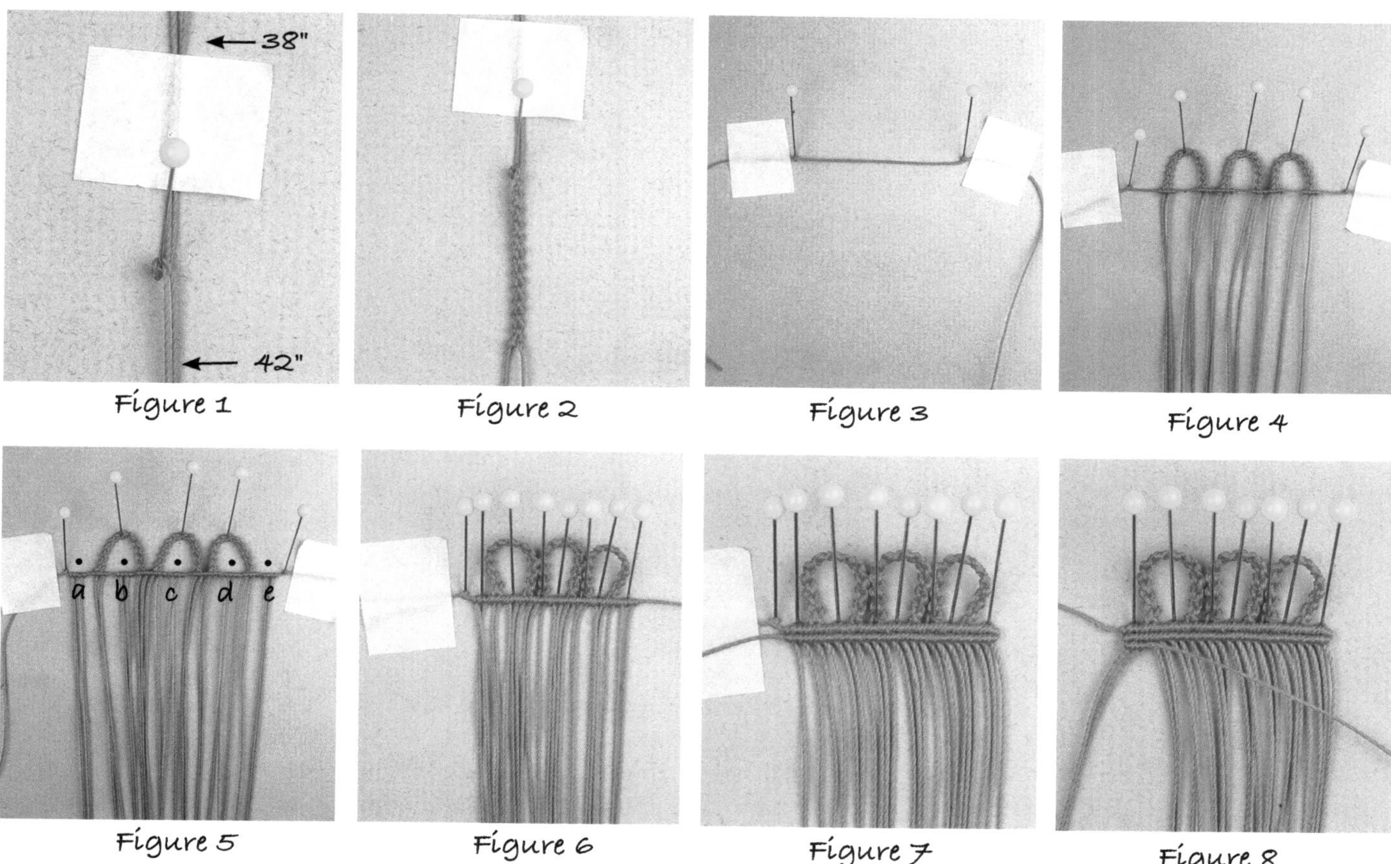

Figure 1 Figure 2 Figure 3 Figure 4

Figure 5 Figure 6 Figure 7 Figure 8

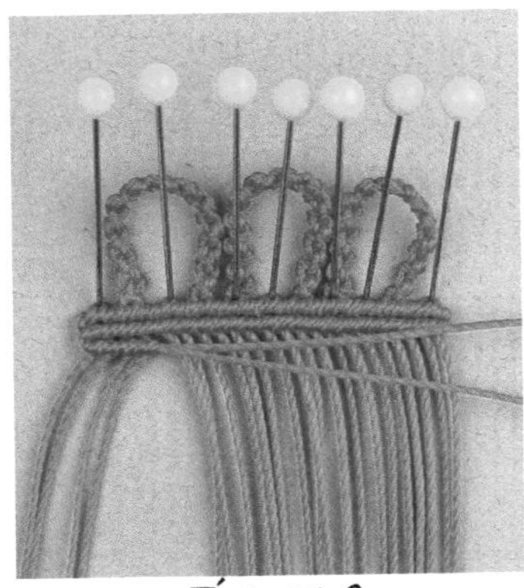
Figure 9

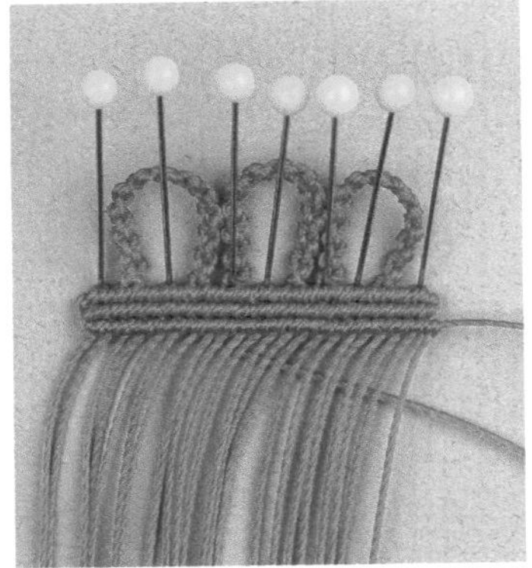
Figure 10

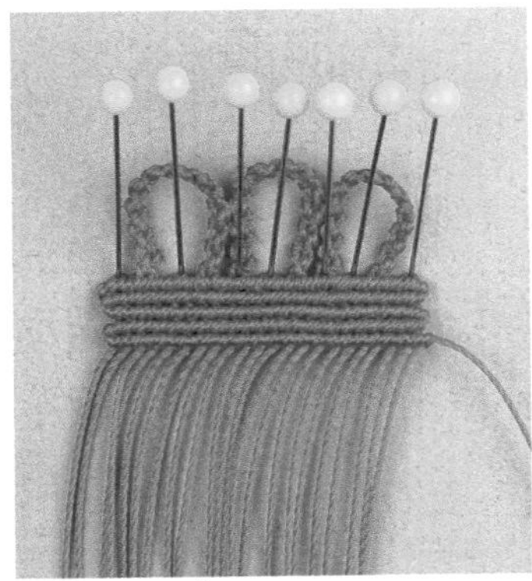
Figure 11

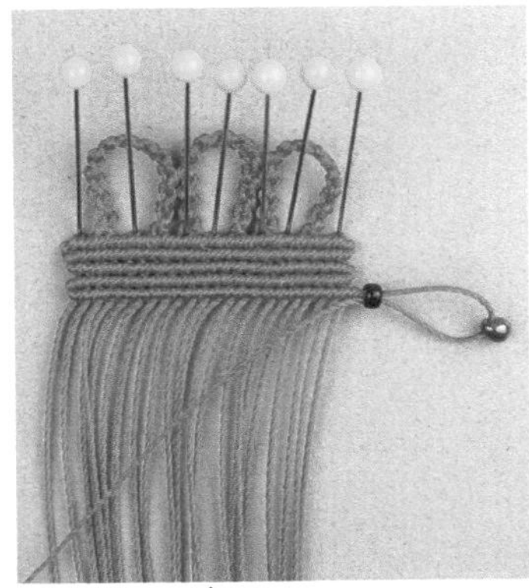
Figure 12

7. Attach the next cord to the bar with a **MTK**, positioning it in the center (in between the two ends) of the first loop (see Fig. 5b).

8. Attach the next cord to the bar with a **MTK**, positioning it in the center of the second loop. Attach the next cord to the bar with a **MTK**, positioning it in the center of the third loop (see Fig. 5c and d).

9. Attach the last cord to the bar with a **MTK**, positioning it to the right of the third loop (see Fig. 5e).

10. Unpin the loops and push all of the cords to the left closely together against the left-hand pin. Retighten and neaten the knots if necessary. They should form a neat horizontal row about 1 ⅜" (or 35mm) wide. Pin the knots in place (see Fig. 6).

- There are 22 warp (hanging) cords to work with. I will refer to each one as Cd. (Cord) #1 - 22 according to it's position from left to right. Cords can change position (and therefore number) from row to row.

11. Release the **AC** from the right-hand pin and bring it to the left horizontally. Make a row of **DHH**s working from right to left (see Fig. 7).

12. Bring the **AC** back around to the right and make **DHH**s with Cd #1 and Cd #2 only (see Fig. 8).

13. Release the short 4" tail of **AC** from the left-hand pin and bring it to the right underneath Cds #1 and 2. Bring it out to the front over Cd #3. It should be parallel with the longer **AC**. Make tight **DHH**s around the two **AC**s (treating them as a single unit) with Cds #3 and 4 (see Fig. 9).

14. Bring the 4" cord to the back again behind the remaining warp cords. Continue making **DHH**s across the rest of the row using only the longer **AC** (see Fig. 10). Trim off the 4" cord at the back of the tab.

15. Bring the **AC** back around to the left and make a row of **DHH**s. Bring the **AC** back around to the right and make a row of **DHH**s (see Fig. 11). Now is the time to add more rows if you want a longer bracelet. The pattern is for a 7" bracelet. Each addition pair of rows will add ⅛". You can add rows here and also on the bottom tab if desired.

Part 2 - The Beaded Pattern

Note - Most Japanese seed beads are fairly uniform in size, however it is possible that some will be slightly shorter or longer than normal. Be aware that there may be size differences which may distort the bead pattern (for instance, too many short beads or too many long beads on one strand). Occasionally it may be necessary to adjust the pattern slightly by using some shorter or longer beads.

Top Half-Wedge

16. Thread an 8° bead and a 3.4mm fringe bead onto the **AC**, leaving the fringe bead about ½" from the 8° bead. Bring the **AC** back around to the left and pass it through the 8° bead again, pulling the cord out to the left (see Fig. 12). Pull the **AC** snugly around the fringe bead so that it sits up against the 8° bead (see Fig. 13).

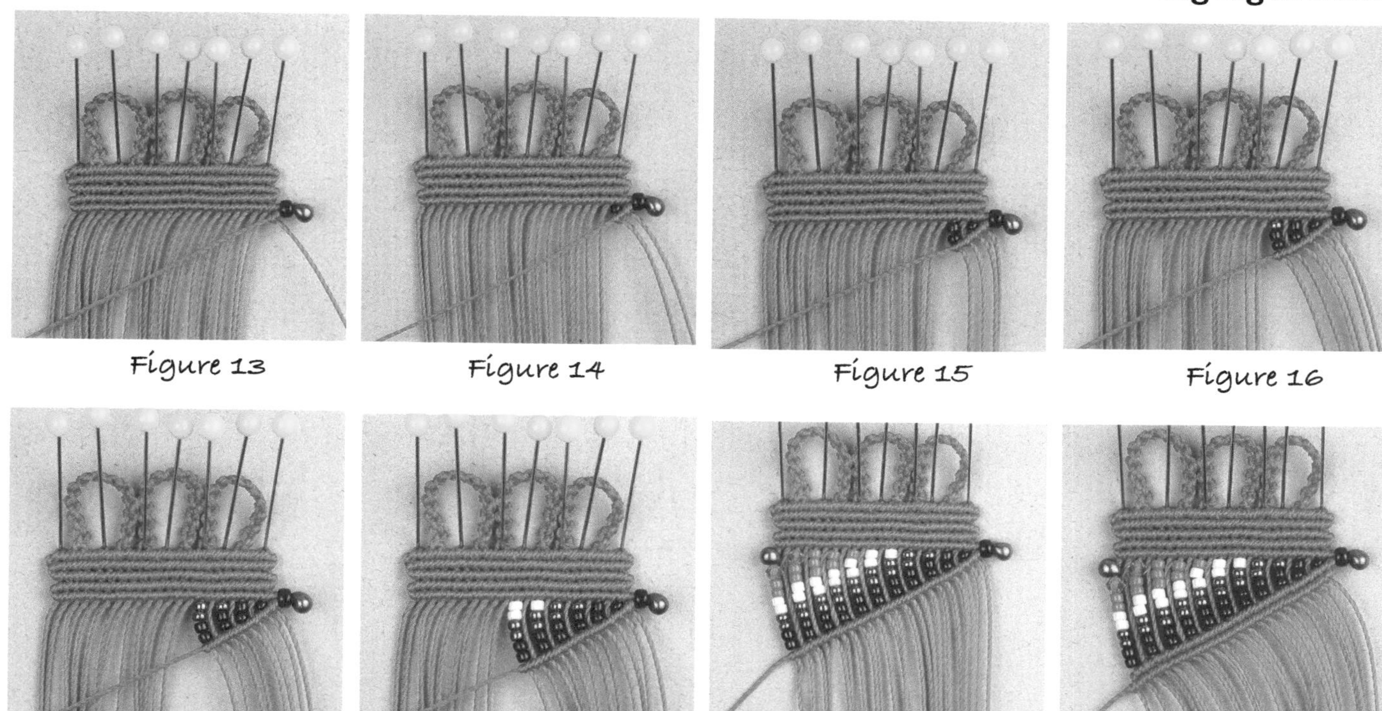
Figure 13 Figure 14 Figure 15 Figure 16

Figure 17 Figure 18 Figure 19 Figure 20

17. Make a **DHH** around the **AC** with Cd #22 (see Fig. 13) **Note - each cord will be attached to the AC with a Double Half Hitch**. Thread a black 11° seed bead onto Cd #21 and attach it to the **AC** (see Fig. 14).

18. Attach Cd #20 to the **AC**. There will be no beads on Cords #20, 18, 16, 14, 12, 10, 8, 6, 4, and 2. Thread (2) black 11° seed beads onto Cd #19 and attach it to the **AC** (see Fig. 15).

19. Attach Cd #18 to the **AC**. Thread (1) bronze and (2) black 11° seed beads onto Cd #17 and attach it to the **AC** (see Fig. 16).

20. Attach Cd #16 to the **AC**. Thread (2) bronze and (2) black 11° seed beads onto Cd #15 and attach it to the **AC** (see Fig. 17).

21. Attach Cd #14 to the **AC**. Thread (1) white, (2) bronze, and (2) black 11° seed beads onto Cd #13 and attach it to the **AC** (see Fig. 18). **Note - the pictures may illustrate more than one Step.**

22. Attach Cd #12 to the **AC**. Thread (2) white, (2) bronze, and (2) black 11° seed beads onto Cd #11 and attach it to the **AC** (see Fig. 18).

23. Attach Cd #10 to the **AC**. Thread (1) red, (2) white, (2) bronze, and (2) black 11° seed beads onto Cd #9 and attach it to the **AC** (see Fig. 19).

24. Attach Cd #8 to the **AC**. Thread (2) red, (2) white, (2) bronze, and (2) black 11° seed beads onto Cd #7 and attach it to the **AC** (see Fig. 19).

25. Attach Cd #6 to the **AC**. Thread (3) red, (2) white, (2) bronze, and (2) black 11° seed beads onto Cd #5 and attach it to the **AC** (see Fig. 19).

26. Attach Cd #4 to the **AC**. Thread (1) 3mm bicone bead, (2) red, (2) white, (2) bronze, and (2) black 11° seed beads onto Cd #3 and attach it to the **AC** (see Fig. 19).

27. Attach Cd #2 to the **AC**. Thread (1) 3.4mm fringe bead, (1) 3mm bicone bead, (2) red, (2) white, (2) bronze, and (2) black 11° seed beads onto Cd #1 and attach it to the **AC** (see Fig. 19).

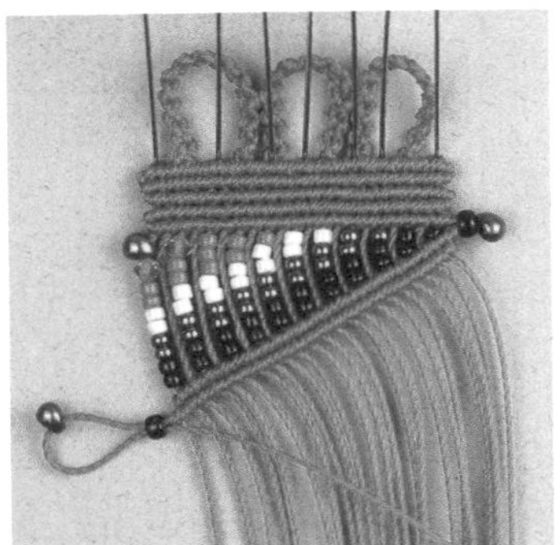

Figure 21

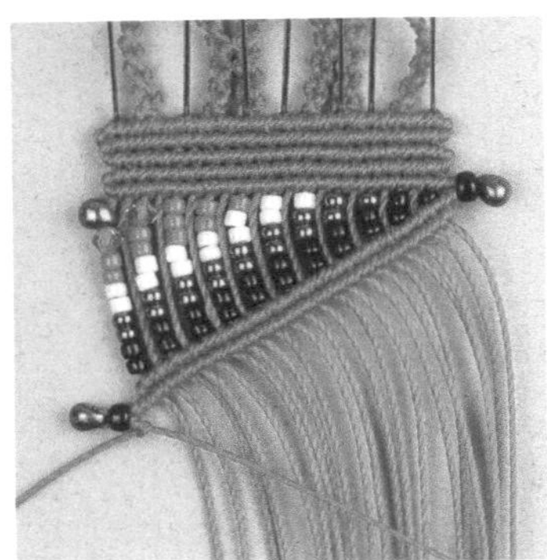

Figure 22

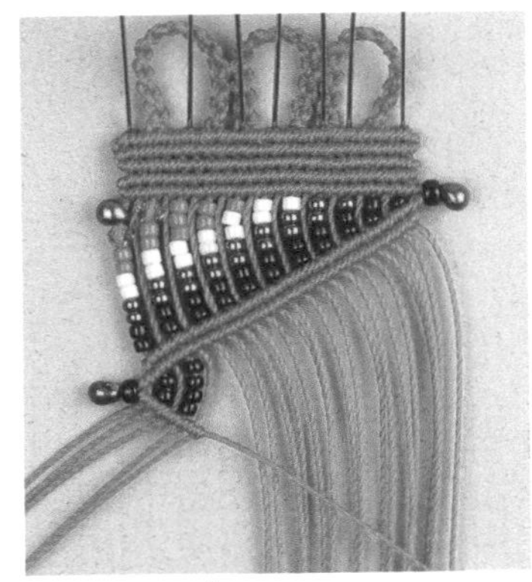

Figure 23

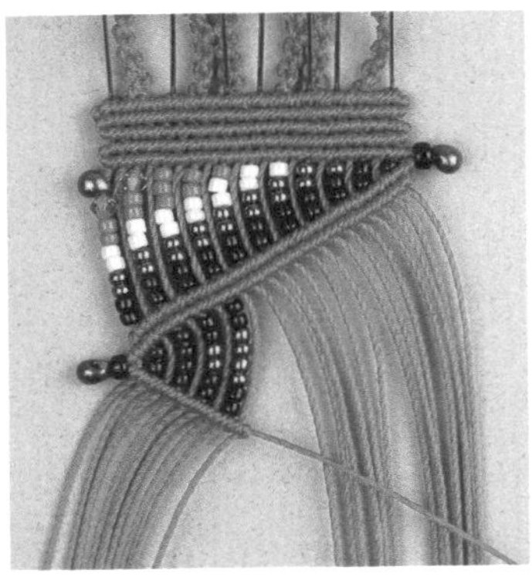

Figure 24

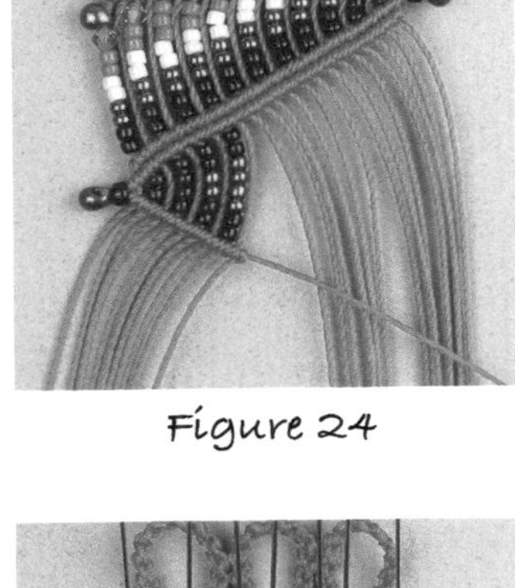

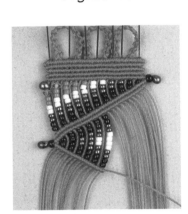

Figure 25

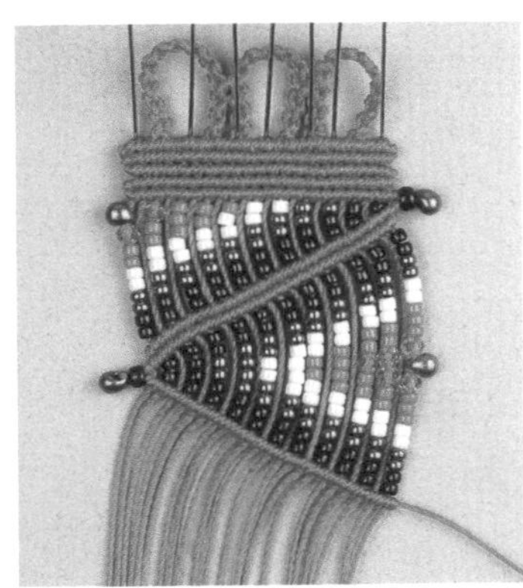

Figure 26

28. Bring Cd #22 diagonally to the left and using it as an **AC**, make a row of **DHH**s working from right to left. The **AC** from the previous row will be knotted into this row as the last **DHH** (see Fig. 20).

Right-facing Wedge

29. Thread an 8° bead and a 3.4mm fringe bead onto the **AC**, leaving the fringe bead about $\frac{1}{2}$" from the 8° bead. Bring the **AC** back around to the right and pass it through the 8° bead again, pulling the cord out to the right (see Fig. 21). Pull the **AC** snugly around the fringe bead so that it sits up against the 8° bead (see Fig. 22).

30. Make a **DHH** around the **AC** with Cd #1 (see Fig. 22) There will be no beads on Cords #1, 3, 5, 7, 9, 11, 13, 15, 17, 19 and 21.

31. Thread (2) black seed beads onto Cd #2 and attach it to the **AC**. Attach Cd #3 to the **AC**. Thread (4) black seed beads onto Cd #4 and attach it to the **AC**. Attach Cd #5 to the **AC** (see Fig. 23).

32. Thread (2) black, (2) bronze, and (2) black seed beads onto Cd #6 and attach it to the **AC**. Attach Cd #7 to the **AC** (see Fig. 24).

33. Thread (2) black, (4) bronze and (2) black seed beads onto Cd #8 and attach it to the **AC**. Attach Cd #9 to the **AC** (see Fig. 24).

34. Thread (2) black, (2) bronze, (2) white, (2) bronze, and (2) black seed beads onto Cd #10 and attach it to the **AC**. Attach Cd #11 to the **AC** (see Fig. 25)

35. Thread (2) black, (2) bronze, (4) white, (2) bronze, and (2) black seed beads onto Cd #12 and attach it to the **AC** (see Fig. 25). Attach Cd #13 to the **AC**.

36. Thread (2) black, (2) bronze, (2) white, (2) red, (2) white, (2) bronze, and (2) black seed beads onto Cd #14 and attach it to the **AC**. Attach Cd #15 to the **AC** (see Fig. 26 for Steps #36 - 40).

37. Thread (2) black, (2) bronze, (2) white, (4) red, (2) white, (2) bronze, and (2) black seed beads onto Cd #16 and attach it to the **AC**. Attach Cd #17 to the **AC**.

38. Thread (2) black, (2) bronze, (2) white, (2) red, (1) 3mm bicone, (2) red, (2) white, (2) bronze, and (2) black seed beads onto Cd #18 and attach it to the **AC**. Attach Cd #19 to the **AC**.

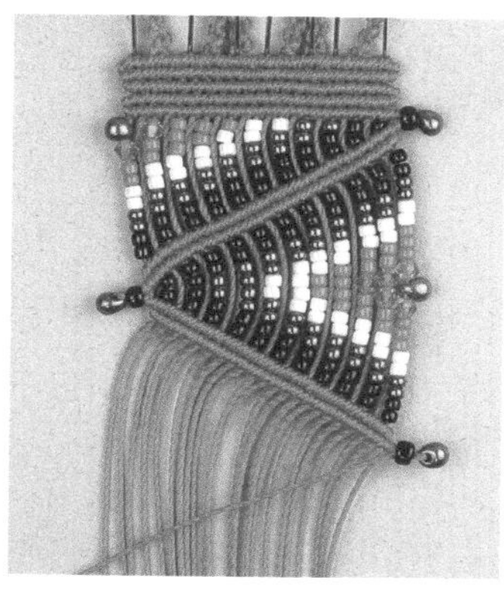
Figure 27

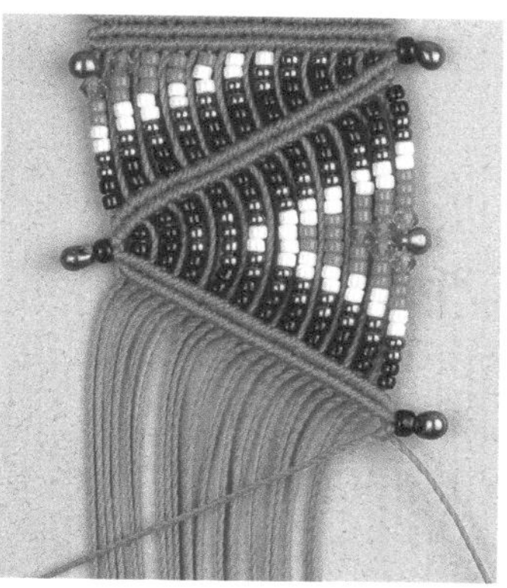
Figure 28

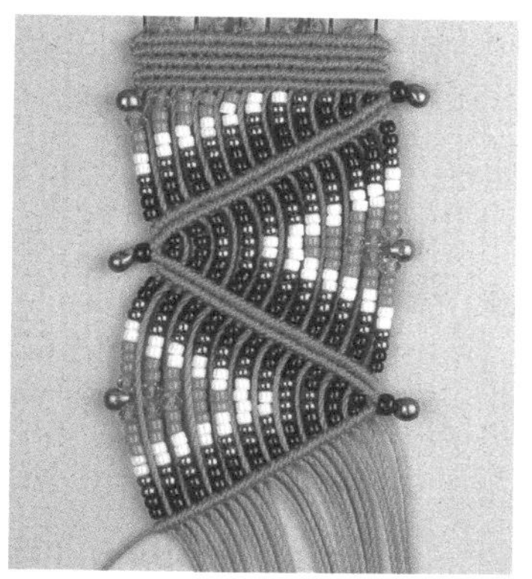
Figure 29

39. Thread (2) black, (2) bronze, (2) white, (2) red, (2) 3mm bicones, (2) red, (2) white, (2) bronze, and (2) black seed beads onto Cd #20 and attach it to the **AC**. Attach Cd #21 to the **AC**.

40. Thread (2) black, (2) bronze, (2) white, (3) red, (1) 3mm bicone, (1) fringe bead, (1) 3mm bicone, (3) red, (2) white, (2) bronze, and (2) black seed beads onto Cd #22 and attach it to the **AC**.

41. Bring Cd #1 diagonally to the right and using it as the **AC**, make a row of **DHH**s working from left to right. The **AC** from the previous row will be knotted into this row as the last **DHH** (see Figure 27).

Left-facing Wedge

42. Thread an 8° bead and a 3.4mm fringe bead onto the **AC**, leaving the fringe bead about ½" from the 8° bead. Bring the **AC** back around to the left and pass it through the 8° bead again, pulling the cord out to the left. Pull the **AC** snugly around the fringe bead so that it sits up against the 8° bead (see Figure 27).

43. Make a **DHH** around the **AC** with Cd #22 (see Figure 28). There will be no beads on Cords #22, 20, 18, 16, 14, 12, 10, 8, 6, 4, and 2.

44. Thread (2) black seed beads onto Cd #21 and attach it to the **AC**. Attach Cd #20 to the **AC** (see Figure 29 for the left-facing wedge, Steps #43 - 54).

45. Thread (4) black seed beads onto Cd #19 and attach it to the **AC**. Attach Cd #18 to the **AC**.

46. Thread (2) black, (2) bronze, and (2) black seed beads onto Cd #17 and attach it to the **AC**. Attach Cd #16 to the **AC**.

47. Thread (2) black, (4) bronze and (2) black seed beads onto Cd #15 and attach it to the **AC**. Attach Cd #14 to the **AC**.

48. Thread (2) black, (2) bronze, (2) white, (2) bronze, and (2) black seed beads onto Cd #13 and attach it to the **AC**. Attach Cd #12 to the **AC**.

49. Thread (2) black, (2) bronze, (4) white, (2) bronze, and (2) black seed beads onto Cd #11 and attach it to the **AC**. Attach Cd #10 to the **AC**.

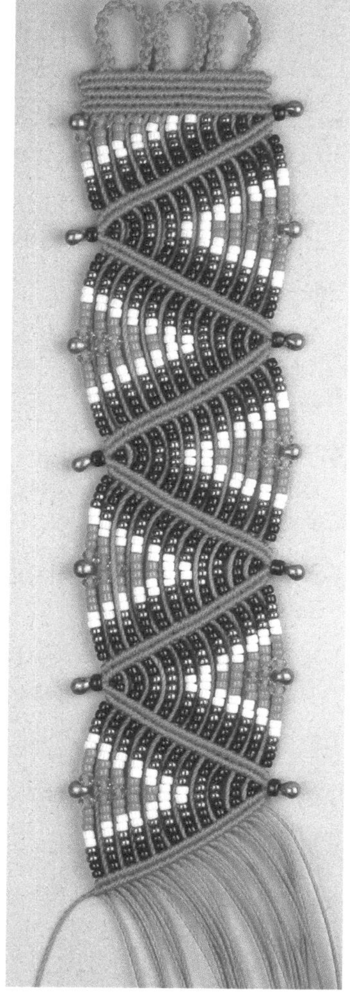
Figure 30

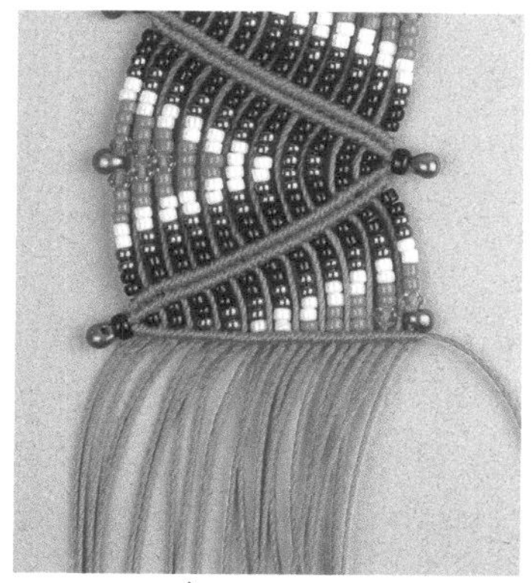
Figure 31

50. Thread (2) black, (2) bronze, (2) white, (2) red, (2) white, (2) bronze, and (2) black beads onto Cd #9 and attach it to the **AC**. Attach Cd #8 to the **AC**.

51. Thread (2) black, (2) bronze, (2) white, (4) red, (2) white, (2) bronze, and (2) black seed beads onto Cd #7 and attach it to the **AC**. Attach Cd#6 to the **AC**.

52. Thread (2) black, (2) bronze, (2) white, (2) red, (1) 3mm bicone, (2) red, (2) white, (2) bronze, and (2) black seed beads onto Cd #5 and attach it to the **AC**. Attach Cd #4 to the **AC**.

53. Thread (2) black, (2) bronze, (2) white, (2) red, (2) 3mm bicones, (2) red, (2) white, (2) bronze, and (2) black seed beads onto Cd #3 and attach it to the **AC**. Attach Cd #2 to the **AC**.

54. Thread (2) black, (2) bronze, (2) white, (3) red, (1) 3mm bicone, (1) fringe bead, (1) 3mm bicone, (3) red, (2) white, (2) bronze, and (2) black seed beads onto Cd #1 and attach it to the **AC**.

55. Bring Cd #22 diagonally to the left and using it as the **AC**, make a row of **DHH**s working from right to left. The **AC** from the previous row will be knotted into this row as the last **DHH**.

56. Repeat Steps #29 - 55 twice, making 4 more "wedge" segments (see Figure 30).

Bottom Half-Wedge

57. Thread an 8° bead and a 3.4mm fringe bead onto the **AC**, leaving the fringe bead about ½" from the 8° bead. Bring the **AC** back around to the right and pass it through the 8° bead again, bringing it out to the right. Pull the **AC** snugly around the fringe bead so that it sits up against the 8° bead.

58. Bring the **AC** to the right horizontally. Make a **DHH** around the **AC** with Cd #1. There will be no beads on Cords #1, 3, 5, 7, 9, 11, 13, 15, 17, 19 and 21.

59. Thread (1) black seed bead onto Cd #2 and attach it to the **AC**. Attach Cd #3 to the **AC** (see Figure 31 for the bottom half-wedge).

60. Thread (2) black seed beads onto Cd #4 and attach it to the **AC**. Attach Cd #5 to the **AC**.

61. Thread (2) black and (1) bronze seed beads onto Cd #6 and attach it to the **AC**. Attach Cd #7 to the **AC**.

62. Thread (2) black and (2) bronze seed beads onto Cd #8 and attach it to the **AC**. Attach Cd #9 to the **AC**.

63. Thread (2) black, (2) bronze, and (1) white seed beads onto Cd #10 and attach it to the **AC**. Attach Cd #11 to the **AC**.

64. Thread (2) black, (2) bronze, and (2) white seed beads onto Cd #12 and attach it to the **AC**. Attach Cd #13 to the **AC**.

65. Thread (2) black, (2) bronze, (2) white, and (1) red seed beads onto Cd #14 and attach it to the **AC**. Attach Cd #15 to the **AC** with a **DHH**.

66. Thread (2) black, (2) bronze, (2) white, and (2) red seed beads onto Cd #16 and attach it to the **AC**. Attach Cd #17 to the **AC**.

67. Thread (2) black, (2) bronze, (2) white, and (3) red seed beads onto Cd #18 and attach it to the **AC**. Attach Cd #19 to the **AC**.

68. Thread (2) black, (2) bronze, (2) white, (2) red seed beads and (1) 3mm bicone bead onto Cd #20 and attach it to the **AC**. Attach Cd #21 to the **AC**.

69. Thread (2) black, (2) bronze, (2) white, (2) red seed beads, (1) 3mm bicone bead, and (1) drop bead onto Cd #22 and attach it to the **AC**.

Part 3 - The Bottom Tab

70. Bring the **AC** back around to the left and make a row of **DHH**s. Continue to use the same **AC** and make 6 more rows of **DHH**s (see Fig. 34).

Adding Cord - If the **AC** starts to get too short to work with comfortably, add a replacement cord (35") in the following way: Start a row working from left to right and make **DHH**s across about one half of the row. Tape the end of the replacement cord to the left side of the tab leaving a 1" or 2" tail. Bring the replacement cord underneath the knotted part of the row and then out to the front parallel to the **AC** (see Fig. 32). Treating the **AC** and the replacement cord as a single unit, make a tight **DHH** around both cords (see Fig. 33). Repeat, making another **DHH** with the next cord to the right. Bring the shorter **AC** to the back of the piece underneath the remaining hanging cords (you can trim off this excess cord now or later). Continue using the new replacement cord as the **AC** for the rest of the piece.

71. Check the bracelet around your wrist for fit. The loops should overlap the bottom tab at least $\frac{1}{4}$" but no more than $\frac{1}{2}$". If more rows are needed, add them now.

72. Flip the piece to the back. Fold all of the cords (except the **AC**) to the back as if making a hem. With matching beading or sewing thread, sew the cords down securely to the back of the tab (see Fig. 35). To keep the thread unnoticeable at the front, stitch only in the "ditches" between the knotted rows.

73. Thread the **AC** onto a narrow embroidery needle. Sew the three 8mm round beads (or buttons) to the tab, placing them so that they correspond with the loops. Knot off the **AC** and trim. Trim off the rest of the hanging cords below the stitching (see Fig. 36).

74. Optional - Cut a small piece of ultra suede to fit the bottom tab. Sew it onto the tab to cover up the cord ends and the stitching (see Fig. 37).

75. Figure 38 shows the finished closure.

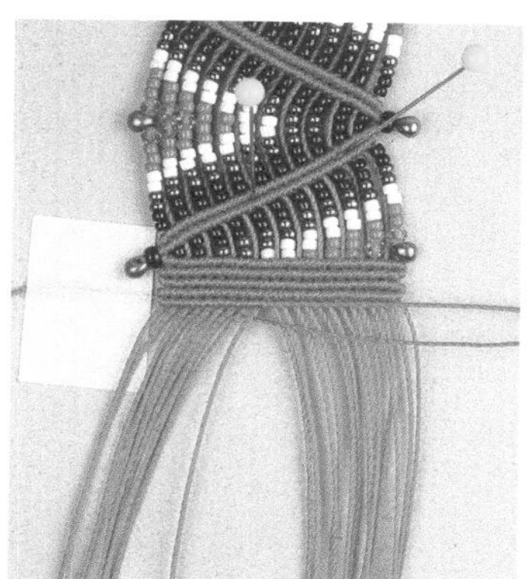

Figure 32

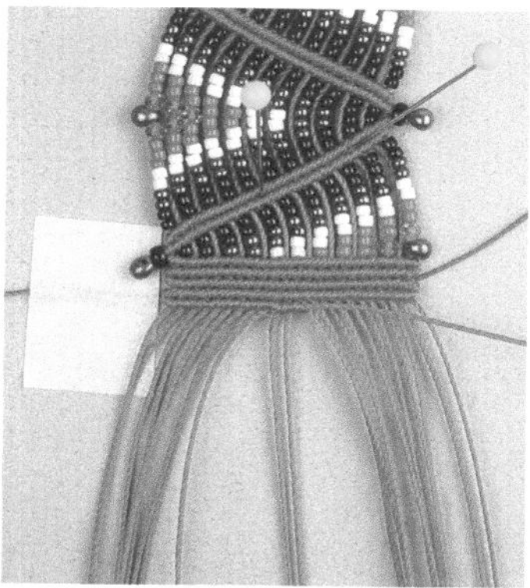

Figure 33

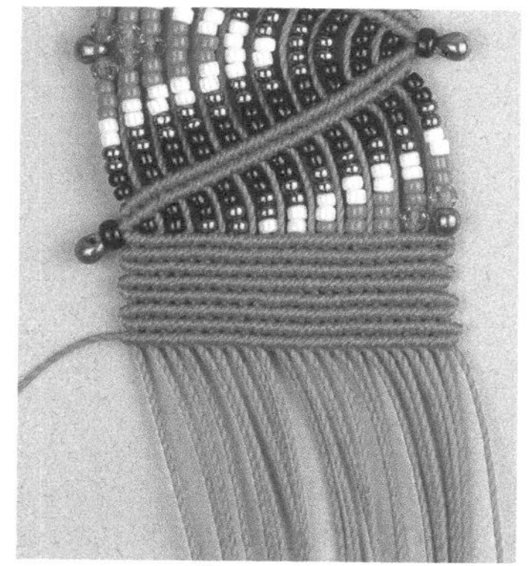

Figure 34

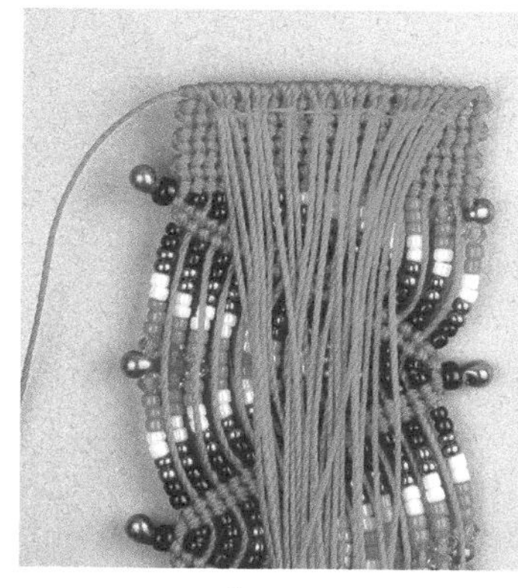

Figure 35

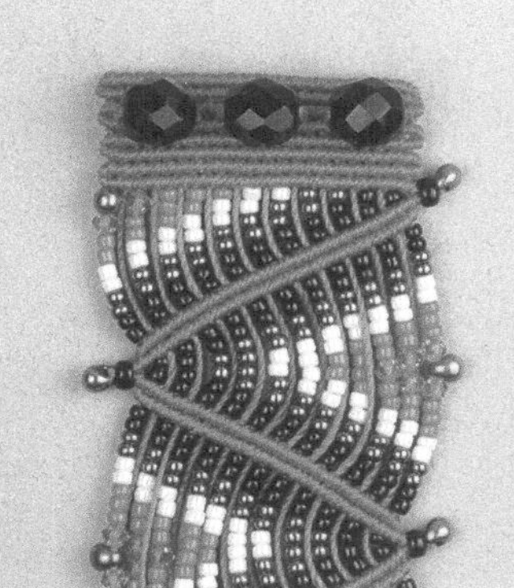

Figure 36

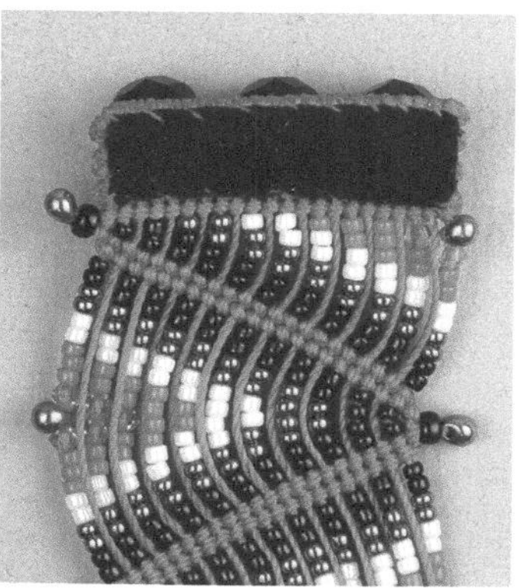

Figure 37

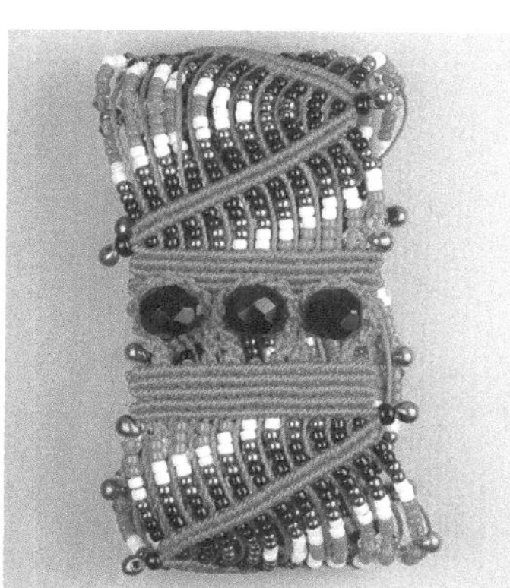

Figure 38

Crossing Paths Bracelet

This detailed bracelet is lacy and textured, with contrasting colors which move from side to side forming a checkerboard pattern where they cross paths.

Materials

Cord:
18g. Nylon Cord:
3 lengths @ 78" Color A (warp cords)
3 lengths @ 78" Color B (warp cords)
1 length @ 48" (Anchor Cord)

Beads :
Note -The beads in the sample echo the two cord colors. Other effects can be achieved with contrasting colors.

- (6) 8mm round beads
- (10) 10° seed beads
- (46) 8° seed beads Color #1
- (36) 8° seed beads Color #2
- (20) 4mm round Color #1
- (20) 4mm round Color #2
- (16) 3.4mm drop/fringe beads Color #1
- (16) 3.4mm drop/fringe beads Color #2

Other :

- (1) Slide Lock Clasp with 3 attachment rings (21x6mm)
- Embroidery Needle
- Clear nail polish

Part 1 - Top Tab

1. Put 2 pins in your board spaced about 3 - 4" apart. Wrap the 48" **AC** (Anchor Cord) once around each pin, making a cord "bar" on which to attach the warp cords. Tape down the cord on the outsides next to the pins so that it doesn't slip. The center point of the **AC** should be in the center of the pins so that the cord is of equal length to the left and right of center (see Figure 1).

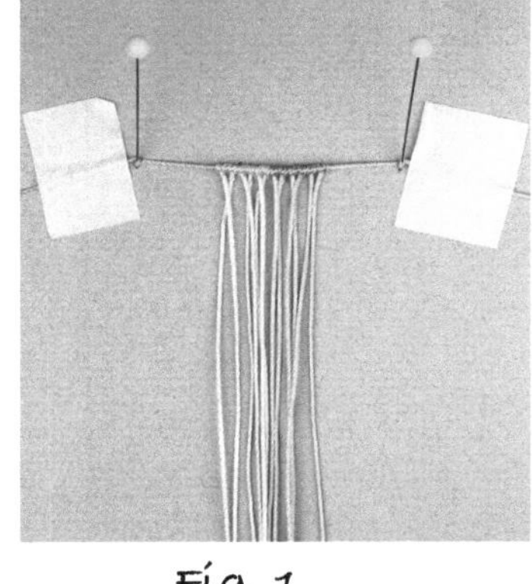
Fig. 1

2. Row 1 - Attach the three Color A (pink) cords to the bar with **MTK**s (Mounting Knots). Next to them, attach the three Color B (green) cords to the bar (see Figure 1).

3. Push all 6 **MTK**s closely together at the center of the bar. Tighten the **MTK**s if needed and pin them to the board in a neat horizontal row. Pin through the "bump" at the top/back/center of each **MTK** (see Figure 2).

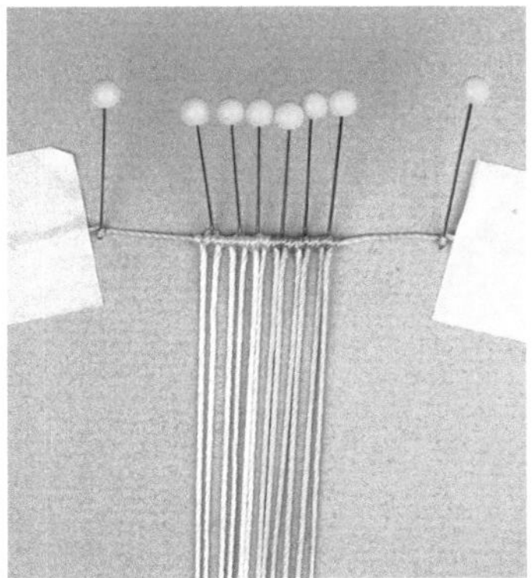
Fig. 2

Note - There are 12 warp cords to work with for the top tab. I will refer to each one as Cd (cord) #1 - 12 according to it's sequence from left to right.

4. Release the bar cord from the tape and pins on both sides (see Figure 3). The left part of the bar cord will be called the left-hand **AC** and the right part will be called the right-hand **AC**.

5. Row 2 - Bring the left-hand **AC** back around towards the center and working from left to right, make a row of **DHH**s (Double Half Hitches) with Cds #1 - 6. Bring the right-hand **AC** back around towards the center and working from right to left, make a row of **DHH**s with Cds #12 - 7 (see Figure 3). The two **AC**s will meet at the center.

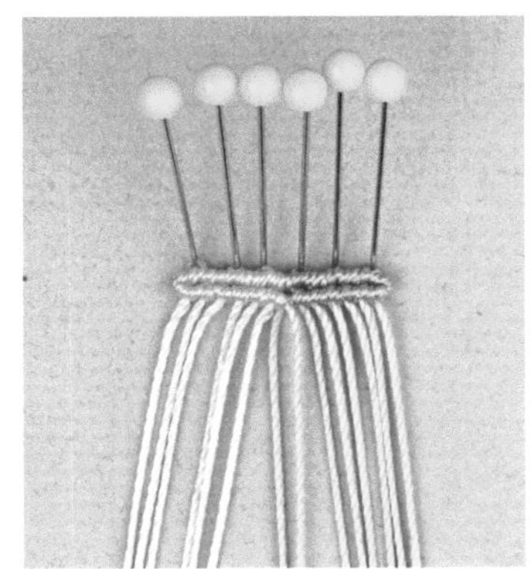
Fig. 3

6. Row 3 - Bring the left-hand **AC** back towards the left and working from right to left, make **DHH**s with Cds #6 - 1. Bring the right-hand **AC** back towards the right and working from left to right, make **DHH**s with Cds #7 - 12 (see Figure 4).

7. Row 4 - Repeat Step 5. The **AC**s should end up at the center of the bracelet (see Figure 5). **Note -** The bracelet will measure approximately 7". If you want a longer bracelet, add more rows as necessary. Each two row segment will add approximately 1/8" to the bracelet's length. For balance, it is preferable to make the same number of extra rows on the top tab and on the bottom tab. It will also be possible to add more length by adding extra beads between the bracelet ends and the clasp in Part 7.

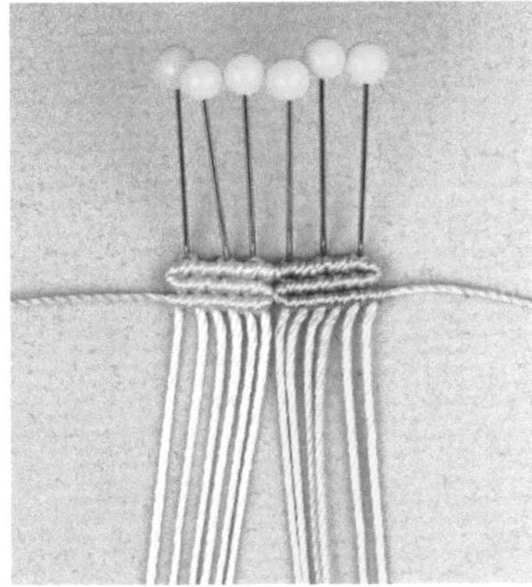
Fig. 4

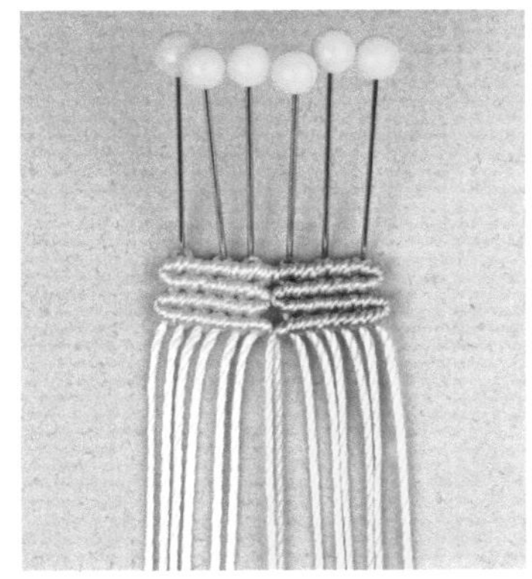
Fig. 5

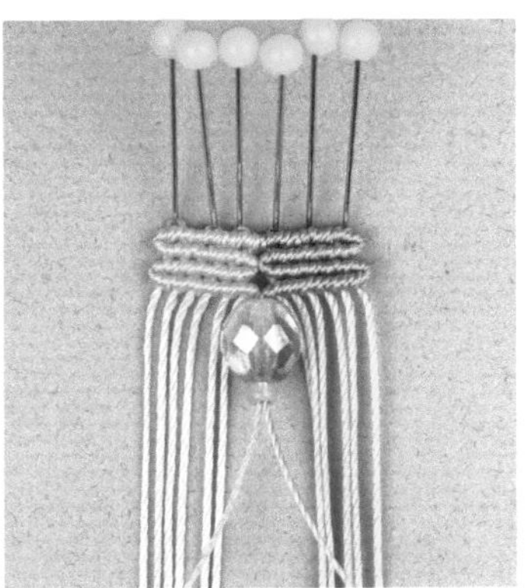
Fig. 6

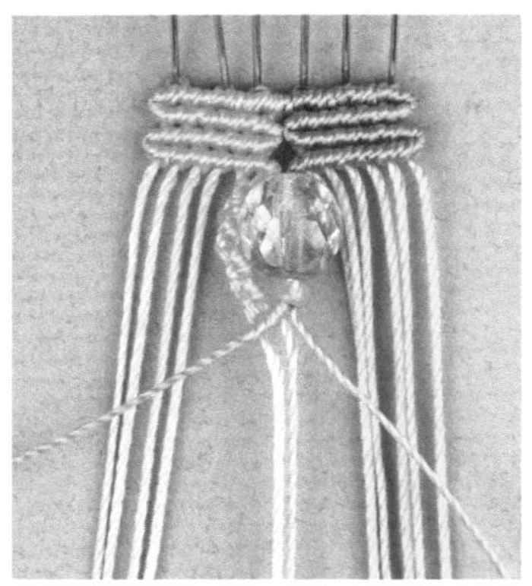
Fig. 7

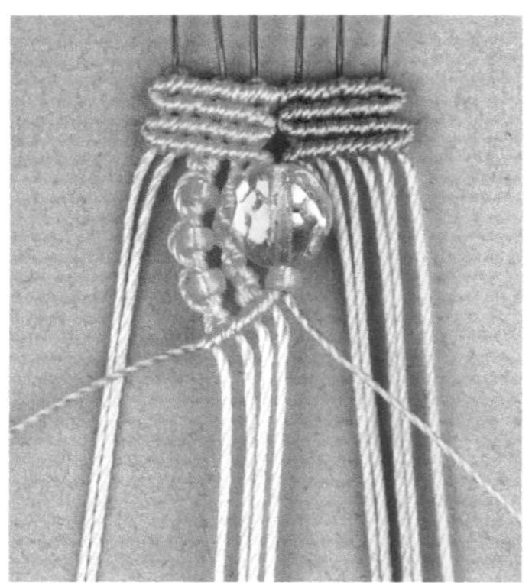
Fig. 8

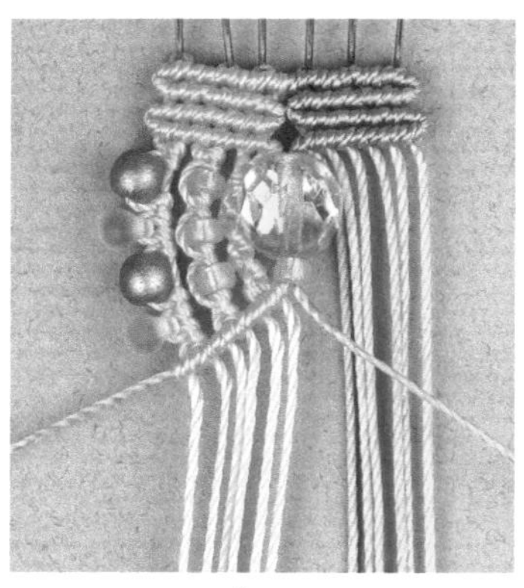
Fig. 9

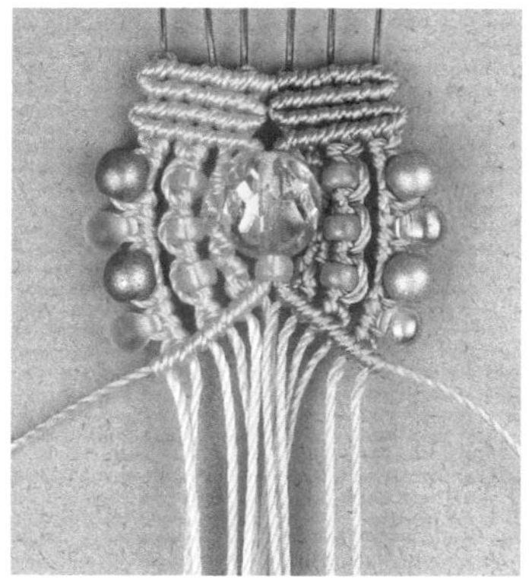
Fig. 10

Part 2 - Knotted Pattern, Section #1

Note - For Parts 2 - 5, I will refer to the cords as Cds #1 - 14 (this now includes the two **AC**s) according to their sequence from left to right.

8. Thread (1) 8mm bead and (1) 8° seed bead onto the two joined **AC**s (Cds #7 and 8). Push them all of the way up the cords. The two cords should come out diagonally to each side below the 8° bead and each will serve as an **AC** (left-hand and right-hand) for the next row (see Figure 6).

9. Left Side - Make an **AHHch** (Alternating Half Hitch Chain) with Cds #5 and 6. There should be about 10- 11 **HH**s in the chain. Bring the left-hand **AC** towards the outside edge at a 45° angle. Bring the two cords of the chain behind the **AC** and attach each to the **AC** with a **DHH** (see Figure 7).

10. Left Side (continued) - For the next chain, Cd #3 will act as the **KC** (Knotting Cord) and Cd #4 will act as the **AC**. All of the beads in this chain will be threaded onto the **Anchor Cord**. Make a **LHK** chain in the following way: Make (1) **LHK**, thread an 8° seed bead onto the **AC**. Make (1) **LHK**, thread an 8° seed bead onto the **AC**. Make (1) **LHK**, thread an 8° seed bead onto the **AC**. Make (1) **LHK**. Attach the **LHK** chain cords to the main **AC** with **DHH**s (see Figure 8).

Note - The knotted and beaded chains here (and in Part 4) should form graceful curves that frame the center 8mm beads. The bead and knot counts can be adjusted by adding or subtracting beads and/or knots if necessary to achieve the best fit.

11. For the next chain, Cd #1 will act as the **KC** and Cd #2 will act as the **AC**. All of the beads in this chain will be threaded onto the **Knotting Cord**. Make a **LHK** chain in the following way: Make a **LHK** around the **AC.** Thread (1) 4mm bead onto the **KC**, followed by a **LHK** around the **AC.** Thread (1) drop bead onto the **KC**, followed by a **LHK**. Thread (1) 4mm bead onto the **KC**, followed by a **LHK**. Thread (1) drop bead onto the **KC**, followed by a **LHK**. Attach the **LHK** chain cords to the main **AC** with **DHH**s (see Figure 9).

12. Right Side - Make an **AHHch** with Cds #9 and 10. There should be about 10 - 11 **HH**s in the chain. Bring the right-hand **AC** to the outside edge at a 45° angle. Bring the two cords of the chain behind the **AC** and attach each to the **AC** with **DHH**s (see Figure 10 for Steps 12 - 14).

13. For the next chain, Cd #12 will act as the **KC** and Cd #11 will be the **AC**. All of the beads in this chain will be threaded onto the **Anchor Cord**. Make a **LHK** chain in the following way: Make (1) **LHK**, thread an 8° seed bead onto the **AC** and push it up. Make (1) **LHK**, thread an 8° seed bead onto the **AC**. Make (1) **LHK**, thread an 8° seed bead onto the **AC**. Make (1) **LHK**. Attach the **LHK** chain cords to the **AC** with **DHH**s.

14. For the next chain, Cd #14 will act as the **KC** and Cd #13 will be the **AC**. All of the beads in this chain will be threaded onto the **Knotting Cord**. Make a **LHK** chain in the following way: Make a **LHK** around the **AC.** Thread (1) 4mm bead onto the **KC**, followed by a **LHK** around the **AC.** Thread (1) drop bead onto the **KC**, followed by a **LHK**. Thread (1) 4mm bead onto the **KC**, followed by a **LHK**. Thread (1) drop bead onto the **KC**, followed by a **LHK**. Attach the **LHK** chain cords to the main **AC** with **DHH**s.

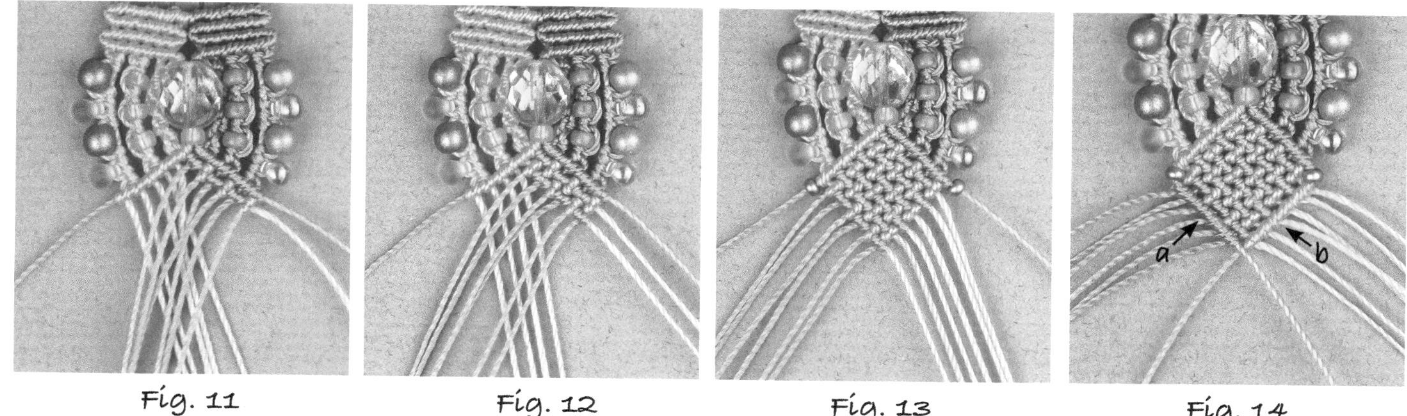

Fig. 11 Fig. 12 Fig. 13 Fig. 14

Part 3 -The "Checkerboard" Diamond Shape

15. Make the first row of knots as follows: Using Cd #7 as the **RC** (Runner Cord) for the row and working from left to right, bring Cd #8 underneath the **RC** and make a **DHH** around the **RC**. Next, bring the **RC** underneath Cd #9 and make a **VDHH** (Vertical Double Half Hitch) around Cd #9. Continue across the row in the same way, alternating **DHH**s and **VDHH**s. There will be 6 knots in the row. Do not include the outer right-hand cord (Cd #14) (see Figure 11).

16. Next row - Use Cd #6 (the next cord to the left) as the **RC** and working from left to right, make a row alternating **VDHH**s and **DHH**s starting with a **VDHH** this time. There will be 6 knots in the row. **Note -** The order of the **VDHH**s and **DHH**s in this row will be the opposite of the previous row (see Figure 12).

17. Next row - Using Cd #5 as the **RC**, make a **DHH**, **VDHH**, **DHH**, etc... across the row. There will be 6 knots in the row (see Figure 13).

18. Next row - Using Cd #4 as the **RC**, make a **VDHH**, **DHH**, **VDHH**, etc... across the row (see Figure 13).

19. Next row - Using Cd #3 as the **RC**, make a **DHH**, **VDHH**, **DHH**, etc... across the row (see Figure 13).

20. Next row - Using Cd #2 as the **RC**, make a **VDHH**, **DHH**, **VDHH**, etc... across the row (see Figure 13).

21. Thread (1) seed bead onto Cds #1 and #14 (the **AC**s) and push them all the way up the cords so that they rest at the end of the rows (see Figure 13).

22. Bring the left hand **AC** down toward the center at a diagonal angle along the bottom edge of the knotting. Make a row of **DHH**s with the first 6 cords working from left to right (see Figure 14a).

23. Bring the right hand **AC** down toward the center at a diagonal angle along the bottom edge of the knotting. Make a row of **DHH**s with the remaining cords working from right to left (see Figure 14b).

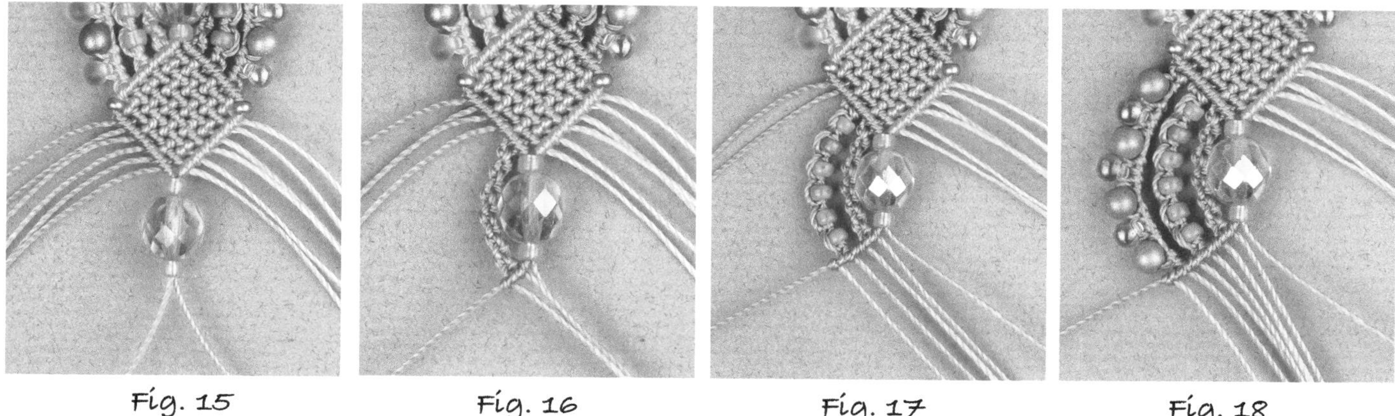

Fig. 15 Fig. 16 Fig. 17 Fig. 18

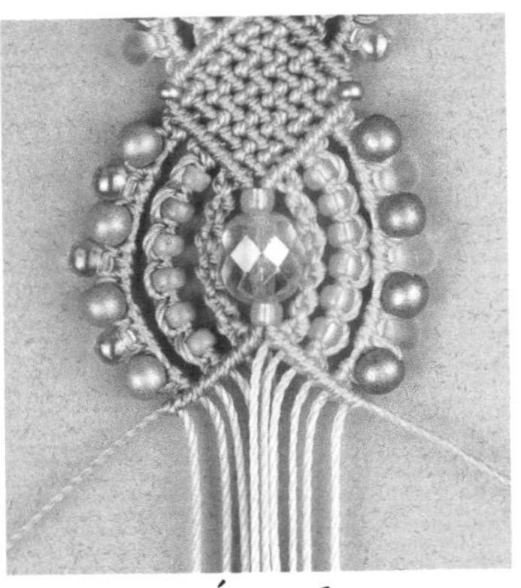

Fig. 19

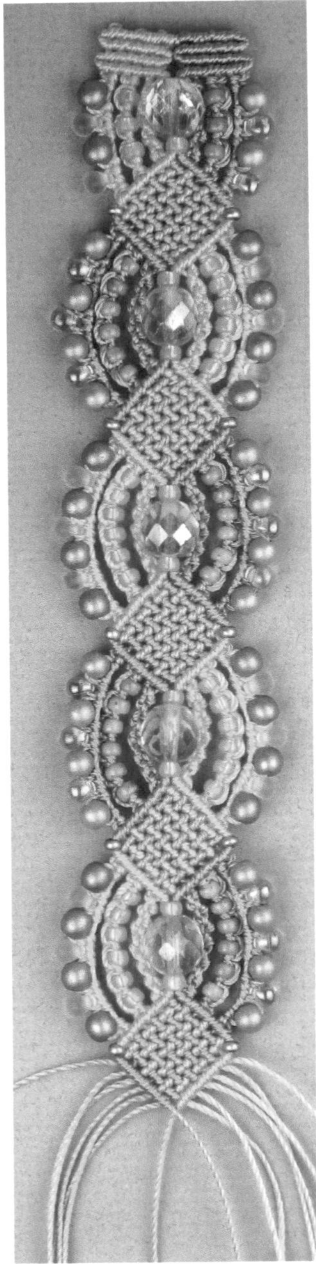

Fig. 20

Part 4 - Knotted Pattern, Sections # 2 - 5

Note - The cord colors will switch sides after each "Checkerboard" section. Be sure to use their corresponding seed bead colors in the following sections.

24. Thread (1) 8° bead, (1) 8mm bead, and (1) 8° bead onto the two joined **AC**s (Cds #7 and 8). Push them all of the way up the cords. The two **AC**s should come out diagonally to each side below the beads and each will serve as an **AC** for the next rows (see Figure 15).

25. Left Side - Make an **AHHch** with Cds #5 and 6. There should be about 12 - 13 **HH**s in the chain. Bring the left-hand **AC** towards the outside edge at a 45° angle. Attach the two cords of the **AHHch** to the **AC** with **DHH**s (see Figure 16).

26. For the next chain, Cd #3 will be the **KC** and Cd #4 will be the **AC**. All of the beads in this chain will be threaded onto the **Anchor Cord**. Make a **LHK** chain in the following way: Make (1) **LHK**, thread an 8° seed bead onto the **AC** and push it up. Repeat five times. Finish the chain with (1) **LHK** (there will be (7) **LHK**s and (6) seed beads in the chain). Attach the **LHK** chain cords to the main **AC** with **DHH**s (see Figure 17). **Note -** Seed beads can vary in size. Subtract beads and **LHK**s if necessary to get the best fit.

27. For the next chain Cd #1 will be the **KC** and Cd #2 will be the **AC**. All of the beads in this chain will be threaded onto the **Knotting Cord**. Make a **LHK** chain in the following way: With Cd #1 make a **LHK** around Cd #2. Thread (1) 4mm round bead onto the **KC**, followed by a **LHK**. Thread (1) drop bead onto the **KC**, followed by a **LHK**. Repeat two times. Thread (1) 4mm bead onto the **KC**, followed by a **LHK**. Attach the **LHK** chain to the **AC** with **DHH**s. There will be (8) **LHK**s, (4) 4mm beads, and (3) drop beads in the chain. Attach the **LHK** chain to the **AC** with **DHH**s (see Figure 18).

28. Right Side - Make an **AHHch** with Cds #9 and 10. There should be about 12 - 13 **HH**s in the chain. Bring the right-hand **AC** towards the outside edge at a 45° angle. Attach the two cords of the **AHHch** to the **AC** with **DHH**s.

29. For the next chain, Cd #12 will be the **KC** and Cd #11 will be the **AC**. All of the beads in this chain will be threaded onto the **Anchor Cord**. Make a **LHK** chain in the following way: Make (1) **LHK**, thread an 8° seed bead onto the **AC** and push it up. Repeat five times. Finish the chain with (1) **LHK**. There will be (7) **LHK**s and (6) seed beads in the chain. Attach the **LHK** chain cords to the **AC** with **DHH**s (see Figure 19).

30. For the next chain Cd #14 will be the **KC** and Cd #13 will be the **AC**. Make a **LHK** chain in the following way: With Cd #14 make a **LHK** around Cd #13. Thread (1) 4mm round bead onto the **KC**, followed by a **LHK**. Thread (1) drop bead onto the **KC**, followed by a **LHK**. Repeat two times. Thread (1) 4mm bead onto the **KC**, followed by a **LHK**. Attach the **LHK** chain cords to the **AC** with **DHH**s. Attach the **LHK** chain to the **AC** with **DHH**s (see Figure 19).

31. To continue the bracelet, repeat Part 3 followed by Part 4 three more times. Then repeat Part 3 one more time. This will give you a total of (5) Checkerboard segments and (5) Knotted Pattern segments which includes the top Knotted Pattern segment in Part 2 (see Figure 20).

Part 5 - Knotted Pattern, Section #6

32. Thread (1) 8° bead and (1) 8mm bead onto Cds #7 and 8. Push them all of the way up the cords. The two cords will come out horizontally to each side below the 8mm bead and each will serve as an **AC** for the rows which form the bottom tab (see Figure 21 for Steps 32 - 34).

33. Left Side - Make an **AHHch** with Cds #5 and 6. There should be about 10 - 11 **HH**s in the chain. Bring the left-hand **AC** out to the left horizontally (this will start the beginning row of the bottom tab). Attach the two cords of the **AHHch** to the left-hand **AC** with **DHH**s.

34. Right Side - Make an **AHHch** with Cds #9 and 10. There should be about 10 - 11 **HH**s in the chain. Bring the right-hand **AC** out to the right horizontally. Attach the two cords of the **AHHch** to the right-hand **AC** with **DHH**s.

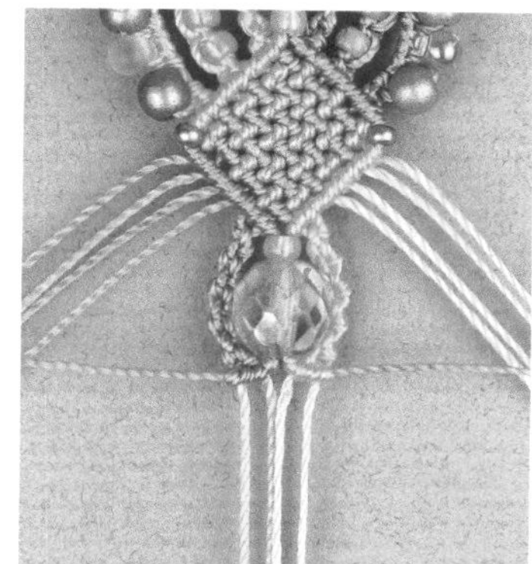

Fig. 21

35. Left Side - For the next chain, Cd #3 will be the **KC** and Cd #4 will be the **AC**. All of the beads in this chain will be threaded onto the **Anchor Cord**. Make a **LHK** chain in the following way: Make (1) **LHK**, thread an 8° seed bead onto the **AC** and push it up. Repeat twice. Make (1) **LHK**. Attach the **LHK** chain cords to the **AC** with **DHH**s (see Figure 22 for Steps 35 and 36).

36. Right Side - For the next chain, Cd #12 will be the **KC** and Cd #11 will be the **AC**. Make a **LHK** chain in the following way: Make (1) **LHK**, thread an 8° seed bead onto the **AC** and push it up. Repeat twice. Make (1) **LHK**. Attach the **LHK** chain cords to the **AC** with **DHH**s.

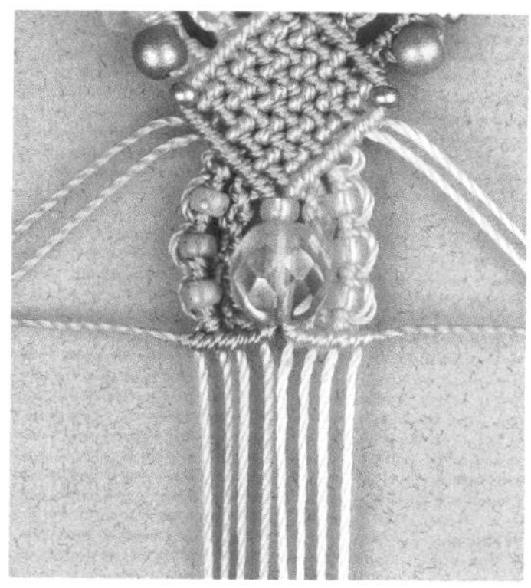

Fig. 22

37. Left Side - For the next chain, Cd #1 will be the **KC** and Cd #2 will be the **AC**. All of the beads in this chain will be threaded onto the **Knotting Cord**. Make a **LHK** chain in the following way: Make a **LHK**. Thread (1) drop bead onto the **KC**, followed by a **LHK**. Thread (1) 4mm bead onto the **KC**, followed by a **LHK**. Thread (1) drop bead onto the **KC**, followed by a **LHK**. Thread (1) 4mm bead onto the **KC**, followed by a **LHK**. Attach the **LHK** chain cords to the **AC** with **DHH**s (see Figure 23 for Steps 37 and 38).

38. Right Side - For the next chain, Cd #14 will act as the **KC** and Cd #13 will be the **AC**. Make a **LHK** chain in the following way: Make a **LHK**. Thread (1) drop bead onto the **KC**, followed by a **LHK**. Thread (1) 4mm bead onto the **KC**, followed by a **LHK**. Thread (1) drop bead onto the **KC**, followed by a **LHK**. Thread (1) 4mm bead onto the **KC**, followed by a **LHK**. Attach the **LHK** chain cords to the **AC** with **DHH**s.

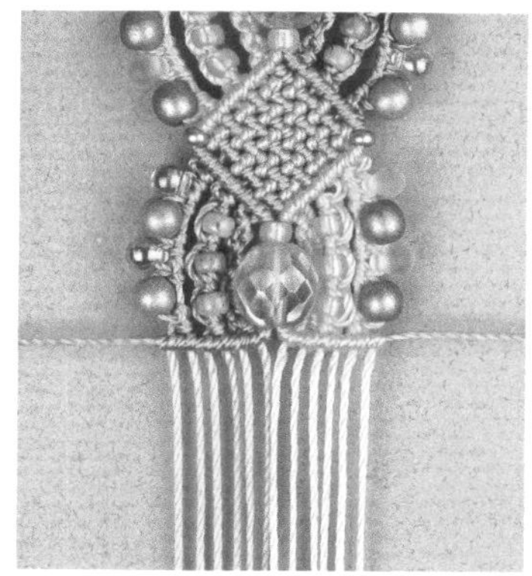

Fig. 23

Part 6- Bottom Tab

Note - For Part 6, I will refer to the cords as #1 - 12 according to their sequence from left to right.

39. Row 2 - Bring the left-hand **AC** back around towards the center and working from left to right, make a row of **DHH**s with Cds #1 - 6 (see Figure 24 for Steps 39 - 43).

40. Row 2 (cont.) - Bring the right-hand **AC** back around towards the center and working from right to left, make a row of **DHH**s with Cds #12 - 7.

Fig. 24

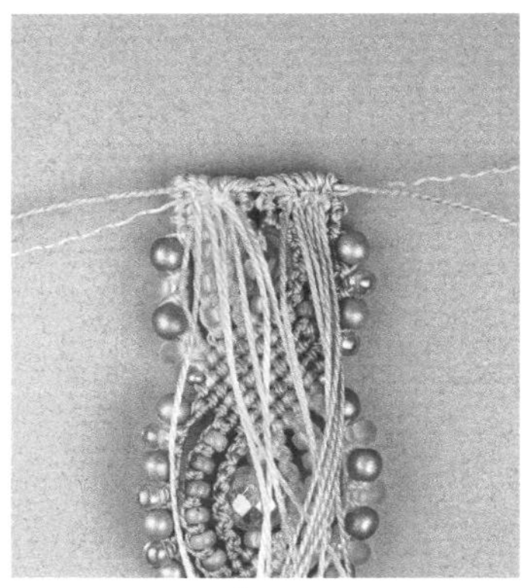

Fig. 25

Fig. 26

Fig. 27

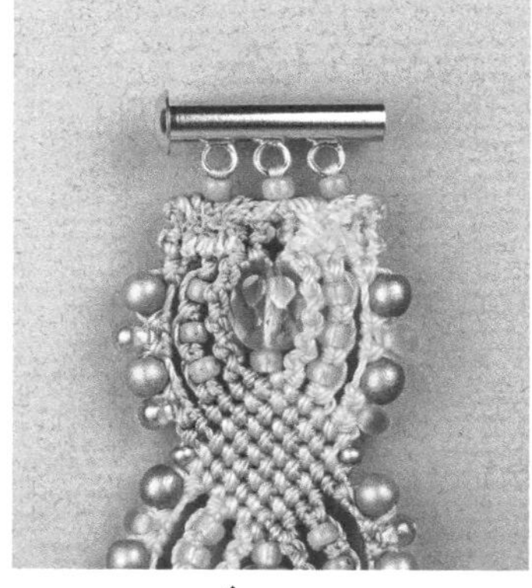

Fig. 28

41. Row 3 - Bring the left-hand **AC** back towards the left and working from right to left, make a row of **DHH**s with Cds #6 - 1.

42. Row 3 (continued) - Bring the right-hand **AC** back towards the right and working from left to right, make a row of **DHH**s with Cds #7 - 12.

43. Row 4 - Repeat Steps #39 and 40. The **AC**s should end up at the center of the bracelet.

Part 7- Adding The Clasp

44. Prepare two 30" lengths of thread, one each to match the colors of the bracelet cords. You can use beading thread or make your own matching threads by untwisting a length of the 18 g. nylon and separating out 1-ply from the other 2 (this way you get a perfect color match). Attach a beading needle to each thread and tie off the end with an Overhand Knot.

45. Flip the bracelet to the back. Cross the two **AC**s over each other at the center and bring them out to the sides. Bring the hanging cords to the back over the **AC**s to make a hem (see Figure 25).

46. Using the matching thread for each side, sew the hem cords down to the back of the tab, going back and forth a few times to make sure they are very secure. To prevent the stitches from showing on the front of the tab, make the stitches only in the "ditches" in between the 2nd and 3rd rows. Sew through the **AC**s once or twice to make sure they are secure and don't slip.

47. Cut off the **AC**s at the sides and the hanging cords closely below the stitching, leaving the sewing threads attached (see Figure 26).

48. Passing under the hem cords, bring the two sewing threads back to the center/top of the tab (see Figure 26a). Pass both threads up through an 8° seed bead, then through the middle ring of the clasp part, then back down through the bead (see Figure 27).

49. Pull the bead close up against the edge of the tab. Sew through some fibers at the back of the tab to secure the bead. Repeat.

50. On the left side bring the matching color thread to the left and pass the needle up through the top of the tab where it aligns with the left ring. Pass the needle up through an 8° seed bead, then through the left ring of the clasp part, then back down through the bead (see Figure 28).

51. Pull the bead close up against the edge of the tab. Sew through some fibers at the back of the tab to secure the bead. Repeat two or three times for added strength. Sew under the hem cords back and forth a few times to secure the thread. Trim off the excess thread.

52. Repeat Steps #50 and 51 on the right side (see Figure 28).

53. Top Tab - Using matching thread for each side, sew the other clasp part to the top edge of the tab. Start by attaching the center bead and ring first as it will position the clasp correctly. **Important -** The top clasp part must face in the opposite direction to the bottom clasp part (see title page picture)!

Dragon Tail Bracelet

Designed with a series of horizontal and diagonal rows, this project uses uncomplicated techniques to produce a striking bracelet with movement and flow.

Materials

18g. Nylon Cord:

- 6 lengths @ 100" -2 each of three complimentary colors (Knotting Cords). Color #1 will run down the middle, Color #2 is next, and Color # 3 runs along the outer edges.
- 1 length @ 110" (Anchor Cord) This cord will be mostly hidden. I suggest you use the same color as the outer band color (Color #3).

Beads:

- (4) 8mm briolette pearls (other round beads may be substituted)
- (120)10° seed beads
- (52)3.4mm drop/fringe beads
- (2) bracelet crimp ends (8mm - 10mm)
- (2) 6mm jump rings
- (1) clasp (ball and socket, fishhook, lobster, or magnetic)

Part 1, Right half of the bracelet -

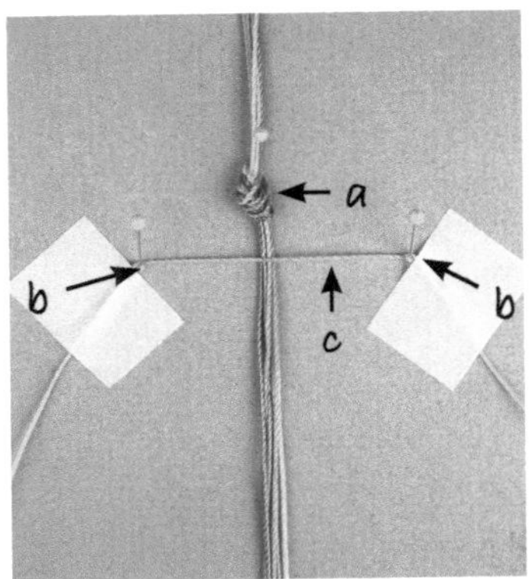

Figure 1

1. Gather the six 100" warp cords together in a bundle with all ends aligned. Locate the center point (50" from the ends) and tie the cords together with a loose (temporary) **OVK** (Overhand Knot). Position the cords vertically on the board and pin through the **OVK** to hold them (see Fig. 1a).

2. Place pins in the board to each side of the bundled cord about 2" apart and ½" below the **OVK** (see Fig. 1b). Take the **AC** (Anchor Cord) and center it between the pins so there are equal lengths of cord (55") to the right and left side of center. Wrap the **AC** around the pins on each side (the **AC** resting on top of the bundled cords). Tape and pin the cord ends in place so they don't slip. This creates a temporary cord "bar" between the pins (see Fig. 1c).

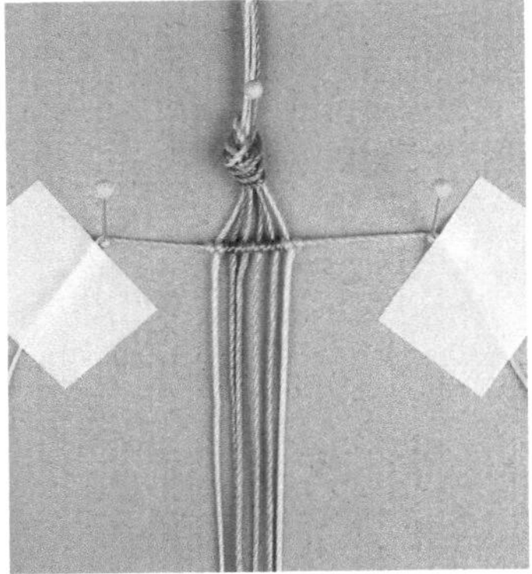
Figure 2

3. Row 1 - Working from left to right, attach each of the six bundled cords to the **AC** with a **DHH** (Double Half Hitch). The color sequence is 1-2-3-3-2-1 (see Fig. 2). Push them closely together at the center of the **AC** and pin in place (see Fig. 3a).

There are 6 warp (hanging) cords to work with. I will refer to each as Cord (Cd) #1 - 6 according to it's sequence from left to right.

4. Row 2 - Release the **AC** from the right-hand pin (see Fig. 3b). Bring this right-hand half of the **AC** horizontally to the left and make a row of **DHH**s (see Fig. 4). Untie the **OVK** and release the left-hand **AC** from the pin. These cords will be used for the second half of the bracelet. Coil and/or tape them together for now to keep them out of the way (see Fig. 4, top).

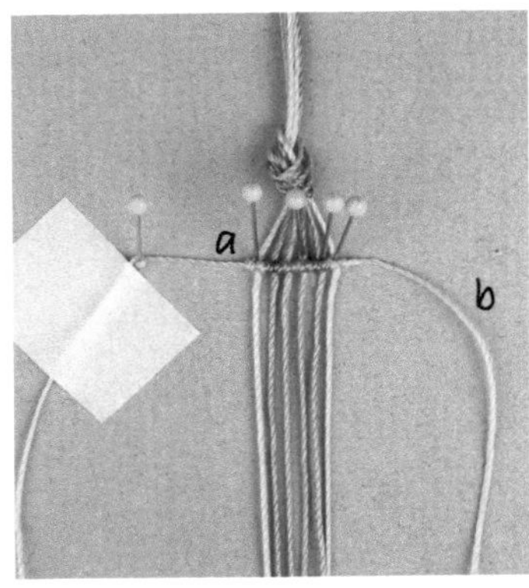

Figure 3

5. Row 3 - Thread a 10° seed bead onto Cd #6 and push it up. Bring the **AC** downward to the right at a slight angle (the width of the bead determining the angle of the row) and make a row of **DHH**s (see Fig. 5).

6. Row 4 - Bring the **AC** to the left and make a row of **DHH**s. This row should be parallel to (touching) the previous row (see Fig. 6).

7. Rows 5 & 6 and 7 & 8 - Repeat Steps #5 and 6 for these rows (see Fig. 7).

Note - Reposition and repin the piece as often as necessary to always have the most comfortable angle for knotting.

8. Row 9 - Thread (1) 3.4mm drop bead onto Cd #6 and push it up. Bring the **AC** over to the right at a slight angle (the width of the drop bead determining the angle of the row) and make a row of **DHH**s (see Fig. 8).

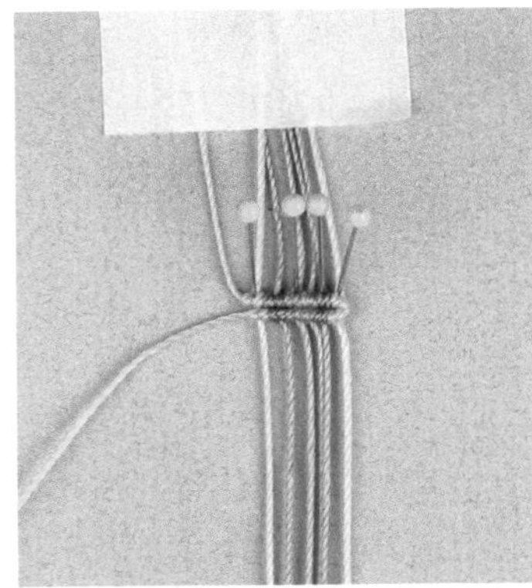
Figure 4

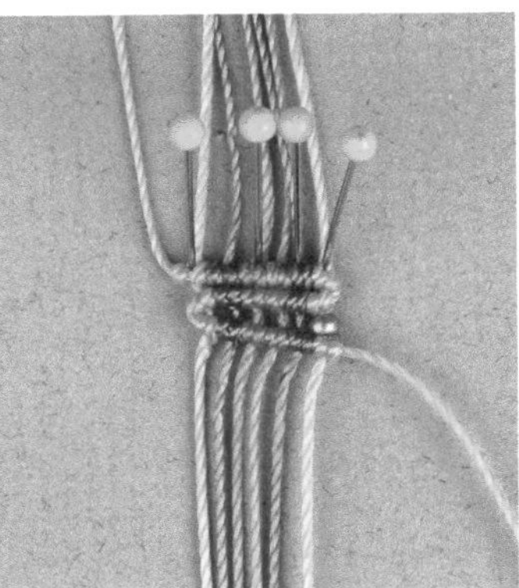
Figure 5

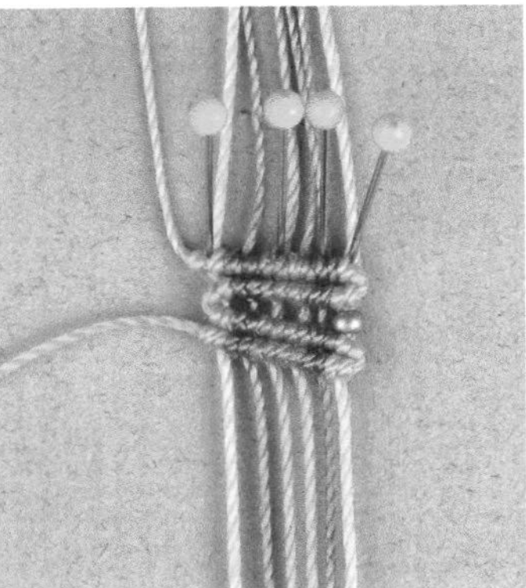
Figure 6

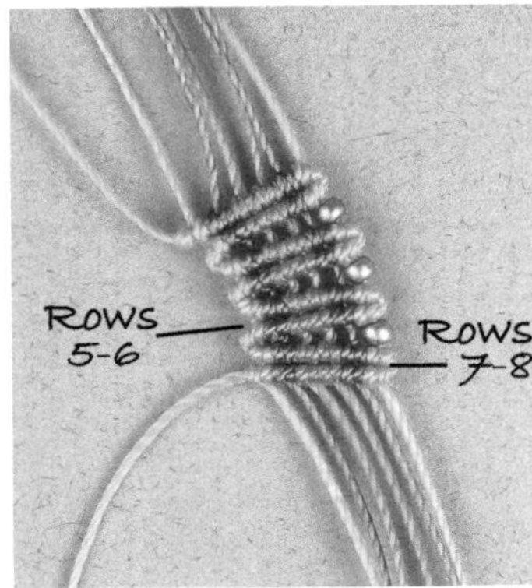

Figure 7

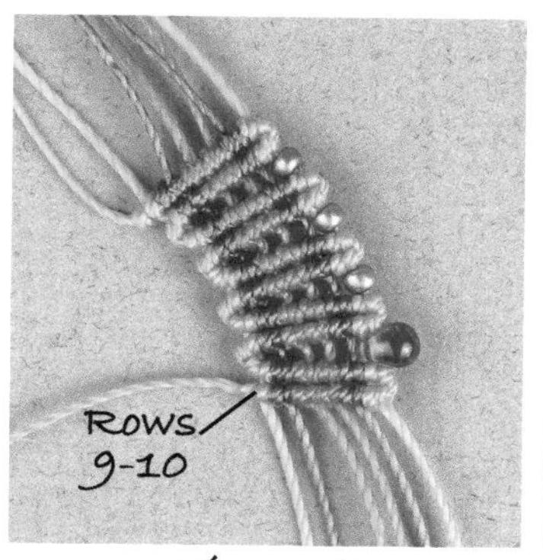

Figure 8

Figure 9

Figure 10

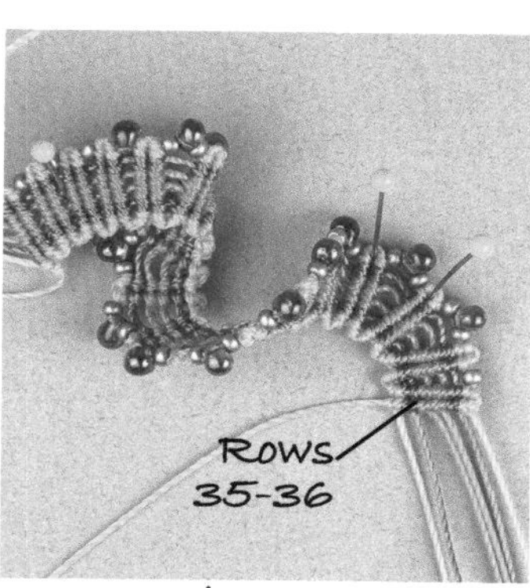

Figure 11

9. Row 10 - Bring the **AC** to the left and make a row of **DHH**s. This row should be parallel to the previous row (see Fig. 8).

10. Row 11 - Thread (1) 10° seed bead, (1) 3.4mm drop bead, and (1) 10° seed bead onto Cd #6. Bring the **AC** over to the right at an angle (the width of the beads determining the angle of the row) and make a row of **DHH**s (see Fig. 9).

11. Row 12 - Bring the **AC** to the left and make a row of **DHH**s. This row should be parallel to the previous row (see Fig. 9).

12. Rows 13 through 34 - Repeat Steps #10 and 11 for these rows. The knotwork will progress in a circular pattern. When completed, there will be a total of 13 drop beads in the circle (see Fig. 10).

Note - When working on overlapping sections, move the bottom section off to the side so that you can pin down the part that you are working on (see Fig. 11 for example).

13. Row 35 - Thread a 10° seed bead onto Cd #6 and push it up. Bring the **AC** over to the right at a slight angle and make a row of **DHH**s (see Fig. 11).

14. Row 36 - Bring the **AC** to the left and make a row of **DHH**s. This row should be parallel to the previous row (see Fig. 11).

15. Rows 37 & 38 and 39 & 40 - Repeat Steps #13 and 14 (see Fig. 12).

16. Rows 41, 42, and 43 - Make 3 parallel rows of **DHH**s. The **AC** should end up on the right-hand side of the knotwork (see Fig. 13).

17. Row 44 - Thread a 10° seed bead onto Cd #1. Bring the **AC** over to the left at a slight angle and make a row of **DHH**s (see Fig. 14).

18. Row 45 - Bring the **AC** to the right and make a row of **DHH**s. This row should be parallel to the previous row (see Fig. 14).

19. Rows 46 & 47 and 48 & 49 - Repeat Steps #17 and 18 (see Fig. 14).

20. Row 50 - Thread (1) 3.4mm bead onto Cd #1. Bring the **AC** over to the left at a slight angle and make a row of **DHH**s (see Fig. 14).

21. Row 51 - Bring the **AC** to the right and make a row of **DHH**s. This row should be parallel to the previous row (see Fig. 14).

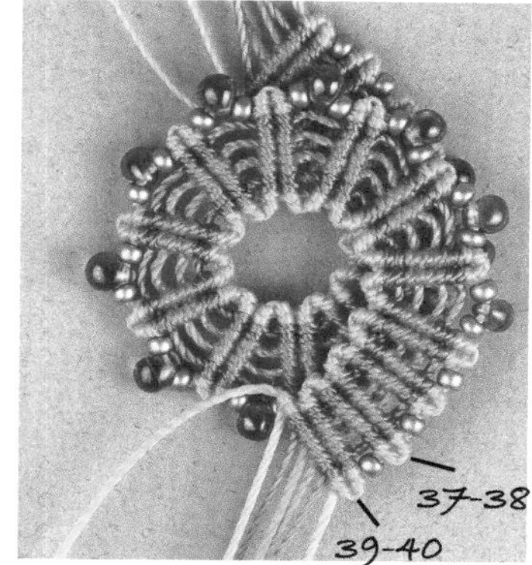

Figure 12

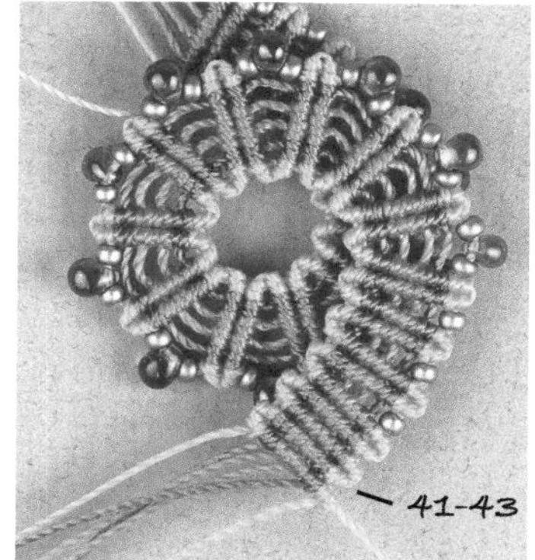

Figure 13

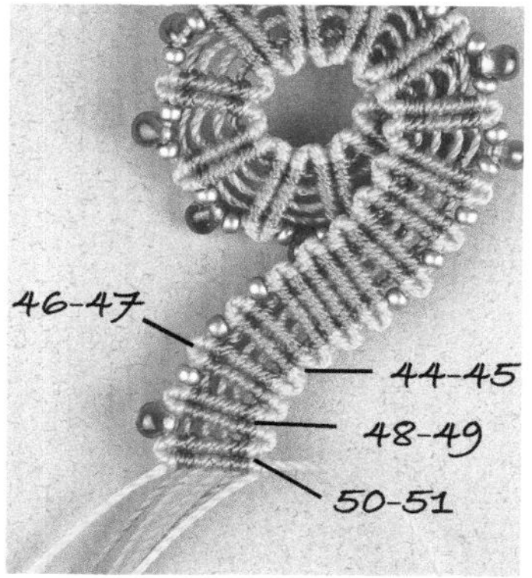

Figure 14

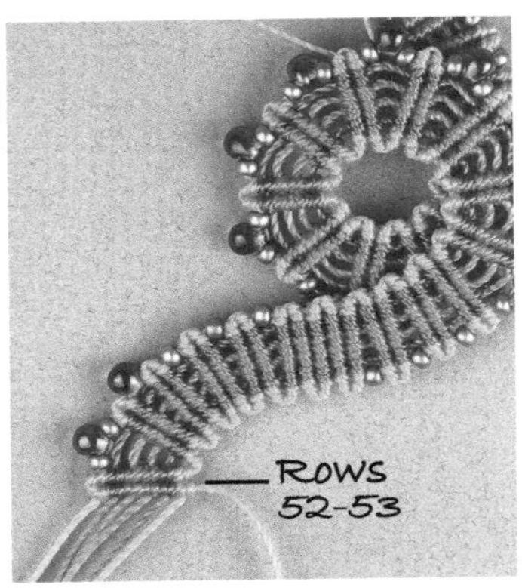

Figure 15

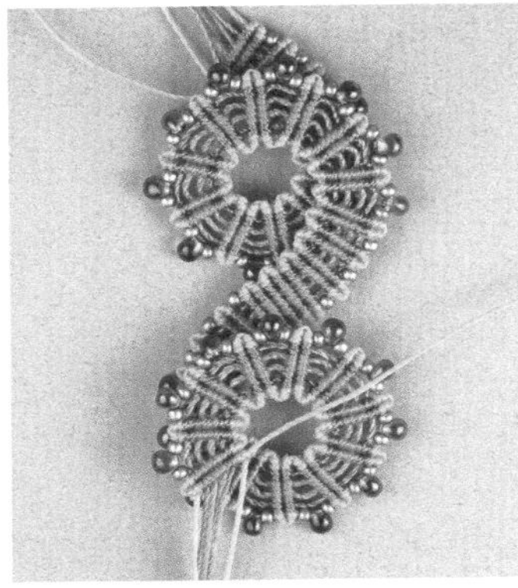
Figure 16

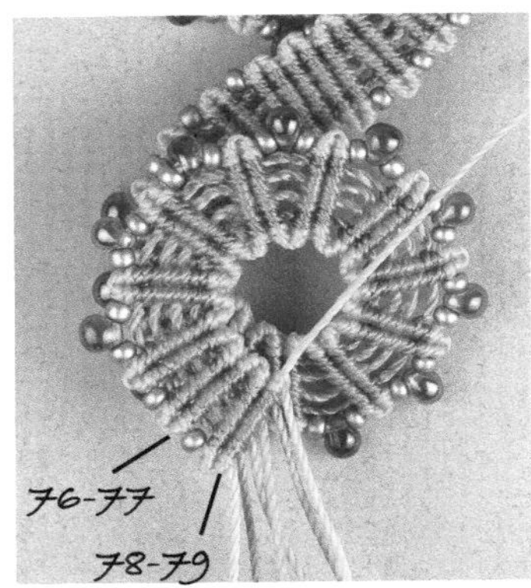

Figure 17

22. Row 52 - Thread (1) 10° seed bead, (1) 3.4mm drop bead, and (1) 10° seed bead onto Cd #1. Bring the **AC** over to the left at an angle and make a row of **DHH**s (see Fig. 15).

23. Row 53 - Bring the **AC** to the right and make a row of **DHH**s. This row should be parallel to the previous row (see Fig. 15).

24. Rows 54 through 75 - Repeat Steps #22 and 23 for these rows. The knotwork will progress in a circular pattern. When completed, there will be a total of 13 drop beads in the circle (see Fig. 16).

25. Row 76 - Thread a 10° seed bead onto Cd #1. Bring the **AC** over to the left at a slight angle and make a row of **DHH**s (see Fig. 17).

26. Row 77 - Bring the **AC** to the right and make a row of **DHH**s. This row should be parallel to the previous row.

27. Rows 78 and 79 - Repeat Steps #25 and 26 (see Fig. 17).

28. Row 80 - Make one parallel row of **DHH**s (see Fig. 18). The **AC** should end up on the left-hand side of the knotwork.

29. Row 81 - Thread a 10° seed bead onto Cd #6. Bring the **AC** over to the right at a slight angle and make a row of **DHH**s.

30. Row 82 - Bring the **AC** to the left and make a row of **DHH**s. This row should be parallel to the previous row.

31. Rows 83 & 84, 85 & 86, and 87 & 88 - Repeat Steps #29 and 30 for these rows (see Fig. 18).

32. Rows 89 through 93 - Make 5 parallel rows of **DHH**s (see Fig. 19). The end will be finished in Part 3.

Part 2, Left half of the bracelet -

33. To work on this half of the bracelet, turn it around 180° and pin in place. Bring the **AC** horizontally to the left and make a row of **DHH**s. The **AC** should end up on the left-hand side.

34. Repeat Steps #5 through #32 from Part 1.

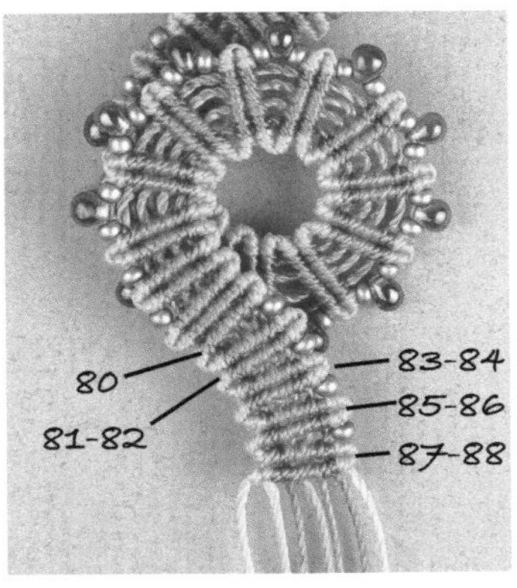

Figure 18

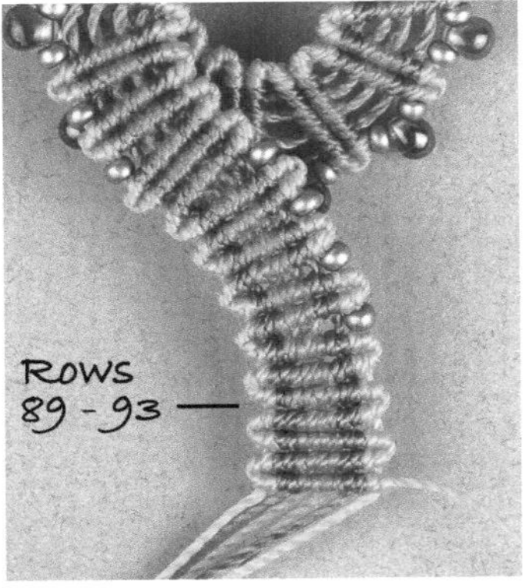

Figure 19

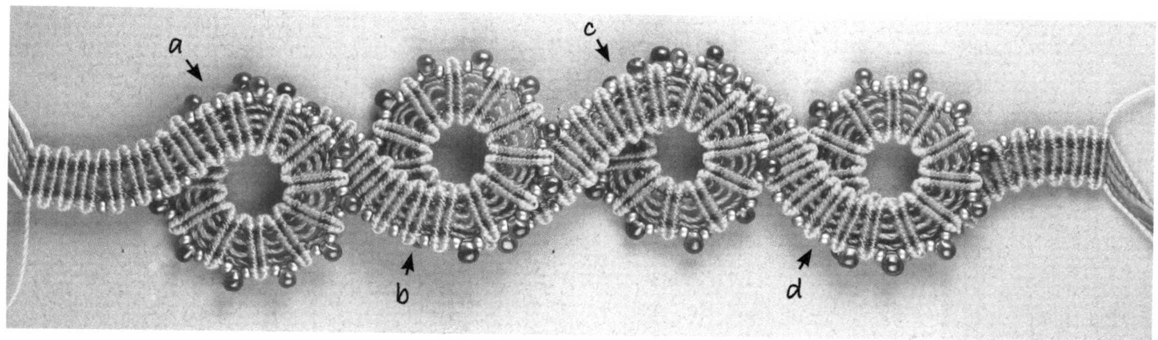

Figure 20

Part 3, Finishing -

35. Compare your bracelet with Figure 20 and arrange the circular sections in the same way. The knotted sections which connect the circular sections should be on top (see Fig. 20 a, b, c, and d).

36. Using the same color thread as the outer edge cord (see note below), tack down (sew) the band at several points to prevent the circular sections from lifting up. Sew the (4) briolette beads onto the band, positioning them in the open spaces (see Fig. 21).

Note - If you don't have the right color beading thread, make your own thread by cutting a 30" - 40" piece of 3-ply nylon cord. Untwist the plies and pull out a single ply from the bunch.

37. Flip the bracelet to the back. On each end - bring the **AC** to the left over the band. Bring the **KC**s to the back over the **AC** to make a hem. Securely sew down the cords to the back near the edge of the band using complimentary colored thread (see Fig. 22). Cut off the excess cords next to the stitching and the **AC** flush with the edge.

38. Attach the crimp ends to the bracelet at each end. Attach the clasp parts to both ends with jumprings (see Fig. 23).

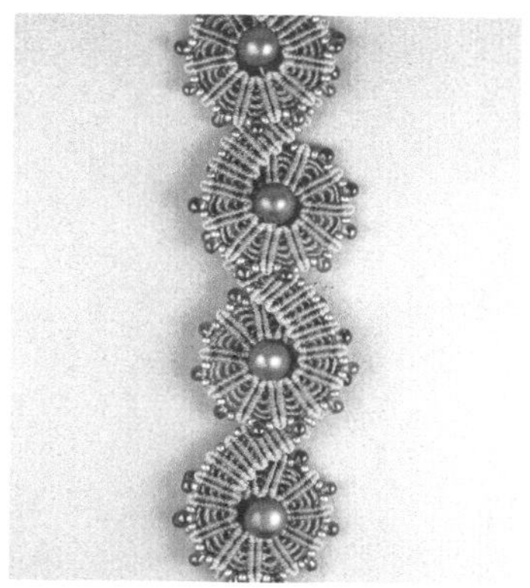

Figure 21

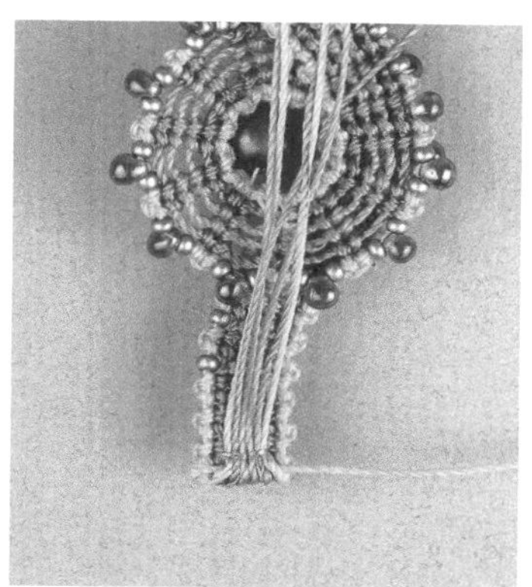

Figure 22

Figure 23

Harlequin Bracelet

The Harlequin Bracelet has two interlacing halves that come together in an engaging design. This is one of my favorite bracelets to wear, I hope it will be yours too!

Materials

- 18 gauge Nylon Cord:
  - 3 lengths of Color A @ 120" ea.
  - 3 lengths of Color B @ 120" ea.
  - 1 length of Color B @ 46" (Runner)
- Beads:
  - (36) size 11° seed beads
  - (9) 4mm round beads
- Findings:
  - (1) Slide Lock Clasp

Part 1 - Top Tab

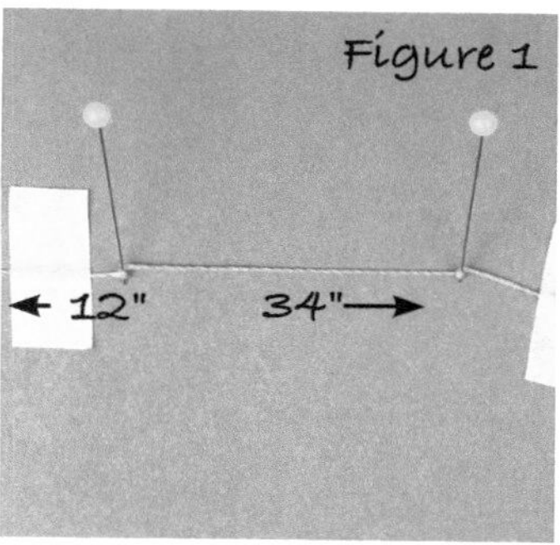

1. Put 2 pins in your board spaced about 3 - 4" apart and angled upwards. Wrap the 46" **RC** (Runner Cord) once around the left-hand pin, leaving only 12" of cord to the left of pin. Bring the longer part of the cord out to the right and wrap it once around the right-hand pin. Tape down the cord on the outsides next to the pins so that it doesn't slip (see Fig. 1). This makes a temporary "bar" on which to attach the warp cords.

2. Fold in half and attach each of the 3 Color-A cords to the **RC** using **MTK**s (Mounting Knots). Attach the 3 Color-B cords to the right of them. Tighten the **MTK**s well and push them close up against the left-hand pin (see Fig. 2).

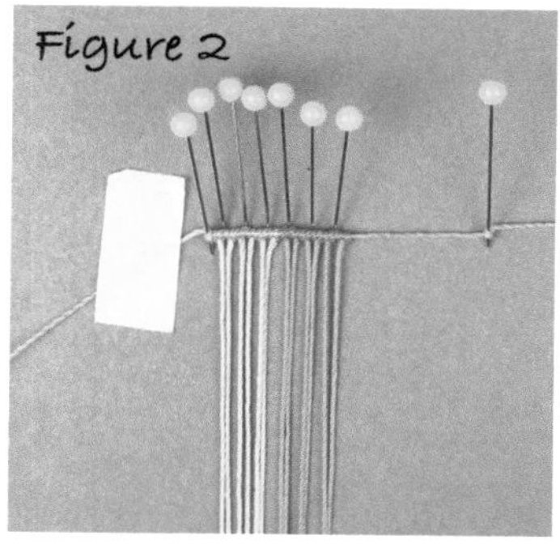

3. Pin the **MTK**s to the board in a neat horizontal row. Pin through the "bump" at the top/back/center of each **MTK** (see Fig. 2).

4. Release the **RC** from the right-hand pin and bring it around to the left horizontally and make a row of Double Half Hitches (**DHH**s) (see Fig. 3).

5. Bring the **RC** back to the right and make the first 3 **DHH**s in the next row. Release the 12" tail of **RC** from the left-hand pin and bring it to the right beneath the 3 **DHH**s and then out to the front parallel to the longer part of the **RC** (see Fig. 4).

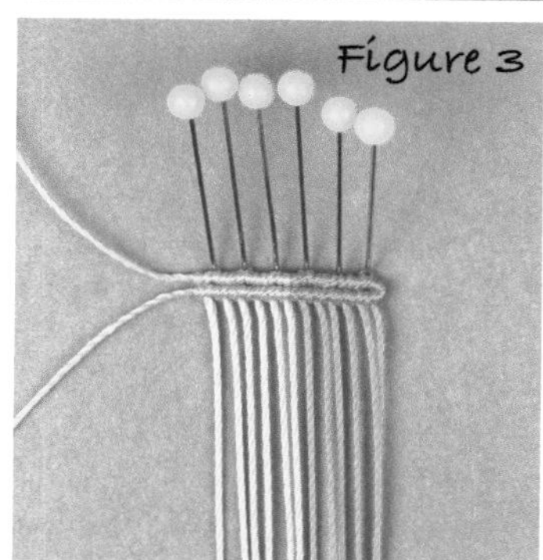

6. Make the next 2 **DHH**s around both **RC**s treating them as a single unit. Bring the 12" **RC** to the back of the piece and finish the row of **DHH**s using only the longer **RC**. Do not cut off the 12" cord, it will be used later to sew on the clasp.

7. The bracelet will measure approximately 7" when finished. If you wish to make a longer bracelet, you can add more rows of **DHH**s here. Add in 2- row increments (each will add about ⅛"). To make the bracelet symmetrical you will need to add the same number of rows to the bottom tab later.

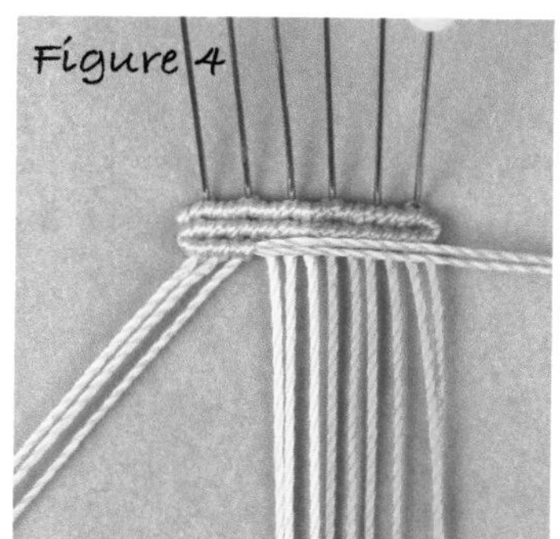

8. Bring the **RC** to the left again and make a row of **VDHH**s (Vertical Double Half Hitches) (see Fig. 5). Bring the **RC** off to the side for now, it will not be used in Part 2.

Part 2 - The Knotting Pattern

9. We will start on the left-hand half of the bracelet and be working with only the first six (Color-A) cords for now. Bring the 1st cord on the left to the right horizontally, using it as an **AC**. Working left to right, make **DHH**s around it with the next 5 cords. Repeat this step 7 more times for a total of 8 horizontal rows. The pattern will naturally make an angle towards the right (see Fig. 6a).

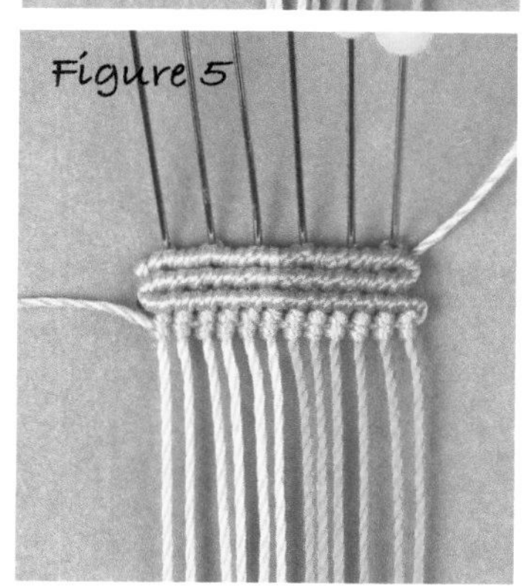

TIP - It's important that these rows be as horizontal as possible. If you notice that they tend to droop downwards toward the end of the row, take the first 2 (left-most) cords in the row and pull downward on them to correct the angle. You may have to do this frequently. Pin the rows in place to maintain the horizontal angle.

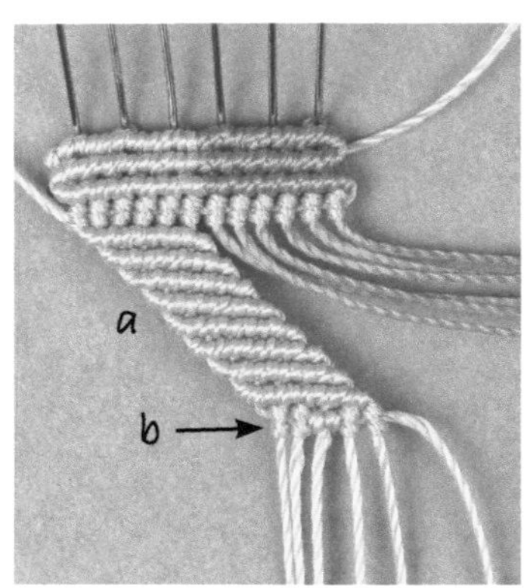

Figure 6

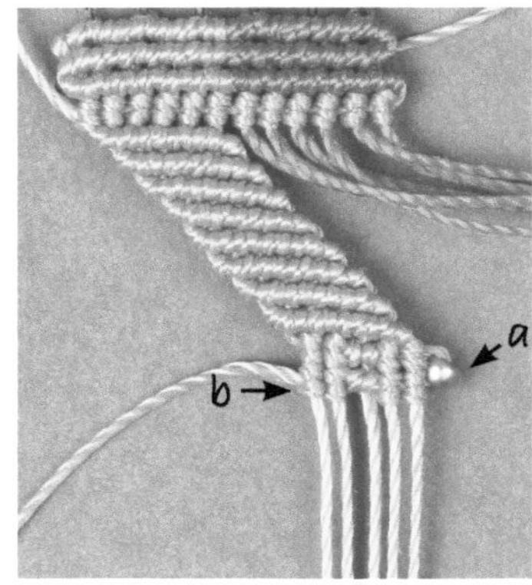

Figure 7

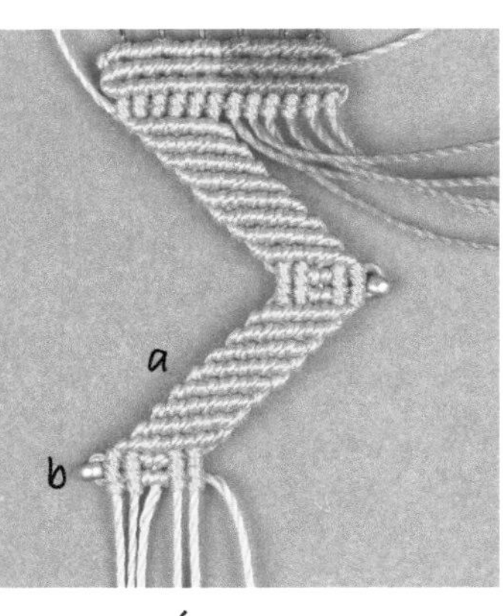

Figure 8

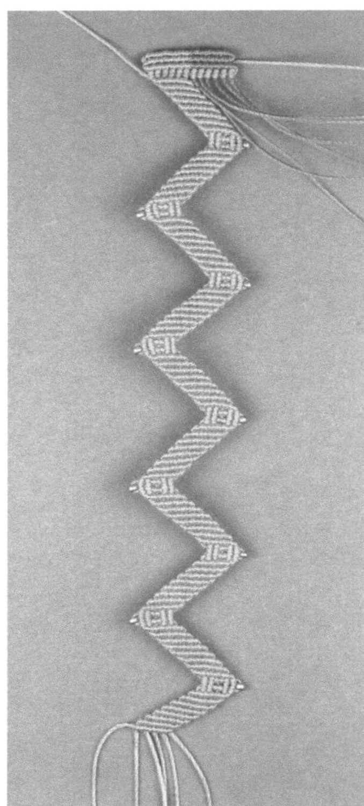
Figure 9

10. Bring Cd #1 (the first cord on the left) to the right again but this time the pattern will be: 2 **VDHH**s, 1 **DHH**, and 2 **VDHH**s (see Fig. 6b). After completing the row, thread a seed bead onto the cord and push it up against the final **VDHH** (see Fig. 7a).

11. Bring the same cord back to the left and working right to left, make a row identical to the previous row with 2 **VDHH**s, 1 **DHH**, and 2 **VDHH**s (see Fig. 7b).

12. Bring Cd. #6 (the right-most cord) to the left horizontally and make a row of 5 **DHH**s. Repeat 7 more times for a total of 8 rows. The pattern will naturally make an angle towards the left (see Fig. 8a). Keep the rows horizontal by pulling down periodically on the 2 right-most cords and pinning the knotwork in place.

13. Bring Cd. #6 horizontally to the left and make a row of 2 **VDHH**s, 1 **DHH**, and 2 **VDHH**s. After completing the row, thread a seed bead onto the cord and push it up against the final knot. Bring the same cord back around to the right and make a row of 2 **VDHH**s, 1 **DHH**, and 2 **VDHH**s (see Fig. 8b).

14. Repeat Steps 9 - 13 three more times. Repeat Steps 9 - 12 one more time. You should end up with nine corners (or points), each with a seed bead at the tip (see Fig. 9).

15. Use the six Color-B cords to knot the right-hand half of the bracelet. Do Steps 12 and 13 to get the pattern started, then follow the pattern as in the left half of the bracelet until the two halves are equal lengths (see Fig. 10).

Note - Knot the right-hand section on top of the completed left-hand section until you have enough finished length that you can move the left-hand section off to one side. Don't worry about joining the 2 sections together when working on them, you will do that when both are complete.

16. Weave the 2 halves together by bringing the Color-B section on top of the Color-A section, then bring the Color A section on top of the Color B section. Alternate in the same way until the whole piece is woven together. It should finish with a Color A section on top of a Color B section. Double check to make sure it looks right (see Fig. 11).

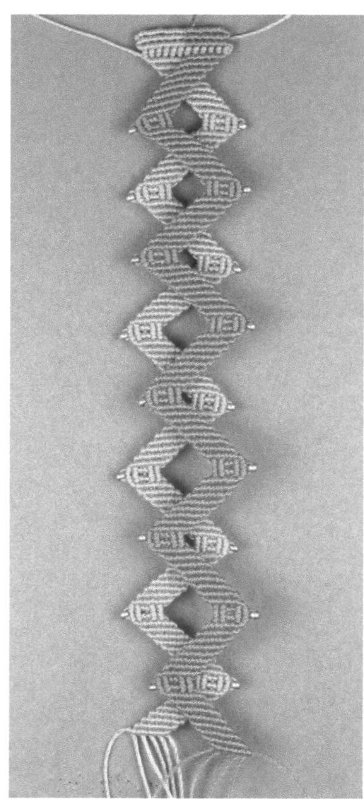
Figure 10

Part 3 - Adding the Center Beads

17. Flip the bracelet to the back. At the top of the bracelet, there are the two parts of the **RC**. Thread the longer part onto an embroidery needle and pass it downward underneath the overlapping (Color-A) knotted section (see Fig. 12).

18. Pass the needle from back to front just to the right of the **VDHH** in the inner right-hand corner and pull through. Flip the bracelet to the front (see Fig. 13 for the front view). At the front, the cord should come out in the "valley" between the two inner **VDHH**s (see Fig. 13a). Remove the needle and thread on (1) 11° seed bead, (1) 4mm bead, and (1) 11° seed bead. Rethread the needle and sew the cord from front to back next to the **VDHH**s on the opposite inner corner of the bracelet (see Fig. 13b).

19. Flip the bracelet to the back again. The cord will be on the left side of the bracelet. Bring it down and to the right under the overlapping (Color B) knotted section. Repeat Steps 18 and 19 until all the center spaces have been filled with beads (see Fig. 14).

20. At the bottom right-hand edge (on the back side of the bracelet), sew the cord under a bit of the knotted cord to hold it in place (see Fig. 14a).

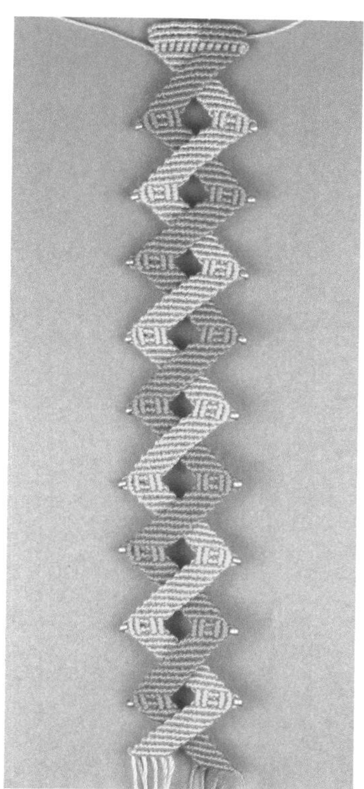

Figure 11

Part 4 - The Bottom Tab and Clasp

21. Flip the bracelet to the front and pin down the two halves so that they meet in the center and the bottom edges are horizontal (see Fig. 15).

22. Bring the **RC** to the right and make a row of **VDHH**s, joining the two halves together (see Fig. 15).

23. Bring the **RC** to the left and make a row of **DHH**s (see Fig. 16).

24. Bring the **RC** to the right and make a row of **DHH**s (see Fig. 16).

25. Bring the **RC** to the left and make a row of **DHH**s (see Fig. 16). Add more rows here if you need a longer bracelet.

26. Flip the bracelet to the back. Untwist the **RC** and separate (pull out) one ply from the 3-ply cord. Carefully cut off the 2-ply section next to the edge of the row and thread the remaining 1-ply cord onto a sturdy sewing needle.

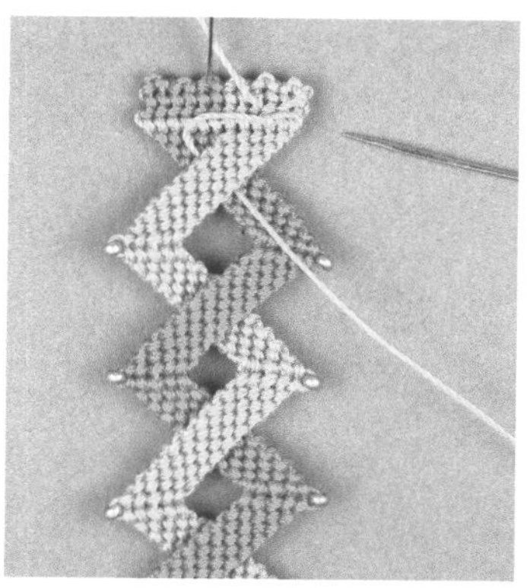

Figure 12

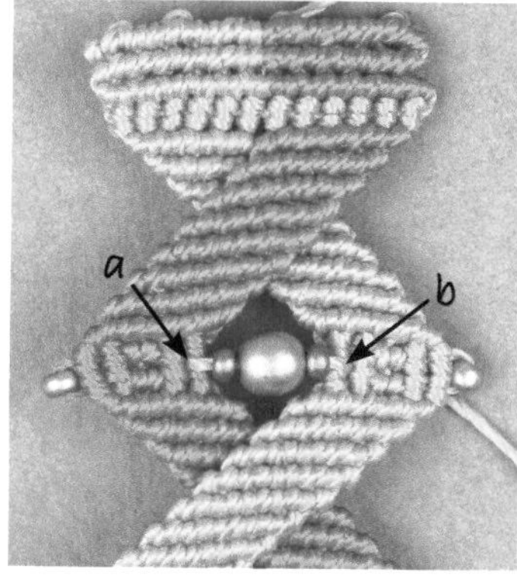

Figure 13

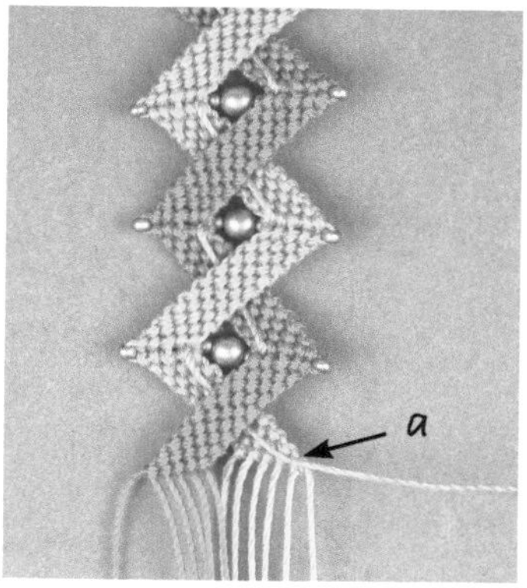

Figure 14

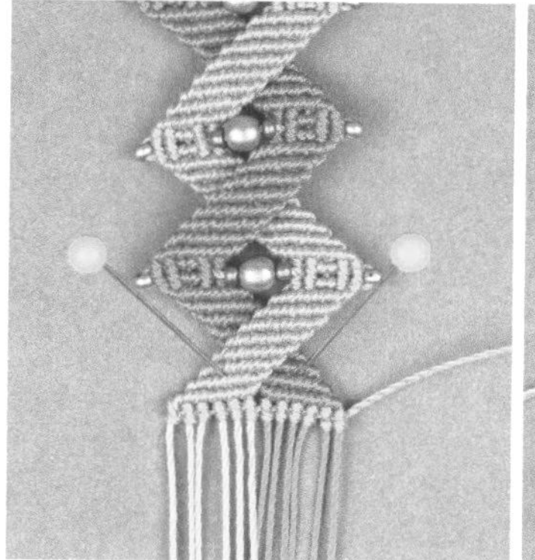

Figure 15

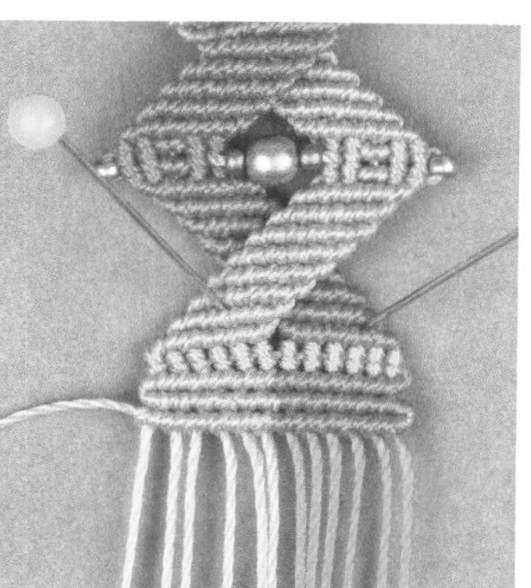

Figure 16

27. Bring the hanging Color A cords to the back as if making a hem. Sew them down securely to the back with the needle and thread (see Fig. 17). **Note -** To prevent the stitches from showing on the front of the bracelet, stitch only in the valleys between the **DHH** rows.

28. Hem up the Color B hanging cords using matching color thread (or make your own thread by separating out one ply from a 24" length of Color B cord) (see Fig. 18).

29. Sew the clasp part to the edge of the tab. First position the center ring at the center of the tab edge and sew it on with both colored threads. Next sew on the outside rings with their corresponding colored threads (see Fig. 19).

30. Trim off the hanging cords close to the stitching (see (see Fig. 20).

31. Sew the remaining clasp part to the edge of the top tab using corresponding colored threads. **Important -** Make sure the clasp part is centered and that the end faces in the opposite direction of the bottom clasp's end (see Figures 21a and 21b).

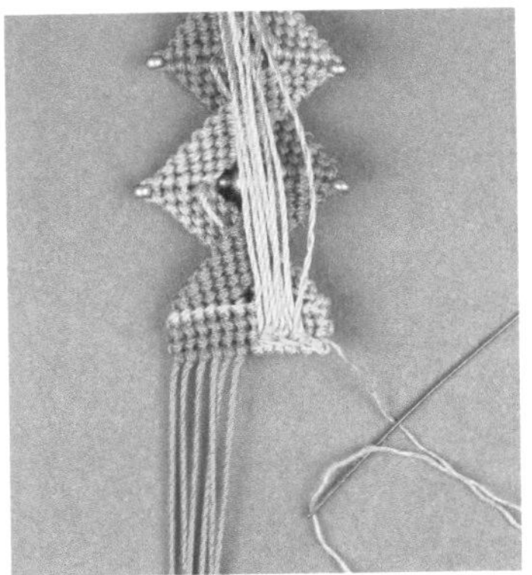

Figure 17

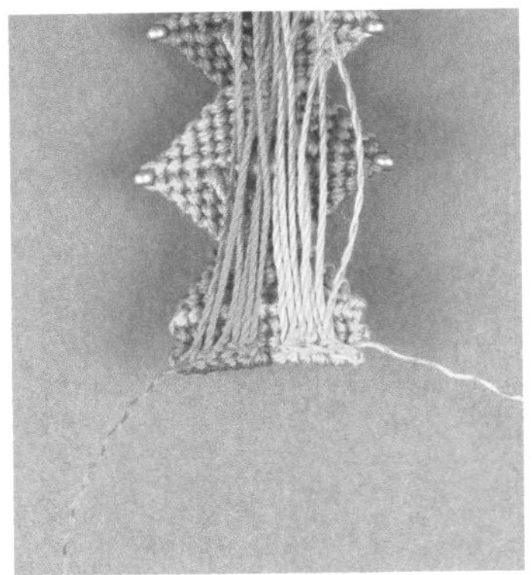

Figure 18

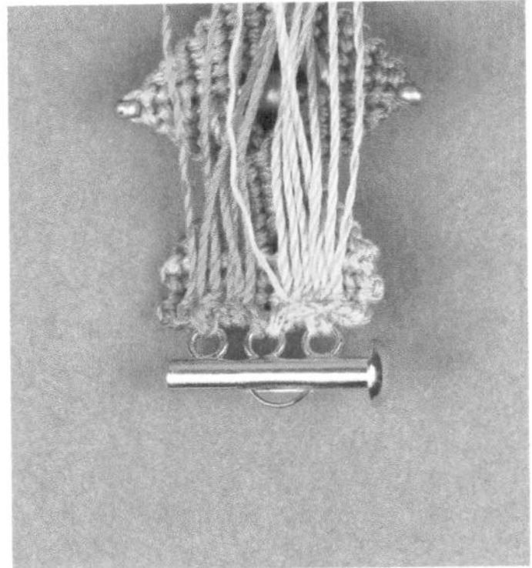

Figure 19

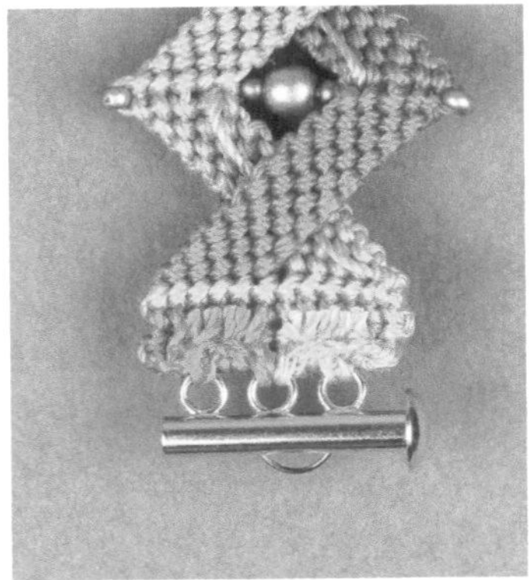

Figure 20

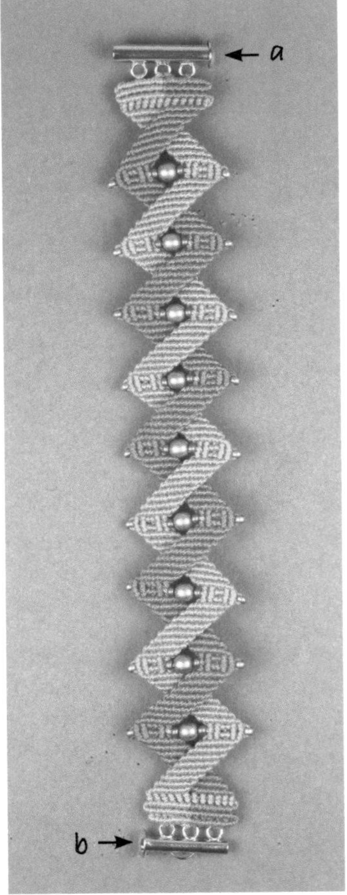

Figure 21

Art Nouveau Bracelet

This fanciful bracelet which evokes the Art Nouveau style is a colorful gem. The cabochon is ringed with a finely textured bezel and capped with beads at both ends. The graceful curves of knotwork lead the eye onward through curving pathways lined with beads.

Materials

- 18g Nylon - 24 @ 48" and 2 @ 46" (bracelet main color), 1 @ 32" (bezel accent color)
- 25mm x 18mm (medium or high dome) Cabochon
- (1) 15mm slide lock clasp
- Sewing needle and thread (matching bracelet main cord color)
- Ultrasuede - 2" x 2"
- Embroidery fabric (Lacy's Stiff Stuff or similar) - 2" x 2"
- E-6000 glue (or similar)

Beads:

(2) 3x6mm metal spacers or rondelles (must have a hole that fits 2 cords)

(4) 4mm round metal spacers (must have a hole that fits 3 cords)

(2) 6mm round faceted crystal or fire polish

(20) 3mm round faceted crystal or fire polish (6° or 8° seed beads may be substituted)

(30) 8° seed beads

(40) 10° seed beads

(12) 3.4mm drop/fringe beads

Part I - Double Bezel

1. Copy (or trace) the oval templates onto a piece of heavy paper and cut them out around the edges (see Fig. 46, templates). Place the larger oval onto a piece of Lacy's Stiff Stuff (or similar bead embroidery fabric) and trace around it (see Fig. 1a). Cut it out. Center the smaller oval within the fabric cut-out and trace around it (see Fig. 1b). Draw (extend) the 4 axis lines onto the fabric at the top, bottom and side points (see Fig. 1c).

2. Spread E-6000 glue onto the back surface of the cab out to the edges. Glue the cabochon onto the fabric, taking time to center it as exactly as possible (see Fig. 1d). Let it dry thoroughly before handling. Check to make sure the cab is completely glued down around the edges!

3. Take the two 46" cords and remove one ply from each, making them into 2-ply cords (these will act as Anchor Cords or **AC**s). Place two pins in the middle of your board $1\frac{3}{8}$" apart and angled slightly outwards (see Fig. 2). Center one of the 2-ply cords underneath the pins and wrap it upwards around the pins, crossing the ends above the pins (see Fig. 2a). Tape down the ends at each side.

4. Center the other 2-ply cord above the pins and wrap it downward around the pins, crossing the ends below the pins (see Fig. 3a). Tape down the ends at each side. Attach 12 (48") cords with **MTK**s (Mounting Knots) to the lower (3) **AC**s, treating them as a single unit (see Fig. 4).

5. Flip your board around and attach the remaining 12 cords to the opposite side **AC**s with **MTK**s (see Fig. 5). Remove it from the board and tighten the ring by pulling outward on the **AC** ends (one at a time). The top and bottom rows of 12 **MTK**s should be of equal lengths (approx. $1\frac{3}{8}$").

6. Turn the cord ring over to show the back (not the smooth) side of the **MTK**s and place it around the edge of the cab, adjusting it to fit closely (see Fig. 6). The **AC** ends should line up with the axis marks on the fabric. Thread the left two **AC** ends onto a needle and sew through the side axis line where it meets the cab edge. Sew the right two **AC** ends through the opposite axis line (see Fig. 6a and 6b). Check to make sure everything looks even.

7. Join the two pairs of cords at the center/back with a **FSQK** (Flat Square Knot). Apply a dab of nail polish to the knot (see Fig. 7). Cut off one of the cords from each side of the knot. There will be two 2-ply cords remaining. Remove one ply from each of these cords and cut it off. There will now be two 1-ply threads remaining. One of these threads will be used to sew on the cord ring and the other will be used to sew on the accent color bezel.

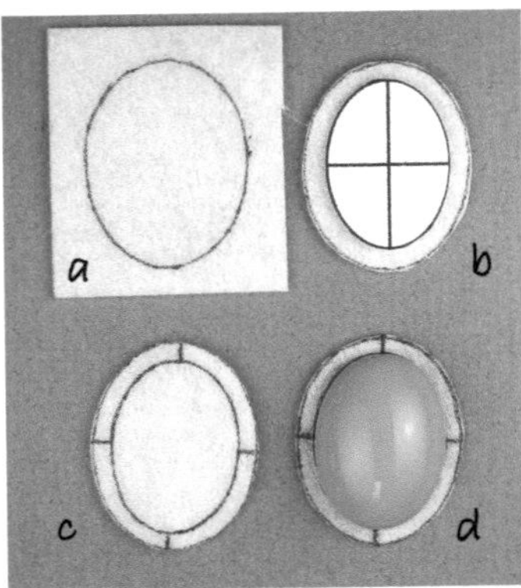

Figure 1

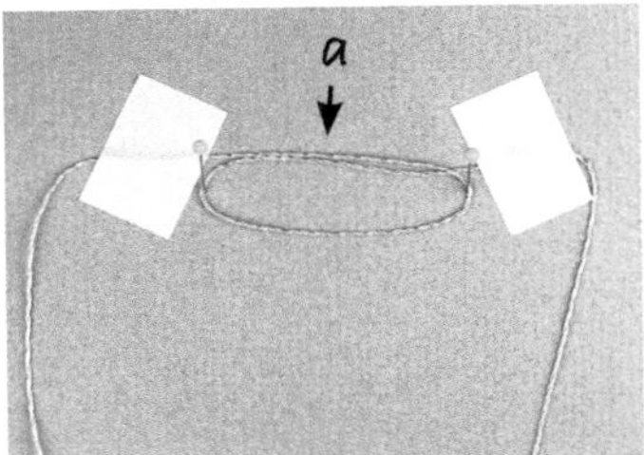

Figure 2

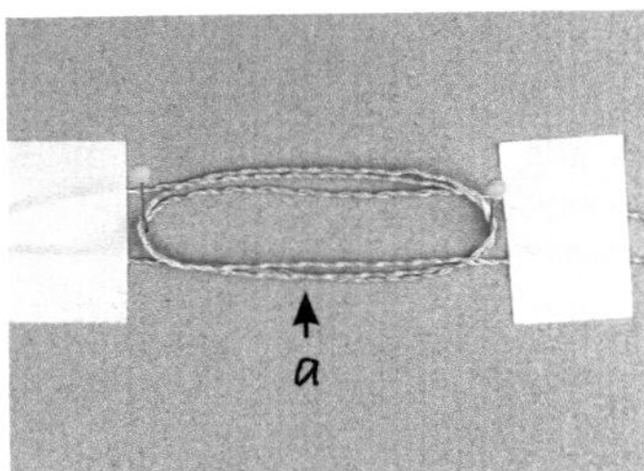

Figure 3

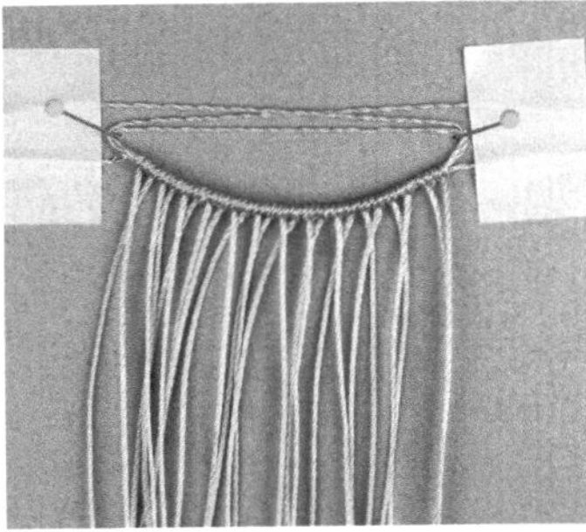
Figure 4

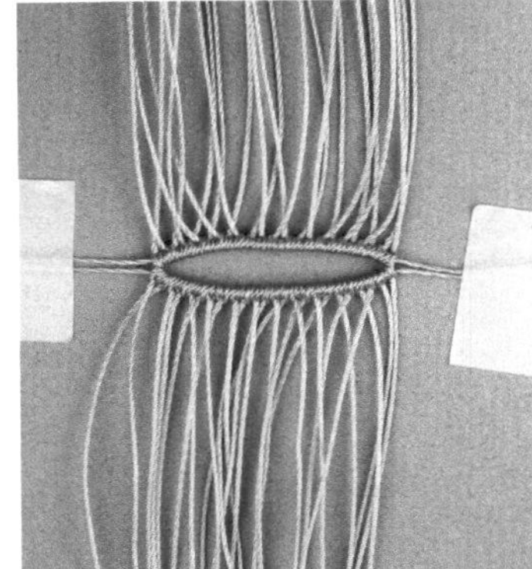
Figure 5

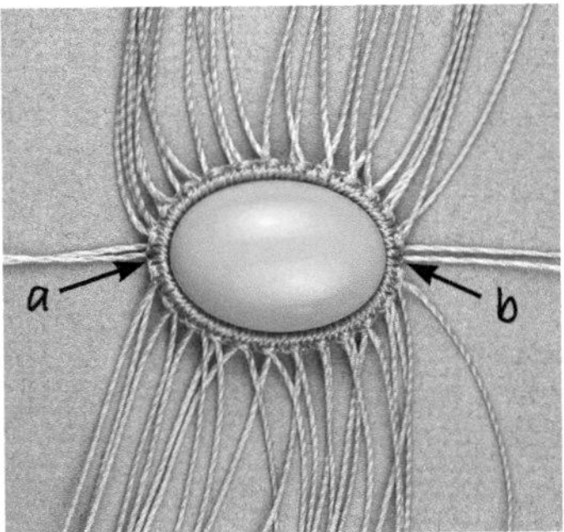

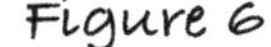
Figure 6

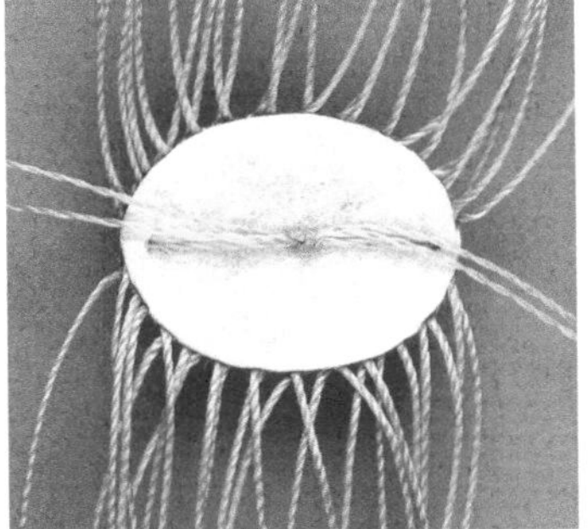
Figure 7

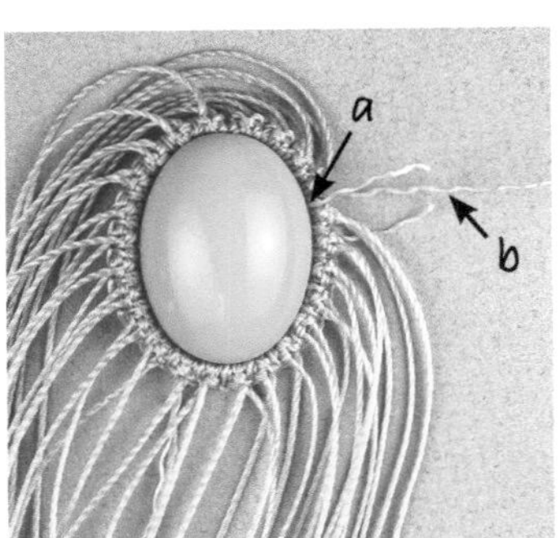

Figure 8

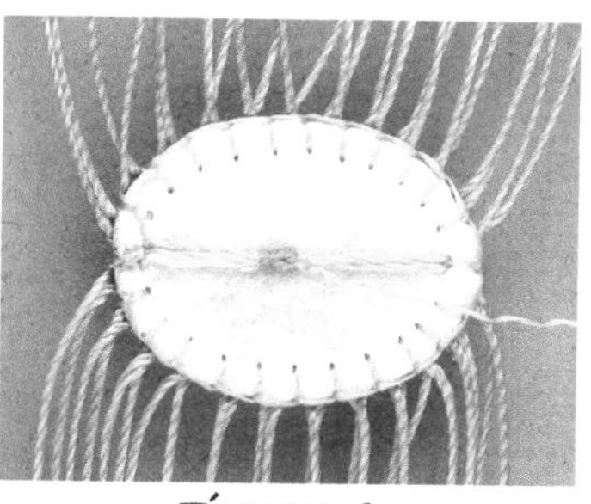
Figure 9

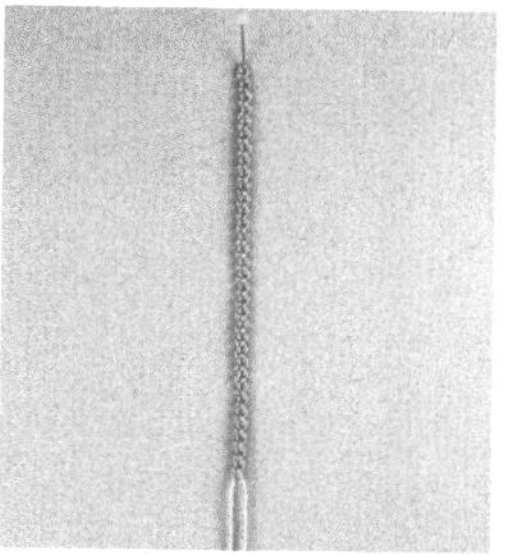
Figure 10

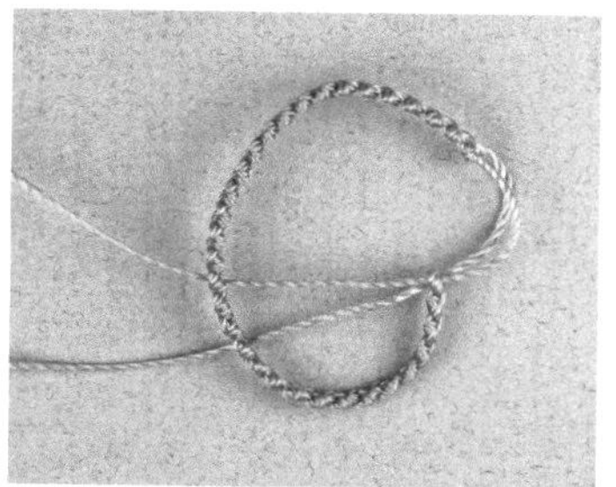
Figure 11

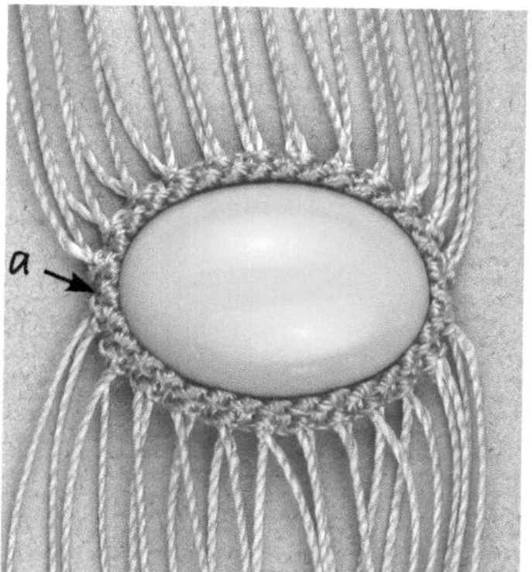

Figure 12

8. Thread one of the 1-ply threads onto a sewing needle. Secure the cord ring to the fabric in the following way: Bring the needle from the back to the front in between 2 **MTK**s (don't sew through the fabric yet). Sew downward between the edge of the cab and the cord ring (see Fig. 8a). To keep the stitch horizontal and in alignment with the ring cords, pass the needle over the thread (see Fig. 8b) before tightening it. Continue around the circle. Tie and cut off the thread when finished (see Fig. 9).

9. Drape the center of the 30" bezel accent cord over a pin. Make an **AHHch** (Alternating Half Hitch Chain) approximately 2 5/8" long (see Fig. 10). Check how it fits around the inside edge of the cord ring and add or subtract **HH**s if necessary. It should be about a **HH** shorter than the circumference. Form the chain into a circle and pass the two ends towards the inside through the top loop in the chain (see Fig. 11). Enlarge the loop with an embroidery needle if necessary. Pull it together to form a ring.

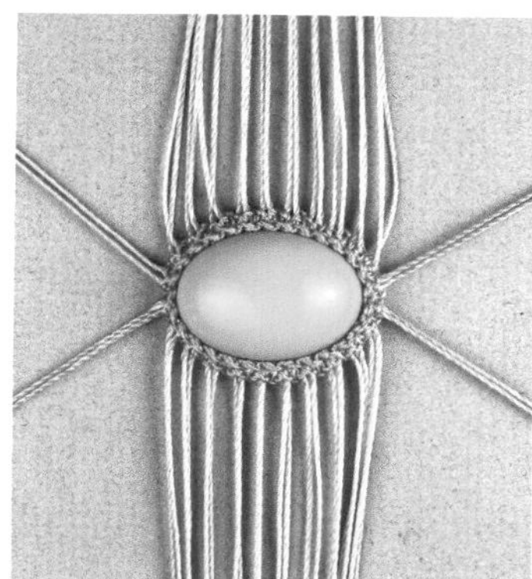
Figure 13

10. Position the **AHH** bezel over the cab and sew the two ends (one at a time) through to the back at the side axis line next to the cab edge (see Fig. 12a). Tie them together at the back with a **FSQK**. Apply a dab of nail polish and cut off the ends. Using the remaining 1-ply thread, sew the bottom edge of the **AHH** bezel to the fabric making small invisible stitches, passing the needle up and down through the space between the cab edge and the cord ring. **Note -** use pliers to pull the needle through if needed.

Part 2 - Main Bracelet

11. Divide the top and lower cords in half (24 each). Bring 4 cords (2 pairs) out to each side (2 pairs per side) leaving 20 cords facing upwards and 20 cords hanging downward. Each of the cord pairs will act as a (double) **AC**. (see Fig. 13).

Figure 14

12. Bring the lower right (double) **AC** towards the center and make a row of 10 **DHH**s (Double Half Hitches). At the center of the **DHH** row, add another **HH** (Half Hitch) to the last (centermost) **DHH**, making it a **THH** (Triple Half Hitch) (see Fig. 14a). The row should turn slightly downwards at the end. Bring the lower left (double) **AC** towards the center and make a row of 9 **DHH**s and 1 **THH** in a mirror image of the right side (see Fig. 14b).

13. Turn the piece upside down and repeat Step 12 on the opposite side of the cabochon (see Fig. 15).

14. On the left-hand side, take the outermost cord from the top **DHH** row and thread on (1) 8° bead, (1) 3x6mm metal spacer, and (1) 8° bead. Take the outermost cord from the lower **DHH** row and thread it in the opposite direction through the same beads and pull together. Repeat on the right-hand side (see Fig. 15a and b).

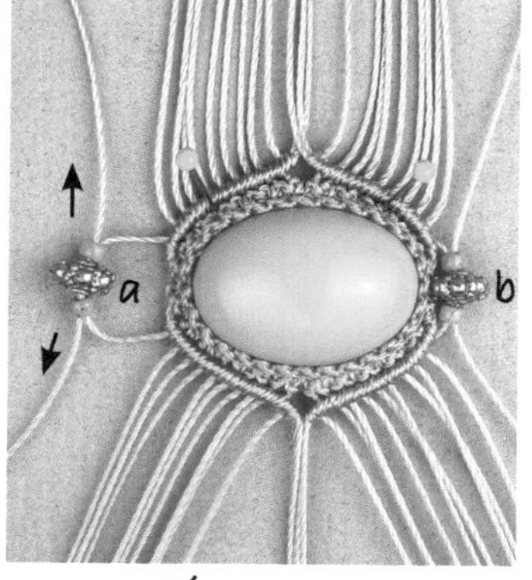

Figure 15

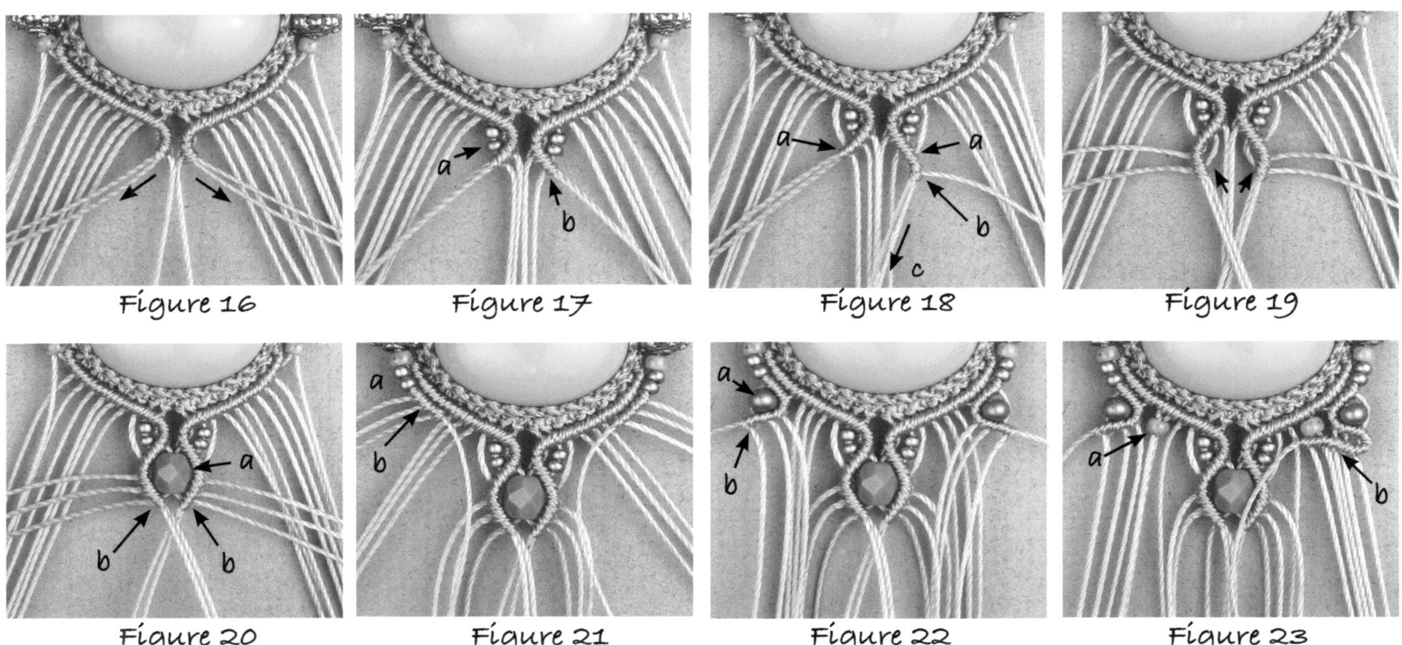

Figure 16 Figure 17 Figure 18 Figure 19

Figure 20 Figure 21 Figure 22 Figure 23

- Although the directions for Steps #15 - 43 are written in the singular (for one side only), make the same pattern on both the left and right sides of the bracelet. They should be mirror images of each other. Some Figures show more than one step. Complete Step "a" on both sides before going on to Step "b".

15. At the center, bring the **THH** cord downward under and to the opposite side of the **AC** and make a **THH** facing in the opposite direction of the first **THH**. The double **AC** should point outwards now (see Fig. 16).

16. Thread (2) 10° seed beads onto the 9th cord from the outer edge (see Fig. 17a). Attach this cord to the **AC** with a **DHH** (see Fig. 17b). The **AC** should point outwards at a downward diagonal angle.

17. Attach the 8th cord from the edge to the **AC** with a **DHH** (see Fig. 18a). Bring this same cord underneath the **AC** and make a **DHH** facing in the opposite direction (see Fig. 18b). The **AC** should point inwards now at a downward diagonal angle (see Fig. 18c).

18. Attach the next cord towards center to the **AC** (see Fig. 19). Thread a 6mm bead onto the two centermost cords and push up (see Fig. 20a). Attach the left-most center bead cord to the left-hand **AC** and the right-most center cord to the right-hand **AC** with **DHH**s (see Fig. 20b).

19. Thread 2 seed beads onto the outermost cord and push them up below the 8° bead (see Fig. 21a). Bring the cord towards the center and using it as an **AC**, attach the next 3 cords with **DHH**s (see Fig. 21b).

20. Thread a 3.4mm drop bead onto the 2nd cord from the edge (see Fig. 22a). Bring the **AC** around horizontally towards the outer edge. Working towards the edge, make **DHH**s with the first two cords. Rotate the drop bead so the wide part faces forward. Make a **THH** with the third (outermost) cord (see Fig. 22b).

21. Thread an 8° bead onto the 5th and 6th cords from the edge (see Fig. 23a). Bring the outer **THH** cord underneath the **AC** and make a **THH** facing in the opposite direction (the **AC** should point towards the center now). Attach the next four cords with **DHH**s, bringing the row up close to the 8° bead (see Fig. 23b).

22. Bringing the **AC** in a downward direction, attach the next cord (the 7th cord from the edge) with a **THH** (see Fig. 24a). Bring the **THH** cord underneath the **AC** and make a **THH** facing in the opposite direction of the first one. The **AC** should point outwards now.

23. Thread a 4mm round spacer bead onto the next three (joined) cords (see Fig. 24b and 25a). Attach these three cords to the **AC** with **DHH**s, positioning the row just below the bead (see Fig. 25). Attach the next cord (2nd from edge) to the **AC** with a **THH** (see Fig. 25b).

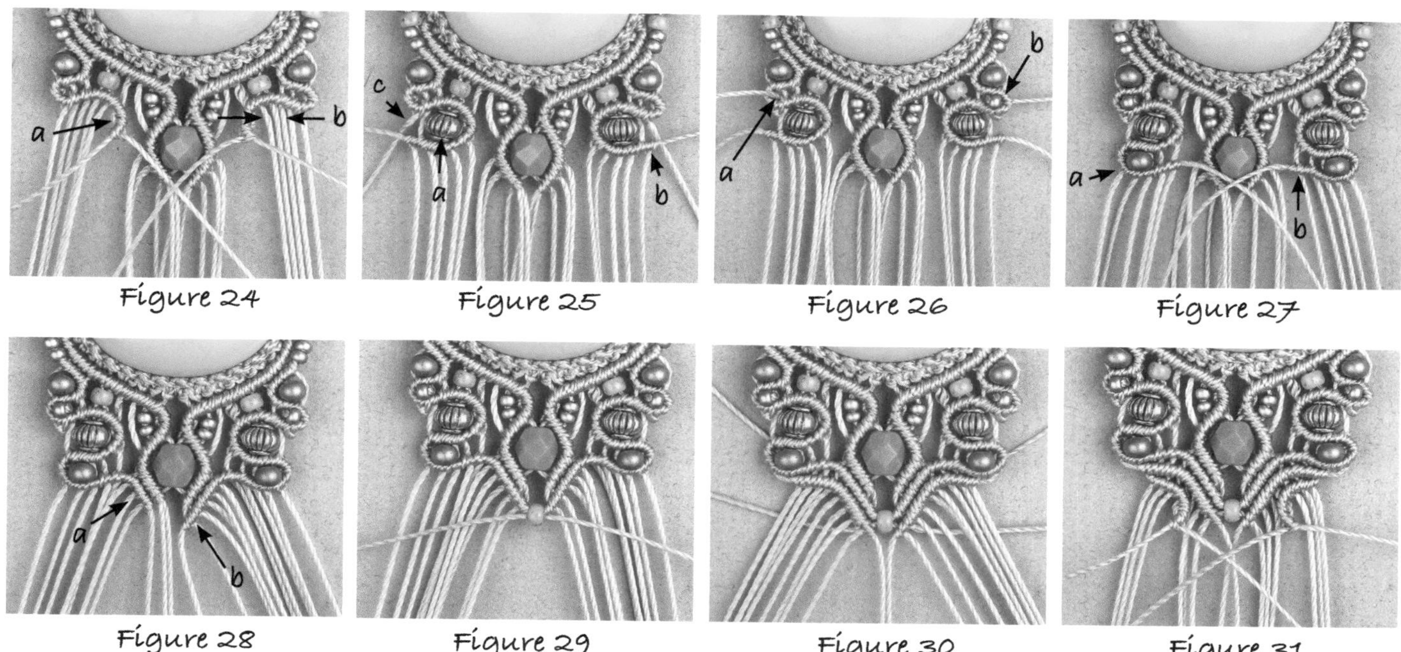

Figure 24 Figure 25 Figure 26 Figure 27

Figure 28 Figure 29 Figure 30 Figure 31

24. Thread the loose outermost cord (see Fig. 25c) onto an embroidery needle and sew it through the space above it so the cord exits to the front (see Fig. 26a). Remove the needle. Thread on a seed bead. Sew back through the same space (see Fig. 26b). Flip the piece to the back and tie off the seed-beaded cord with an **OVK** (Overhand Knot) flush with the knotwork. Apply a dab of nail polish. Let dry and cut off the cord next to the **OVK**.

25. Bring the outer **THH** cord underneath the **AC** and make a **THH** facing in the opposite direction (see Fig. 27a). The **AC** should point towards the center now. Thread a 3.4mm drop bead onto the next cord. Attach this drop bead cord and the next 2 cords to the **AC** with **DHH**s. Attach the next cord with a **THH**, bringing this row upward closer to the row above it (see Fig. 27b).

26. Working towards center, continue the **DHH** row by attaching the 3 cords that come off of the center row that surrounds the 6mm bead (see Fig. 28a). Attach each of the double **AC**s from the center row also (see Fig. 28b). This creates a continuous row from the edge to the center.

27. Thread an 8° bead onto the left-hand center **AC**. Thread the right-hand center **AC** through the same bead going in the opposite direction. Pull out on the cords to center the bead (see Fig. 29).

28. Bring the two outermost cords toward the center and using them as a double **AC**, make **DHH**s with the next 4 cords. Omit the 5th cord and bring it to the back (it will be discarded). Make **DHH**s with the next 3 cords. Using the cord that exits the 8° bead, make a **DHH** around only one of the double **AC**s, the other **AC** will be discarded (see Fig. 30). Flip the piece to the back and cut off the discarded cords.

29. Bring the outermost cord towards the center and using it as an **AC**, make **DHH**s with the next 3 cords. Make a **THH** with the next (4th) cord. Bring this **THH** cord underneath the **AC** and make a **THH** facing in the opposite direction (see Fig. 31). The **AC** should point towards the outer edge now.

30. Thread (1) drop bead onto the 3rd cord from the edge. Bring the **AC** horizontally out to the side and attach the drop bead cord to the **AC** with a **DHH**. Skip the next cord (it will be discarded) and attach the outermost cord with a **DHH** (see Fig. 32). Cut off the discarded cord at the back.

31. Make 2 **SQK**s (Square Knots) using the 4 centermost cords (see Fig. 33a). Thread (3) 10° seed beads onto the 6th cord from the edge, next to the **SQK**s (see Fig. 33b). Bring the outermost cord towards the center and using it as an **AC**, make a diagonal row of 7 **DHH**s (see Fig. 34).

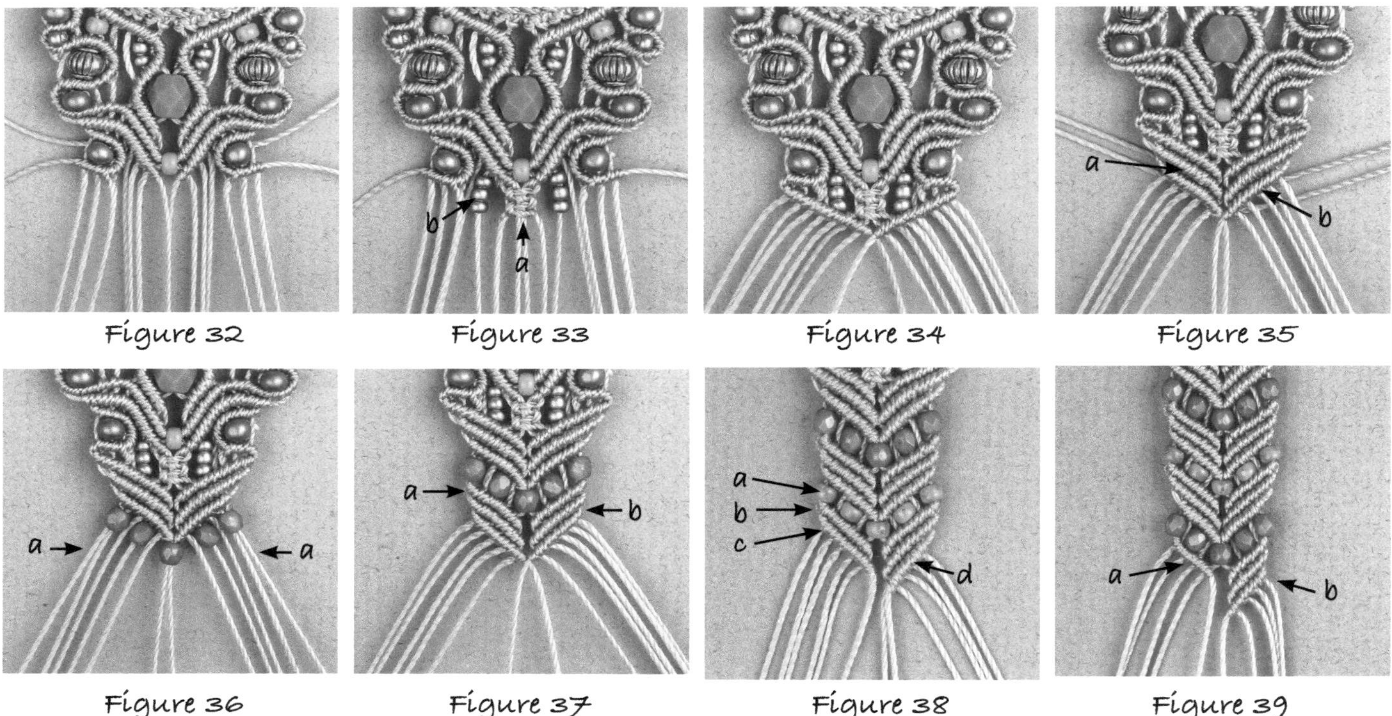

Figure 32 Figure 33 Figure 34 Figure 35

Figure 36 Figure 37 Figure 38 Figure 39

32. Bring the two outermost cords towards the center and using them as a double **AC**, make a row of 6 **DHH**s; the **AC** from the row above should be knotted in as the last **DHH** (see Fig. 35a, middle row). Bring one of the double **AC**s to the back (it will be discarded). Next row - Bring the two outermost cords towards the center and using them as a double **AC**, make a row of 5 **DHH**s (see Fig. 35b, bottom row). Bring one of the double **AC**s to the back (it will be discarded). Flip the piece to the back and cut off the discarded **AC**s flush with the row ends.

Note - if your wrist measurement is 6" or less, skip Steps #33 and 34 and go on to Step #35.

33. Thread (1) 3mm round bead onto the two (joined) centermost cords, the two (joined) outermost cords, and the 4th cord from the edge (see Fig. 36). **Note -** 6° or 8° seed beads may be substituted if the 3mm beads have holes that are too small for 2 cords.

34. Bring one cord from the outer bead (see Fig. 36a) towards the center and use it as an **AC**. Make a row of **DHH**s below the beads with the next 5 cords (this includes the other cord that exits the outer bead) (see Fig. 37a). Next two rows - Bring the outermost cord towards the center and using it as an **AC**, make a row of 5 **DHH**s. Repeat (see Fig. 37b).

35. Thread (1) 8° seed bead onto the two (joined) centermost cords, onto the two (joined) outermost cords, and the 4th cord from the edge (see Fig. 38a). Bring one of the cords that exits the outer bead towards the center and using it as an **AC**, make a row of **DHH**s below the beads with the next 5 cords (see Fig. 38b).

36. Bring the outermost cord towards the center and using it as an **AC**, make a row of 5 **DHH**s (see Fig. 38c). Next row - Bring the two outermost cords towards the center and using them as a double **AC**, make a row of 4 **DHH**s (see Fig. 38d). Bring one of the double **AC**s to the back and cut it off.

37. Thread (1) 3mm round bead onto the two (joined) centermost cords, the outermost cord, and the 3rd cord from the edge. Bring the cord that exits the outer bead towards the center and using it as an **AC**, make a row of **DHH**s below the beads with the next 4 cords (see Fig. 39a).

38. Next two rows - Bring the outermost cord towards the center and using it as an **AC**, make a row of 4 **DHH**s. Repeat (see Fig. 39b).

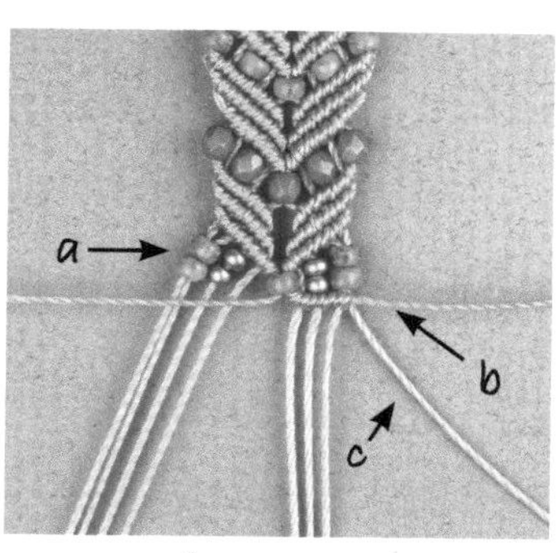

Figure 40

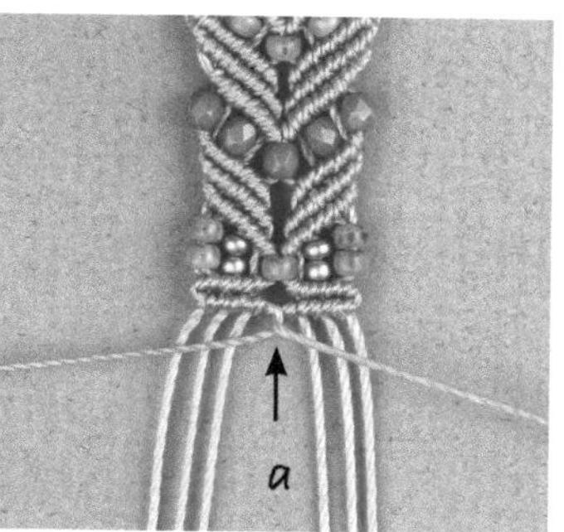

Figure 41

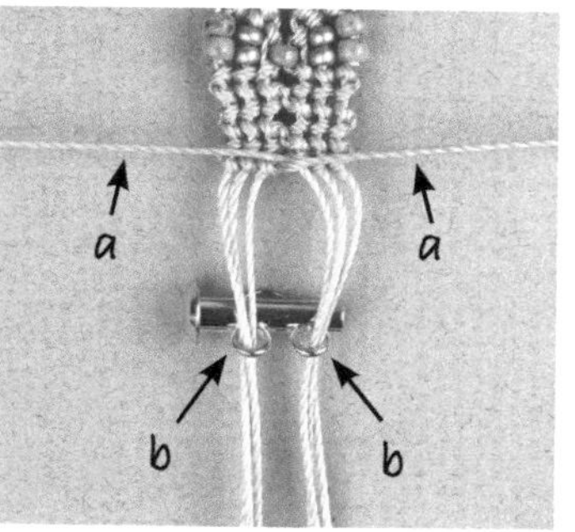

Figure 42

Figure 43

39. Thread (1) 8° seed bead onto the two (joined) centermost cords. Thread (2) 8° beads onto the two (joined) outermost cords (make an **OVK** at the tip of the 2nd cord from the edge to differentiate it from the outermost cord). Thread (2) 10° seed beads onto the 3rd cord from the edge (see Fig. 40a).

40. Bring the two cords that exit the center bead outwards horizontally to each side and use them as **AC**s. Working from the center outwards, attach the next 2 cords with **DHH**s (see Fig. 40b). Attach only the outermost cord of the two cords that exit the (2) 8° beads. At the back, cut off the discarded 2nd cord (see Fig. 40c) flush with the bottom of the outer bead.

41. Bring the **AC**s towards the center and make rows of 3 **DHH**s on each side. Wrap the left **AC** once around the right **AC** and bring them back outwards horizontally (see Fig. 41a). Working from the center outwards, make a row of 3 **DHH**s (not shown).

42. Repeat Step #41 until this half of the bracelet is half the length of the finished bracelet minus $\frac{1}{4}$" (measuring from the center line of the cab to the bottom row of the knotwork). For example - if you'd like your bracelet to be 7", (7" ÷ 2 = 3 $\frac{1}{2}$" – $\frac{1}{4}$" = 3 $\frac{1}{4}$"). Bring the **AC**s inwards towards the center and make one more row of 3 **DHH**s on each side.

43. Turn the bracelet upside down and repeat Steps #15 - 42.

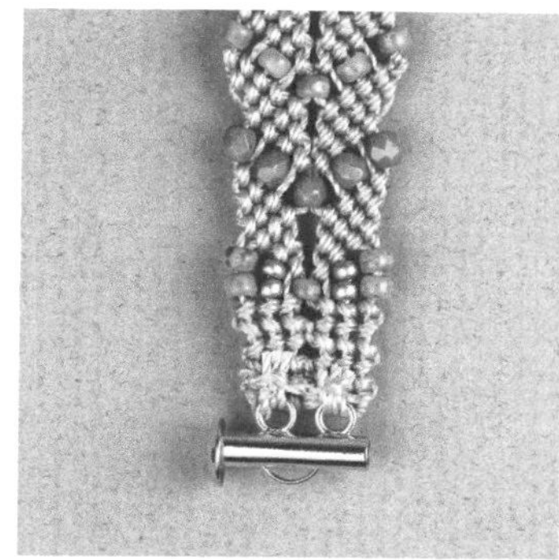

Figure 44

Part 3 - Finishing

Figure 45

44. To sew on the clasp, you'll need a 30" length of matching thread (or a 1-ply piece of the cord) and a sewing needle. Check the bracelet's length around your wrist and adjust if necessary. The clasp will add about $\frac{3}{8}$".

45. At the back of the band, cross the 2 **AC**s over each other and bring them outward horizontally (see Fig. 42a). Thread the remaining cords through the loops of the clasp segment, 3 cords per loop (see Fig. 42b). Fold the cords neatly to the back of the band. Sew them down securely near the bottom edge, passing over and through the cords several times so that they can't pull out (see Fig. 43). Cut off the **AC**s at the outer edges and the other cords below the stitching (see Fig. 44). Repeat on the other end, making sure that the clasp tips face in opposite directions or it won't close properly (see front photo).

46. Use the large template for the Ultrasuede lining. Place the lining over the fabric at the back, and sew around the edge with whip stitching (see Fig. 45).

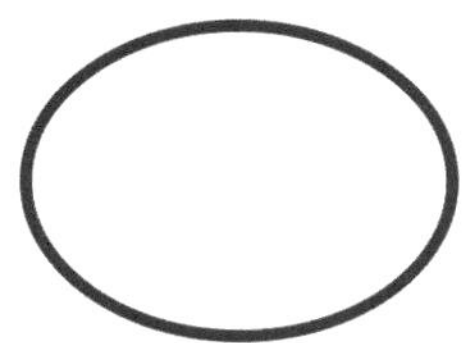

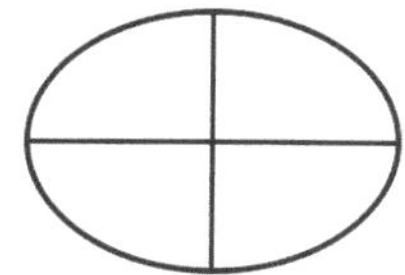

Figure 46
Templates

The Mérida Necklace

Beads take center stage in this lightweight and versatile necklace. From casual to dressy, it's sure to compliment any outfit.

Materials

18g Nylon Cord - 6 lengths @ 70" (all one color or various colors) 2 @ 120" (main neck chain color)

Beads:

6°, 8°, 11° seed beads, assorted beads of your choice (rondelles, rounds, bicones, etc..)

(2) 8mm jumprings

(1) Hook and eye clasp

Part I - Neck Chain, right side

1. Gather together the six 70" cords and thread them through a jumpring. Line up all 12 ends evenly. Temporarily tie the bundle of cords together just below the jumpring with a piece of spare cord (see Fig. 1)

2. Pin the jumping to the board to hold it in place. Fold over 5" of one end of a 120" cord. Make a vertical **MH** (Mounting Hitch) around the bundled cords. The **MH** cords should come out to the right with the 5" cord above the longer cord. Tighten well (see Fig. 2).

3. The longer (lower) cord will act as the **KC** (Knotting Cord). Make a **HH** (Half Hitch) around the bundled cords with the **KC** in this way: Bring the **KC** to the left over the cords (see Fig. 3a), then back to the right under the cords (see Fig. 3b), and pull through, passing the **KC** over the loop (see Fig. 3c). Tighten. Repeat one time.

4. Make a **HH** around the bundled cords with the **KC** in this way: Bring the **KC** to the left under the cords (see Fig. 4a), then back to the right over the cords (see Fig. 4b), and pull through, passing the **KC** under the loop (see Fig. 4c). Tighten. Repeat two times (see Fig. 5). Remove the spare cord and push the knots up to the jump ring. Hide the 5" tail by sewing it downward under the **HH**s at the back of the chain with an embroidery needle (see Fig. 6). Cut off the excess cord.

5. Continue knotting down the neck chain in sets of 6 **HH**s: Make 3 **HH**s (as in Step 3 - over/under/over) followed by 3 **HH**s (as in Step 4 - under/over/under). Repeat this pattern until the chain is about 4.5" long (excluding the jumpring). As the chain progresses you'll see a zig-zag line forming along the outside edge of the neck chain (see Fig. 7a).

6. Divide the 12 bundled cords into two groups of 6 (if you are using different colors, both groups should have some of each color). Bring the **KC** to the left and make 2 **VDHH**s (Vertical Double Half Hitch), one **VDHH** around each group (see Fig. 7b). Bring the **KC** to the right and make 2 **VDHH**s (see Fig. 8).

7. Divide the 12 cords into three groups in the following way: take 4 from the right-hand side, 4 from the left-hand side, and 2 from each side and group them together at the center. Make one row of 3 **VDHH**s going right to left. Make another row of 3 **VDHH**s going left to right (see Fig. 9).

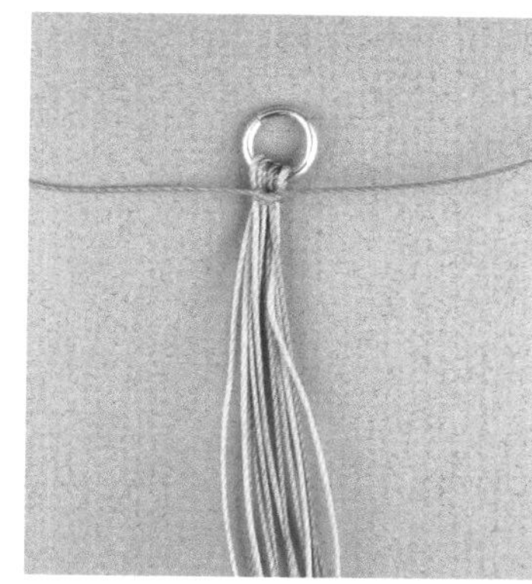

Figure 1

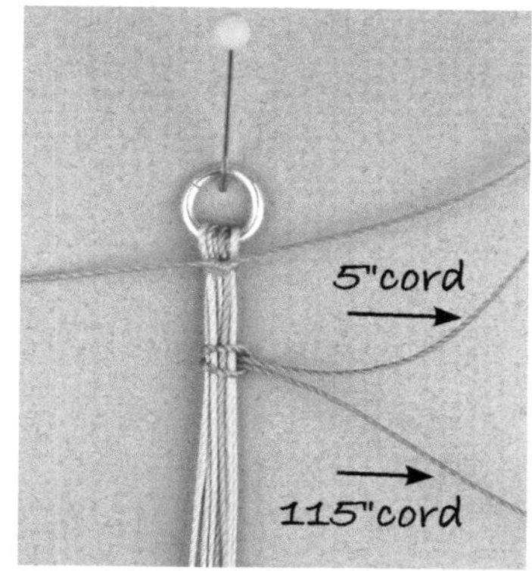

Figure 2

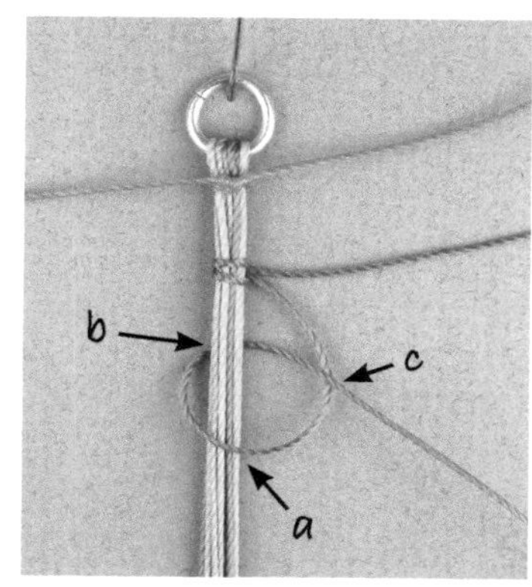

Figure 3

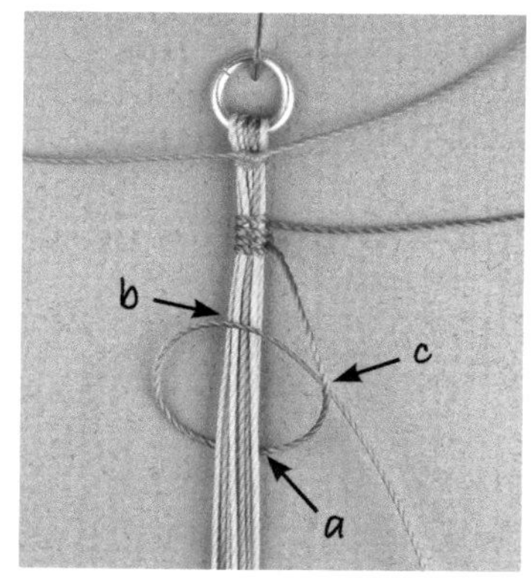

Figure 4

Figure 5

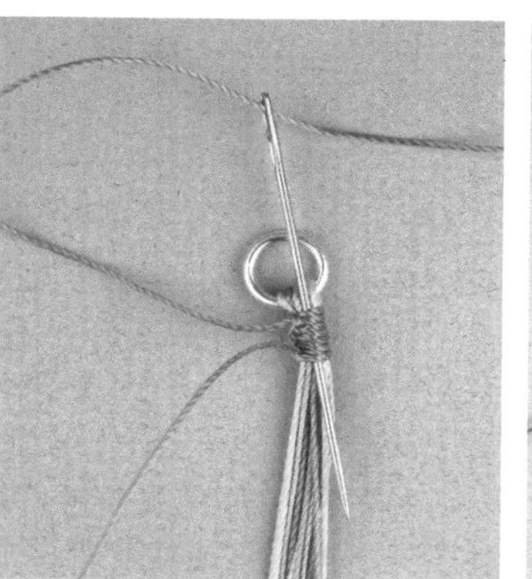

Figure 6

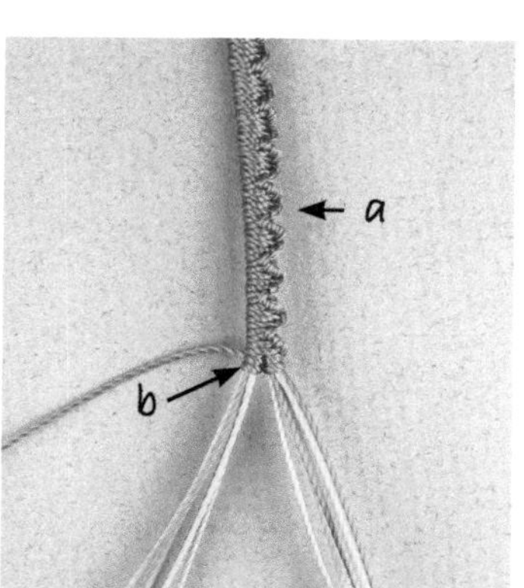

Figure 7

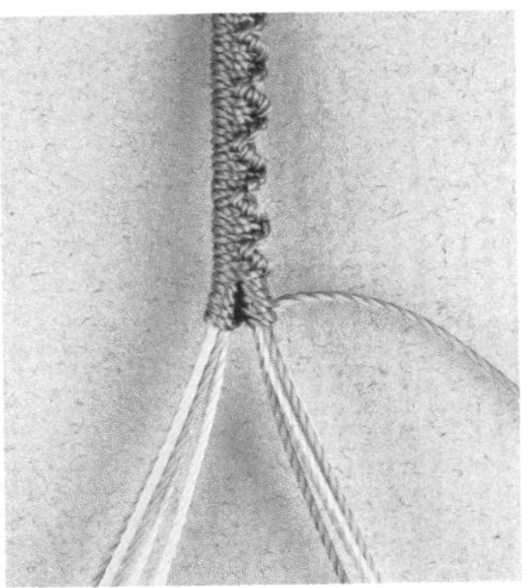
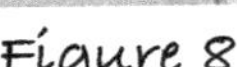

Figure 8

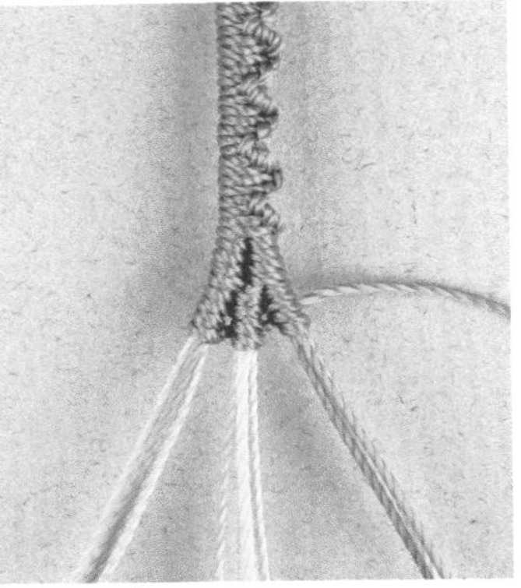

Figure 9

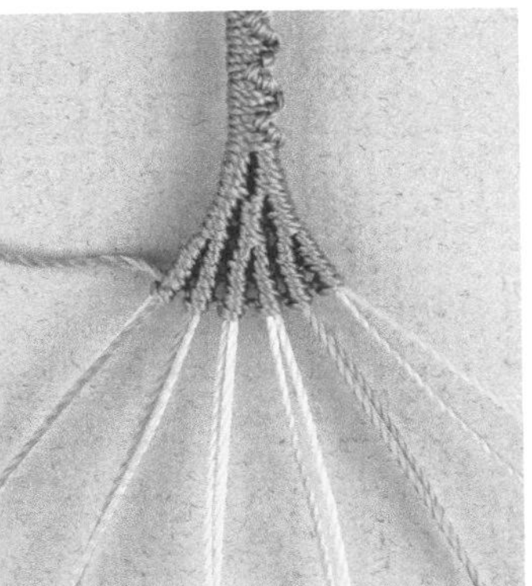

Figure 10

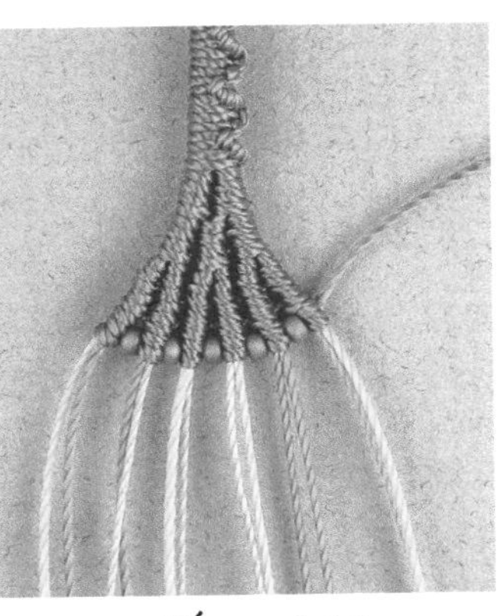

Figure 11

8. Divide the three groups of 4 cords into six groups of 2 cords each. Make one row of 6 **VDHH**s from right to left. Make another row of 6 **VDHH**s from left to right, leaving a small space between each **VDHH**. Make a third row of 6 **VDHH**s from right to left, leaving a little bit more space between the **VDHH**s. In other words, the rows should fan out slightly (see Fig. 10).

9. Bring the **KC** back to the right and make a **VDHH** around the first 2 (grouped) cords. Thread (1) 11° seed bead onto the **KC** and push it up next to the **VDHH**. Make a **VDHH** around the second 2 (grouped) cords. Thread (1) 11° seed bead onto the **KC** and push it up next to the **VDHH**. Continue this pattern across the row, adding beads between the **VDHH**s (see Fig. 11).

Figure 12

10. Bring the **KC** back to the left and make a row of 12 **VDHHs** (one per each cord). Make two more rows of 12 **VDHH**s (see Fig. 12).

11. Flip the piece to the back. Thread the **KC** onto an embroidery needle and sew under a stitch in the center of the knotwork (this is done to position the cord away from the edge, while still keeping it at the back, see Fig. 13a). Pass the needle through the space between the top 2 **VDHH**s where it meets the neck chain and pull through to the front (see Fig. 13b).

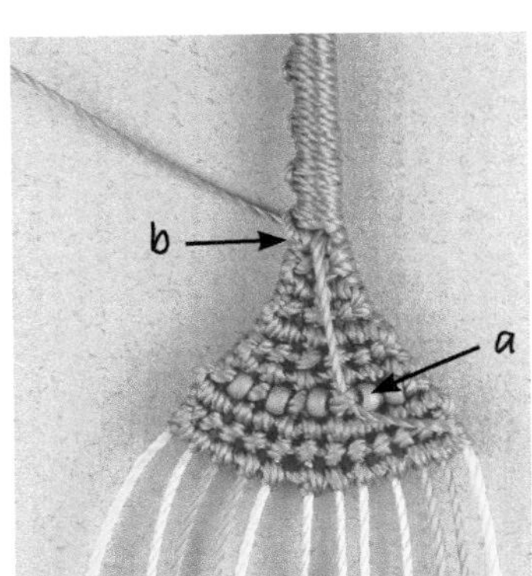

Figure 13, back view

12. Take off the needle and thread an 8° seed bead onto the **KC**. Thread the cord on the needle again and pass it back through the knotwork below the bead (see Fig. 14a). Make an **OVK** (Overhand Knot) in the **KC** flush with the knotwork on the back side. Tighten well and apply a tiny dab of clear nail polish to the **OVK**. Let dry and cut off the excess cord close to the **OVK**.

Part 2 - Center Bead Strands

This section allows you to be creative and choose bead combinations that appeal to you. In general I suggest that you use smaller beads towards the top and leave larger beads for the bottom strands. You can completely cover each cord with beads or make some strands which leave some of the cord exposed as I did in my example (see main photo).

Tips - When using beads larger than 8° seed beads, start and end those strands with a couple of 11° seed beads so that the beads don't get too crowded where they meet the knotwork. Take care when positioning the strands that they are spaced evenly and about $\frac{1}{4}$" to $\frac{1}{2}$" apart at center (unless you desire an effect of more space between strands). It's OK to combine two side by side cords together into one beaded strand to reduce the overall number of strands (I did that twice in my example).

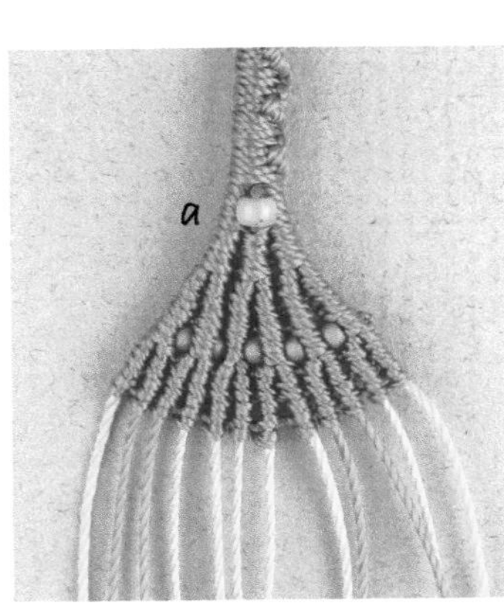

Figure 14

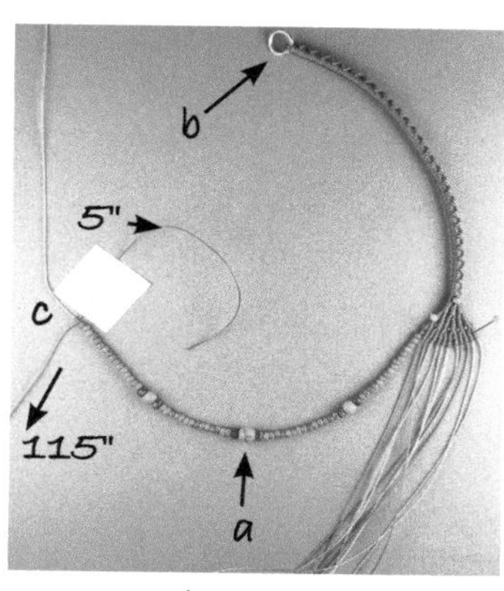

Figure 15

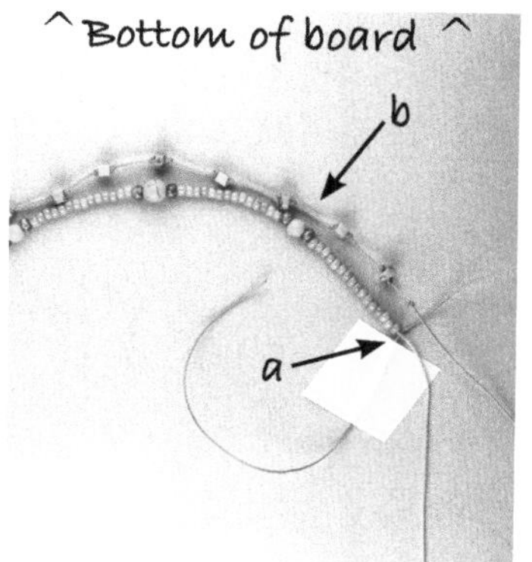

Figure 16

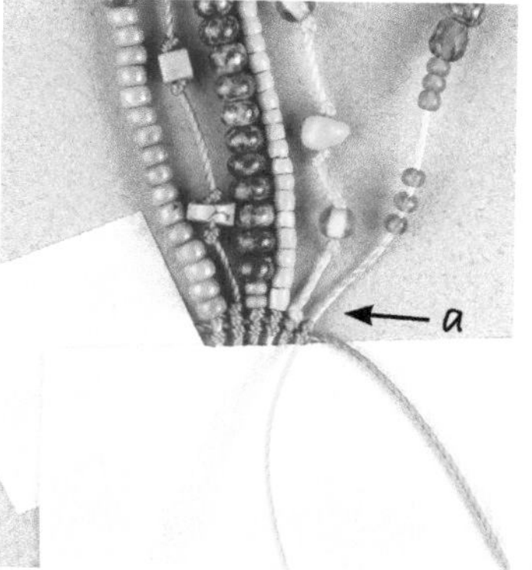

Figure 17

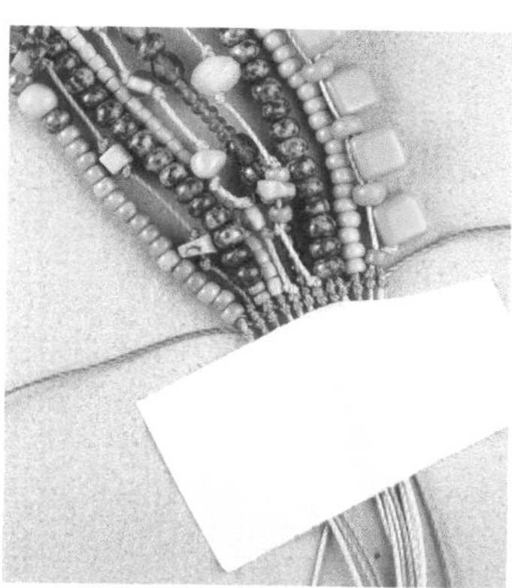
Figure 18

13. Position the necklace on your board as in Fig. 15 and pin in place. The topmost strand will determine the circumference of the necklace. The measurement from the center of this beaded strand (see Fig. 15a) to the end of the completed neck chain (see Fig. 15b) should be half of the length of the finished necklace (minus half the length of your clasp). For example, for an 18" necklace with a 2" clasp - (18"÷ 2 = 9"-1"= 8").

14. The bead strand should droop down in the middle so that it and the neck chain form a continuous rounded half-circle. Tape the end of an 120" cord (**KC**) next to the end of the top bead strand, positioning it as in Fig. 15c. Leave 5" of **KC** to the right of the tape and the longer part to the left.

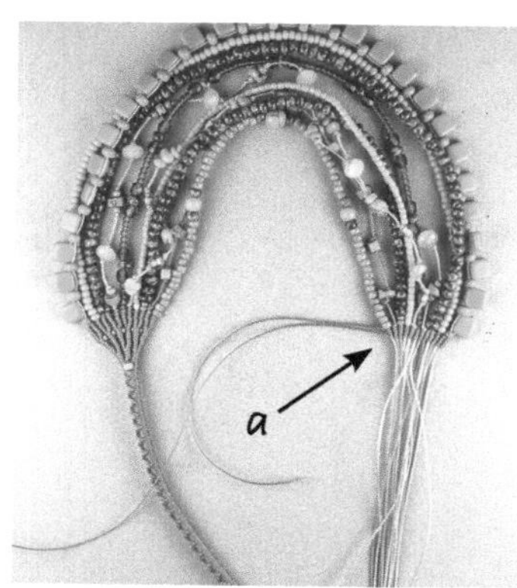

Figure 19

15. Place the board on a flat surface and turn it around so that the bottom of the board is now the top. Working left to right, make a **VDHH** around the bead strand cord with the **KC** (see Fig. 16a). This starts a row of **VDHH**s. All of the remaining cords will be attached to this row one by one after they have been beaded and/or knotted. Tape down the strand ends after each is finished (see Fig. 17 and 18). **Tip -** Since the **KC** is long, it may help to coil most of it up and tie it temporarily (leaving about 20 - 30" to work with).

16. Turn the board back to the correct position (top up and slanted, leaning against the table) and complete the second strand. In my example, I left some cord exposed and placed beads at regular intervals, holding them in place with **OVK**s before and after the bead(s) (see Fig. 16b). Put an **OVK** at the beginning and end of the strand to hold the cord in position.

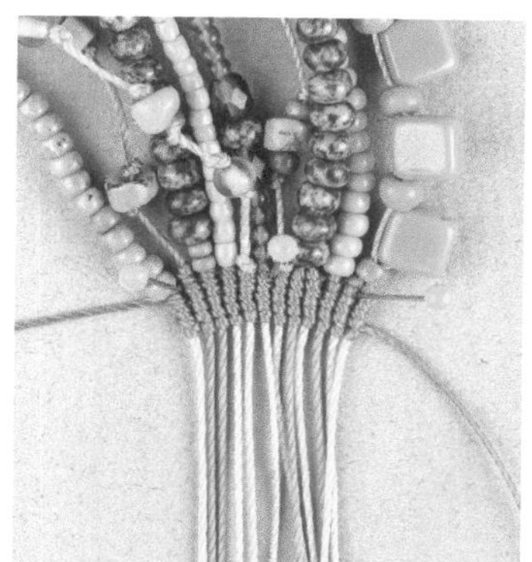
Figure 20

17. Place the board on a flat surface and turn it around again. Make a **VDHH** around the bead strand cord with the **KC**. Turn the board back to the correct position and complete the third strand. Continue attaching each of the strands to the **VDHH** row as you complete them. **Tip** - when attaching solidly beaded strands to this row it helps to make the **VDHH** an inch down (away from) the beads (see Fig. 17a). Then pull the cord taut, bringing the beads even with the **VDHH** row.

Part 3 - Neck Chain, Left Side

18. Turn the board around and make a row of 12 **VDHH**s going right to left (see Fig. 19a). Position the necklace as in Fig. 19 for the next steps. Tape or pin the bead strands so that they stay up and out of the way.

19. Make a row of 12 **VDHH**s going left to right (see Fig. 20).

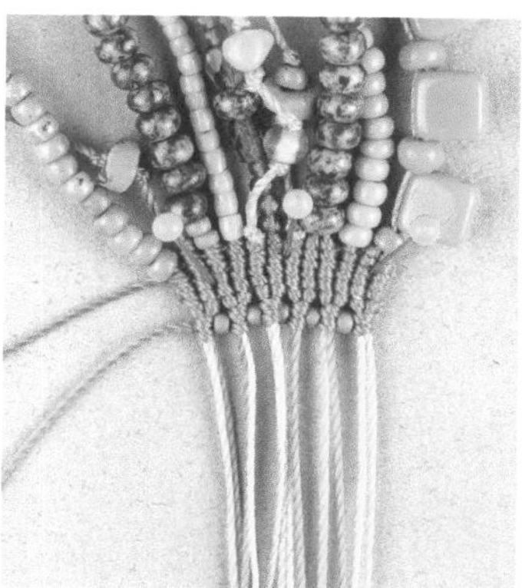
Figure 21

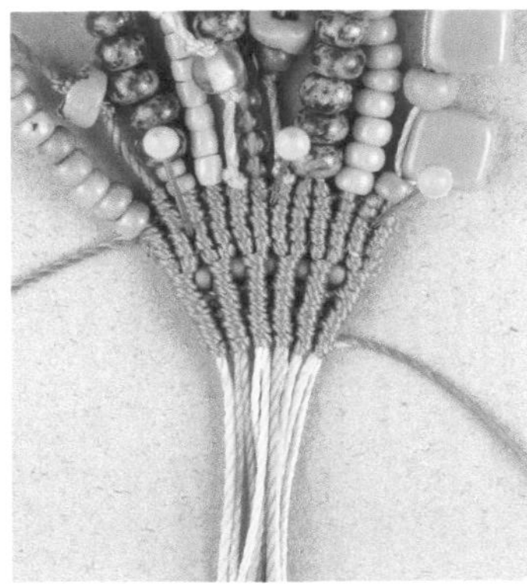

Figure 22

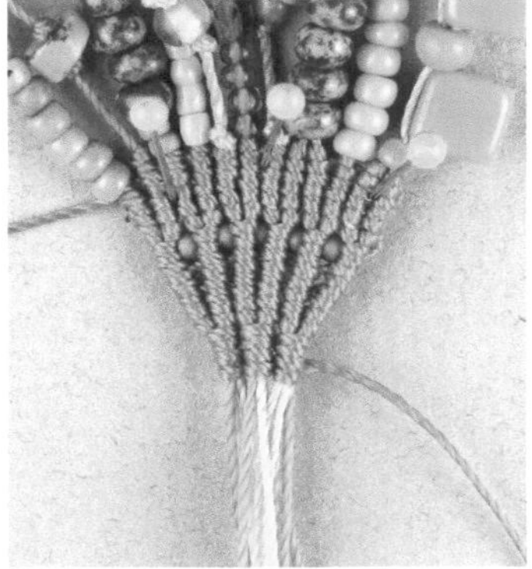

Figure 23

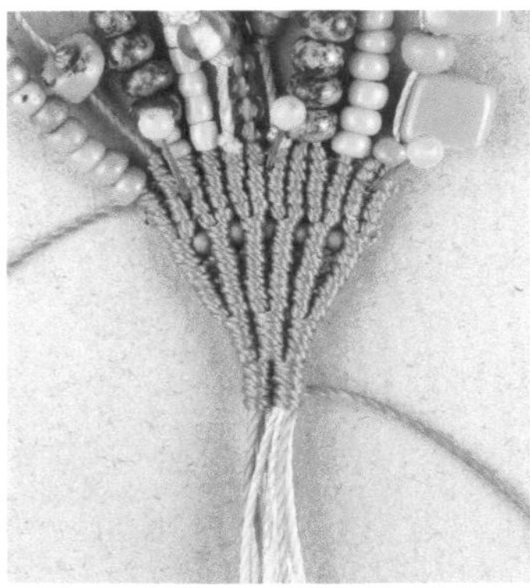

Figure 24

20. The next four rows will each have 6 **VDHH**s (2 cords per **VDHH**). Bring the **KC** back to the left and make a **VDHH** around the first 2 (grouped) cords. Thread (1) 11° seed bead onto the **KC** and push it up next to the **VDHH**. Make a **VDHH** around the next 2 (grouped) cords. Continue this pattern across the row, adding seed beads between the **VDHH**s (see Fig. 21).

21. Make three more rows of 6 **VDHH**s. The **VDHH**s should get closer together with each row (see Fig. 22).

22. Make two rows with 3 **VDHH**s each (4 cords per **VDHH**) (see Fig. 23).

23. Make two rows with 2 **VDHH**s each (6 cords per **VDHH**). The **KC** should end up at the right (outside) edge (see Fig. 24).

24. Remove the piece from the board and repeat Steps 11 and 12 to secure the 5" tail of **KC**.

25. Make knots around the 12 bundled cords of the neck chain in sets of 6 **HH**s: Make 3 **HH**s (as in Step 3 - over/under/over) followed by 3 **HH**s (as in Step 4 - under/over/under). Repeat this pattern until the chain is about 3" long (or 1.5" shorter than the other side neck chain).

26. Thread a jump ring onto 4 of the 12 bundled cords, positioning it 1.5" from the bottom of the knotted chain. Fold the 4 cords upward, leaving 8 loose downward-hanging cords. Tie a temporary cord around the bundle to hold all it in place (see Fig. 25). Make a tight set of 6 **HH**s (3 over/under /over and 3 under/over/under) around all of the bundled cords (see Fig. 26a).

27. Line up the two sides of the neck chain and compare to make sure they are the same length. Adjust the 4 upward facing jump ring cords so that the jump rings are even (see Fig. 26b).

28. Trim off 1 of the 8 downward-hanging cords close to the bottom of the knotting. Make a set of **HH**s (3 over/under/over and 3 under/over/under) around all of the bundled cords. Cut off another cord. Repeat until all 8 downward-hanging cords have been cut off (if you run out of space, cut off any remaining hanging cords just above the jump ring (see Fig. 27).

29. Cut off the 4 upward facing cords as close as possible to the knotwork. To hide the tail of the **KC**, separate it into 3 plies and sew each ply upward under the knotwork with a sewing needle (see Fig. 28). Cut off the excess threads flush with the knotwork. Attach the clasp parts to the jump rings.

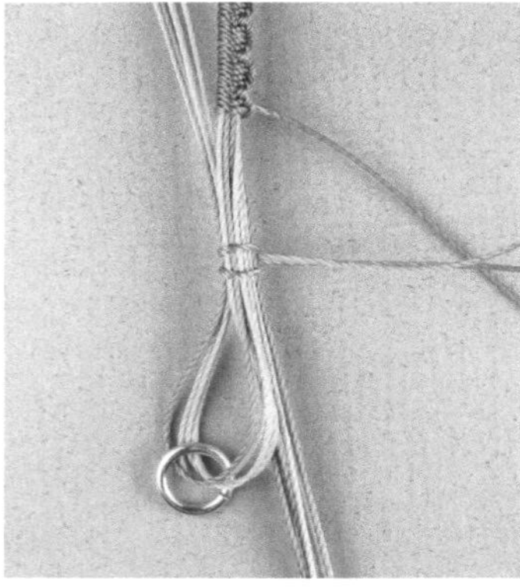

Figure 25

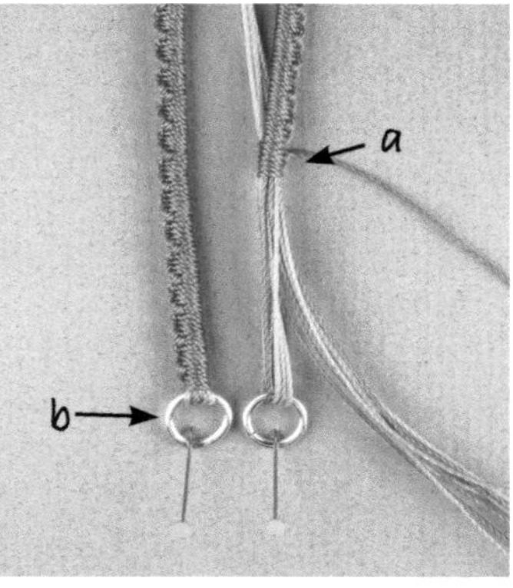

Figure 26

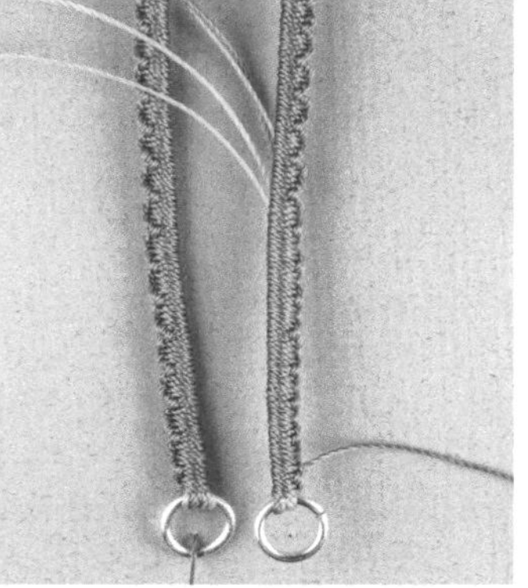

Figure 27

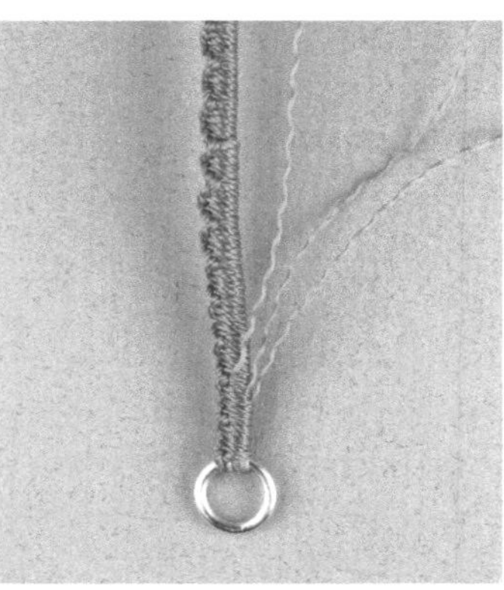

Figure 28

Nile Necklace

This striking necklace features strong elements with an Egyptian flair.
The multiple strands of seed beads give a fluid feeling to the neck chain.

Materials

18g Nylon Cord - 12 @ 70" (4 ea. of three colors), 5 @ 20" (1 ea. of top and lower colors, 3 of the middle color), 1 @ 72" (Runner cord)
(1) Gemstone Donut 40 - 45mm
(2) 8mm soldered jump rings
(1) Hook and Eye clasp
Beads:
(46) 8° Seed Beads
(38) 10° Seed Beads (metallic)
(12) 4mm Cube Beads
(12) Two-holed Square Beads (Tila)
(2) 4mm Bicones
(1) 6mm Round
(1) hank 10° Czech seed beads

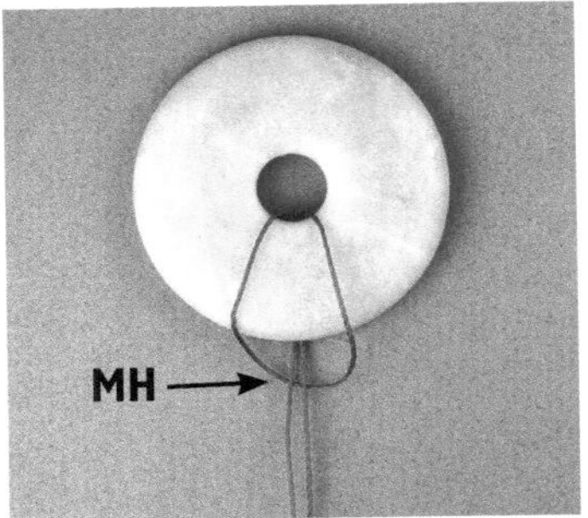

Figure 1

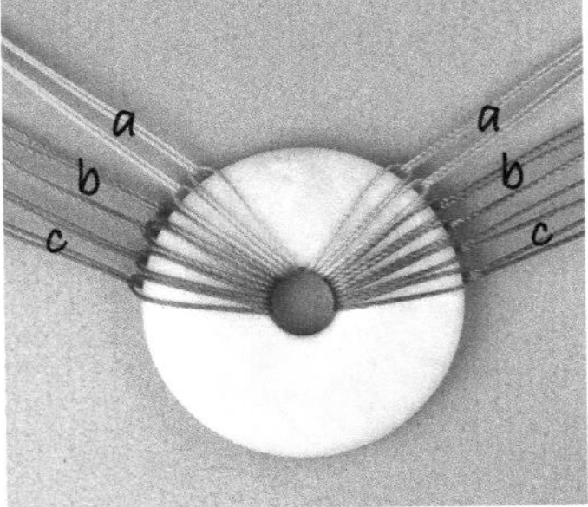

Figure 2

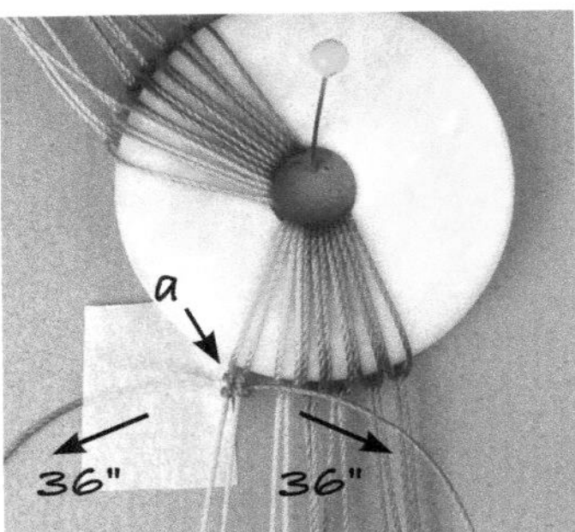

Figure 3

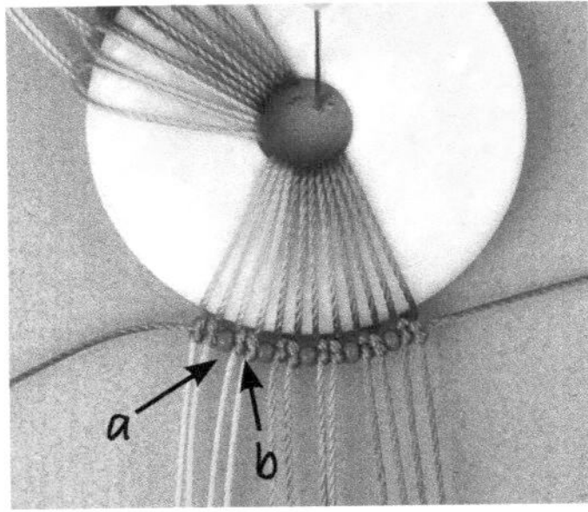

Figure 4

Part I - Main Knotted Sections

1. Fold in half and attach each of the 70" cords to the donut with a **MH** (Mounting Hitch) (see Fig. 1). On each side, attach 2 top color cords (see Fig. 2a), 2 middle color cords (see Fig. 2b), and 2 lower color cords (see Fig. 2c).

Left Side, Section 1:

• There will be 12 warp cords to work with for the first row. I will refer to each as Cd (Cord) #1 - 12 according to it's sequence from left to right•

2. Reposition the donut so that the left-hand 12 cords are now hanging downward (see Fig. 3). Tape the center point of the **RC** (Runner Cord) to the left of Cd #1, just below the donut. **Half of the RC (36") must be to the left side of the tape and the other half on the right.** Working with the right-hand part of the **RC**, make **VDHH**s (Vertical Double Half Hitches) around Cds #1 and 2 (see Fig. 3a).

3. Thread a 10° seed bead onto the **RC** and push it up next to the last **VDHH** (see Fig. 4a). Make **VDHH**s around Cds #3 and 4 (see Fig. 4b). Thread on a seed bead. Repeat the same pattern across the row, ending with **VDHH**s on Cds #11 and 12.

4. Place a pin to the right of the lower edge of the last **VDHH**. Bring the **RC** tightly around the pin and to the left. Make **DHH**s with Cds #12 and 11 (see Fig. 5).

5. Attach a 20" (lower color) cord to the **RC** with a **MH** and push it next to the previous **DHH** (see Fig. 6a). Make **DHH**s with the next 2 cords (see Fig. 7a).

6. Attach a 20" (middle color) cord to the **RC** with a **MH** and push it next to the previous **DHH** (Fig. 7b). Make **DHH**s with the next 2 cords. Attach another 20" (middle color) cord (Fig. 7c), make **DHH**s with the next 2 cords. Attach another 20" (middle color) cord (Fig. 7d).

7. Make **DHH**s with the next 2 cords. Attach a 20" (top color) cord and make **DHH**s with the next 2 cords (see Fig. 7e).

• There are now 22 warp cords. I will refer to each as Cd #1 - 22 according to it's sequence from left to right•

8. Bring the **RC** back around to the right and make a row of **VDHH**s (these will be very close and bow out slightly) (see Fig. 8).

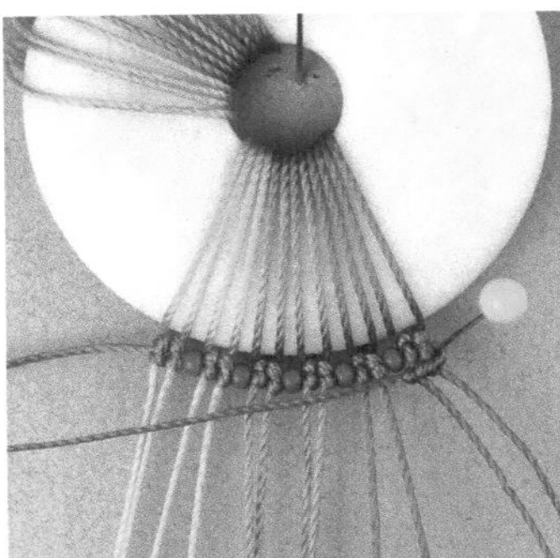
Figure 5

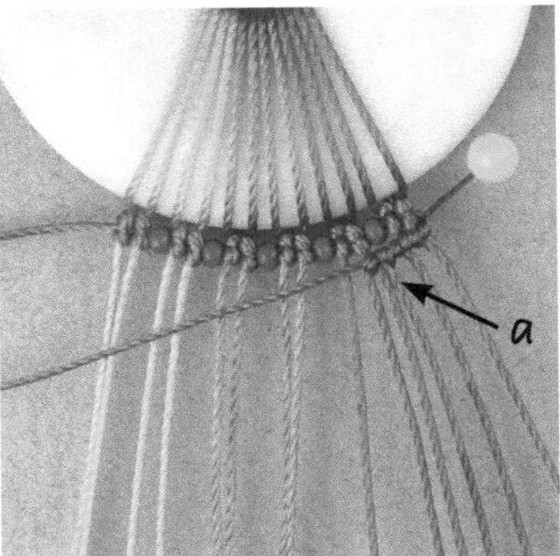

Figure 6

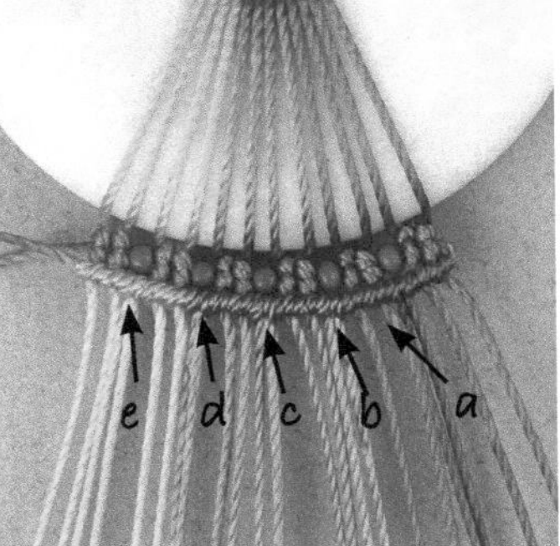

Figure 7

Figure 8

Figure 9

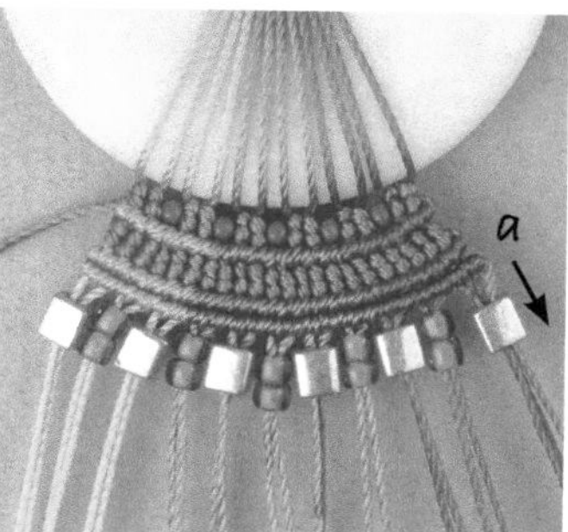

Figure 10

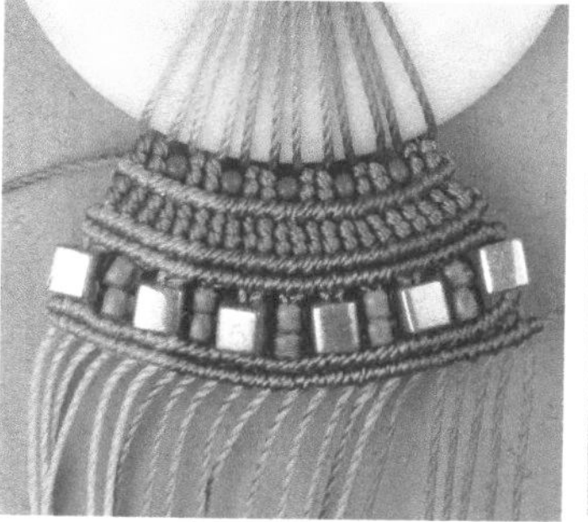
Figure 11

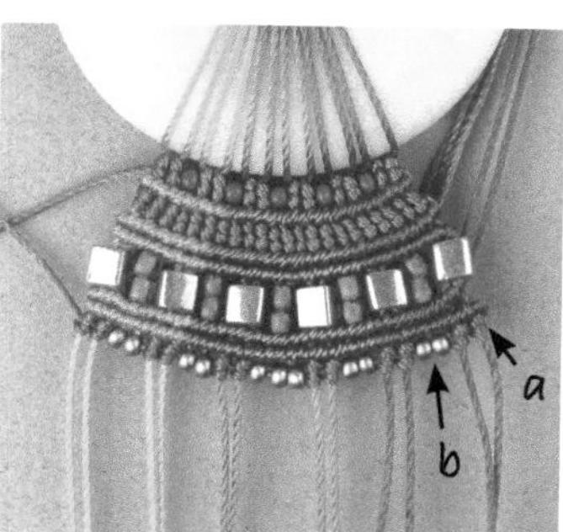

Figure 12

9. Bring the **RC** back around to the left and make a row of **DHH**s. Bring the **RC** back around to the right and make another row of **DHH**s (see Fig. 9).

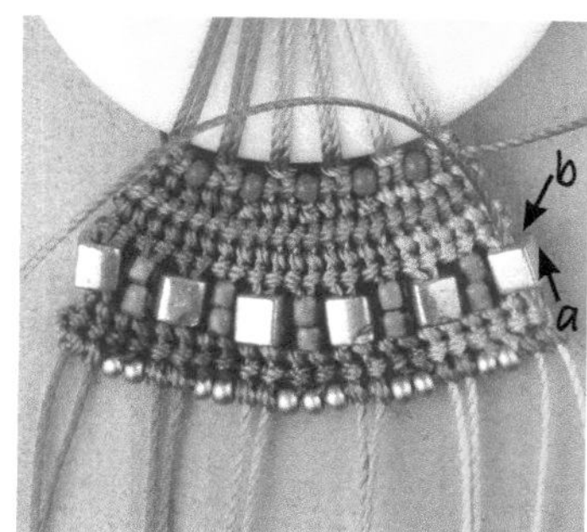

Figure 13

10. Thread a 4mm cube bead onto (joined) Cds #1 - 2, 5 - 6, 9 - 10, 13 - 14, 17 - 18, and 21 - 22. Thread (2) 8° seed beads onto (joined) Cds #3 - 4, 7 - 8, 11 - 12, 15 - 16, and 19 - 20 (see Fig. 10).

11. Thread the **RC** downward through the rightmost cube bead (see Fig. 10a). Working right to left, make a row of **DHH**s just below the beads (place a pin at the edge of the row below the cube bead to prevent the **RC** from pulling inward). Bring the **RC** back around to the right and make another row of **DHH**s (see Fig. 11).

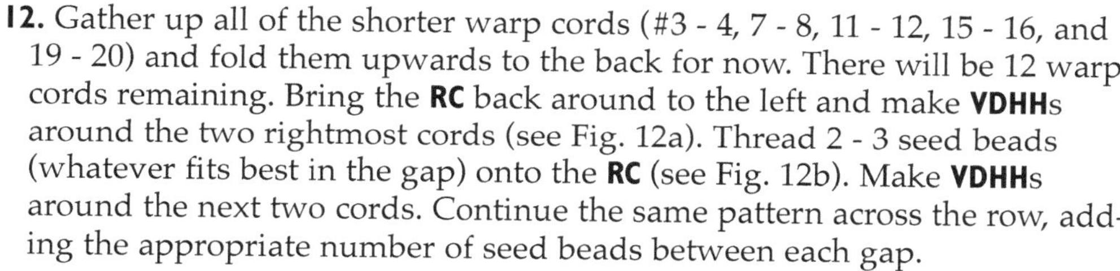

12. Gather up all of the shorter warp cords (#3 - 4, 7 - 8, 11 - 12, 15 - 16, and 19 - 20) and fold them upwards to the back for now. There will be 12 warp cords remaining. Bring the **RC** back around to the left and make **VDHH**s around the two rightmost cords (see Fig. 12a). Thread 2 - 3 seed beads (whatever fits best in the gap) onto the **RC** (see Fig. 12b). Make **VDHH**s around the next two cords. Continue the same pattern across the row, adding the appropriate number of seed beads between each gap.

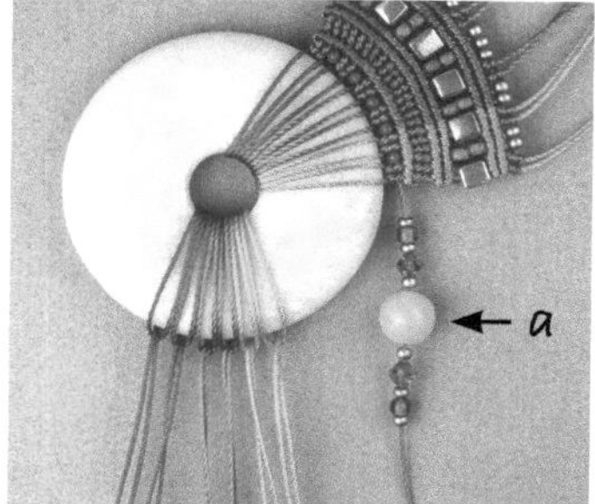

Figure 14

13. Flip the piece to the back. Apply a light dab of clear nail polish to the base of each pair of short cords. Let dry. Cut the short cords off close (but not flush) to the base. Thread the **RC** upwards through the adjacent cube bead (see Fig. 13a) and pull through (use nail polish or Fray Check to stiffen the cord end for easier threading). Make an **OVK** (Overhand Knot) flush with the top of the cube bead (see Fig. 13b). Apply a light dab of clear nail polish to the **OVK**. Let dry. Cut off the excess cord flush with the **OVK**.

Right Side, Section 1:

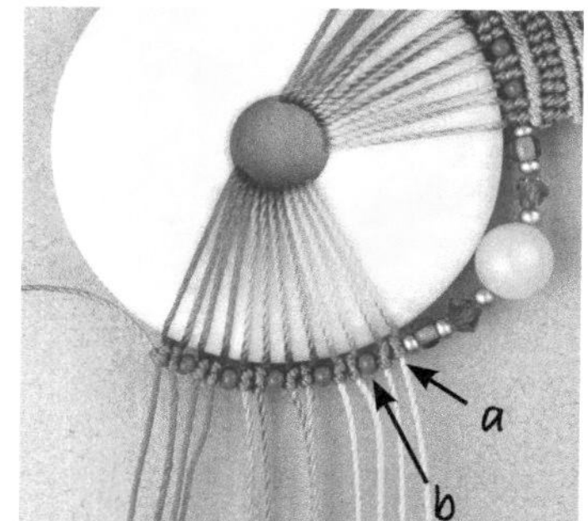

Figure 15

14. Position the piece as in Fig. 14. Onto the right half of the **RC**, thread a strand of beads 1⅛" long in a similar configuration as in Fig. 14. There should be a center focal bead framed by equal and opposite smaller beads on each side.

15. Make a **VDHH** around each of the rightmost two cords to hold the bead strand in place (see Fig. 15a). Thread a 10° seed bead onto the **RC** (see Fig. 15b). Make **VDHH**s around the next two cords. Repeat the same pattern across the row.

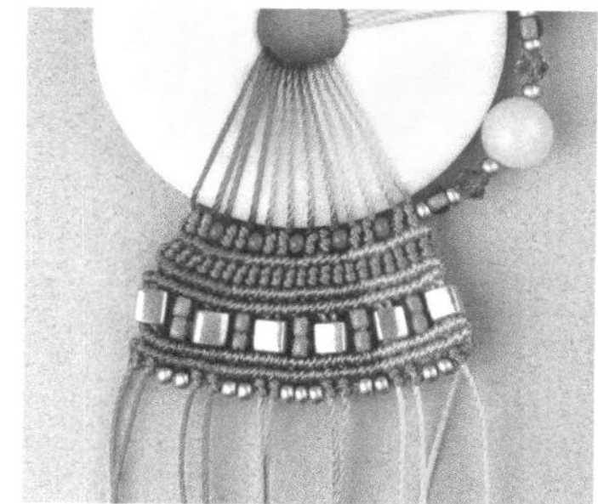
Figure 16

16. This right-hand knotted section of the necklace is a mirror image of the completed (left) side. Repeat the same pattern as on the left side (see Fig. 16). The only difference will be the direction that the knotting moves from row to row (it will be the opposite of the left side).

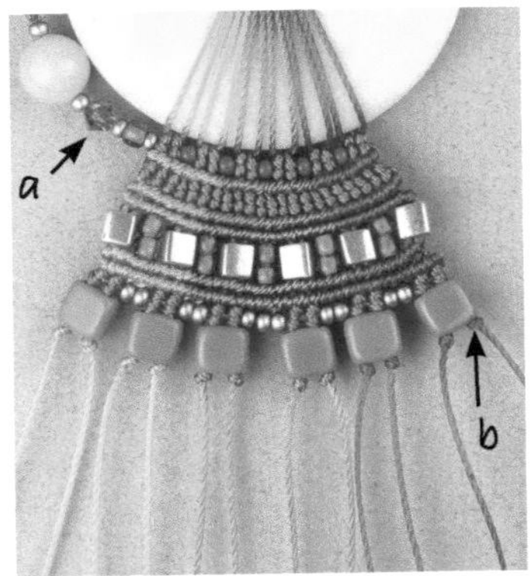

Figure 17

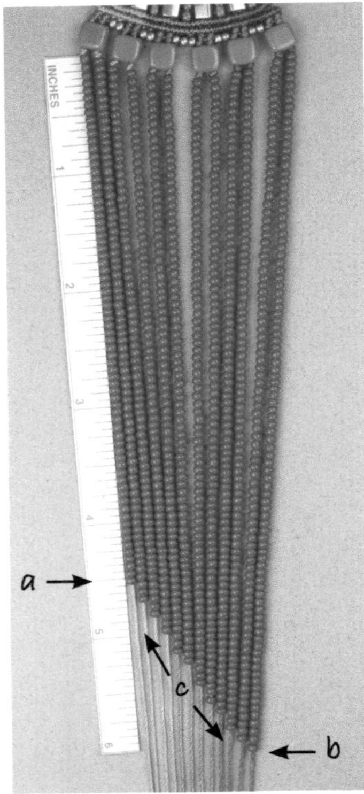

Figure 18

Part 2 - Beaded Neck Chains

Left Side, Neck Chain:

- There are 12 cords on each side of the necklace for the neck chain. I will refer to each as Cd #1 - 12 according to it's sequence from left to right•

17. Position the piece with the beaded strand on the left (see Fig. 17a). Thread a Tila bead onto each of the 6 pairs of cord. Put an **OVK** in each cord flush with the bottom of the Tila bead (see Fig. 17b).

18. Thread 10° seed beads onto each of the 12 cords (lay your board flat on a table so the beads don't slip down). The length of Cd #1 should be 4½" (see Fig. 18a) and the length of Cd #12 should be 6" (see Fig. 18b). The other strands should get gradually longer from Cd #2 to Cd #11, forming an even edge between the two outer cords (see Fig. 18c).

19. Reposition and pin the piece so that the ends of Cds #1 and 12 are on a horizontal plane and all of the strands ends form a straight across horizontal line (to adjust the evenness, add or subtract beads to the strands if necessary). Make an **OVK** at the end of each strand (see Fig. 19a). Thread (2) 8° beads onto (joined) Cds #1 - 2, 3 - 4, 5 - 6, 7 - 8, 9 - 10, and 11 - 12 (see Fig. 20).

20. Place a pin between Cds #1 and 2, just below the beads (see Fig. 21a). Bring Cd #1 to the right and using it as a **RC**, make a **VDHH** around Cd #2. Thread a 10° bead onto the **RC** and push it up next to the **VDHH** (see Fig. 21b). Make one **VDHH** around (joined) Cds #3 and 4 (see Fig. 21c). Repeat the pattern across the entire row.

21. Bring the **RC** around to the left and make a horizontal row of **DHH**s. Make four more rows of **DHH**s (see Fig. 22).

22. Bring Cd #1 to the right and make **VDHH**s around Cds #2 - 6. Bring Cd #12 to the left and make **VDHH**s around Cds #11 - 7 (see Fig. 23). Bring the two **KC**s (which meet at the middle) to the back of the piece (see Fig. 24).

23. There are now 10 warp cords. Bring Cd #1 to the right and make **VDHH**s around Cds # 2 - 5. Bring Cd #10 to the left and make **VDHH**s around Cds #9 - 7. Bring the two **KC**s which meet at the middle to the back of the piece (see Figure 24 for Steps 23 - 25).

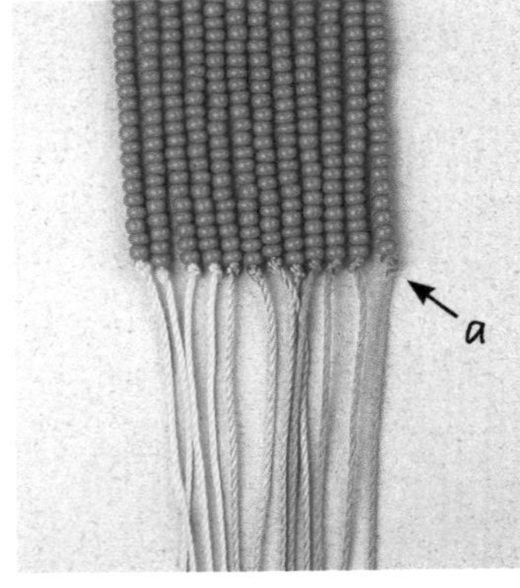

Figure 19

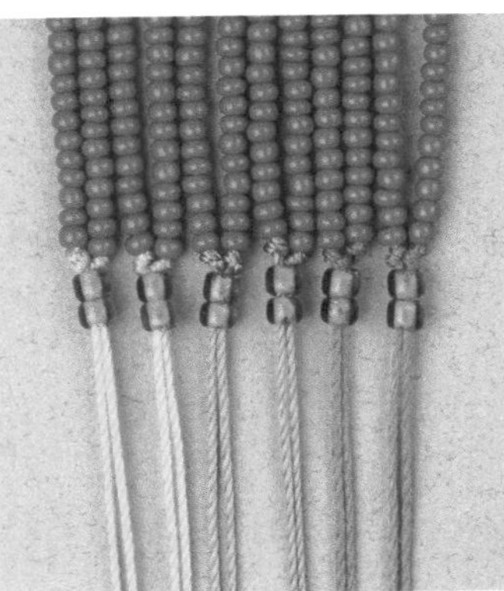
Figure 20

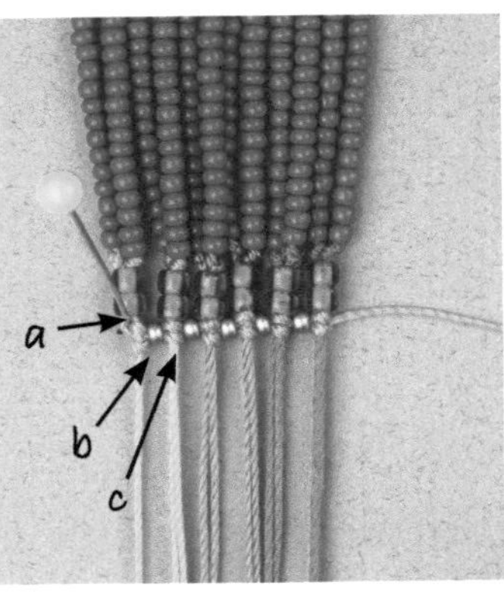

Figure 21

Figure 22

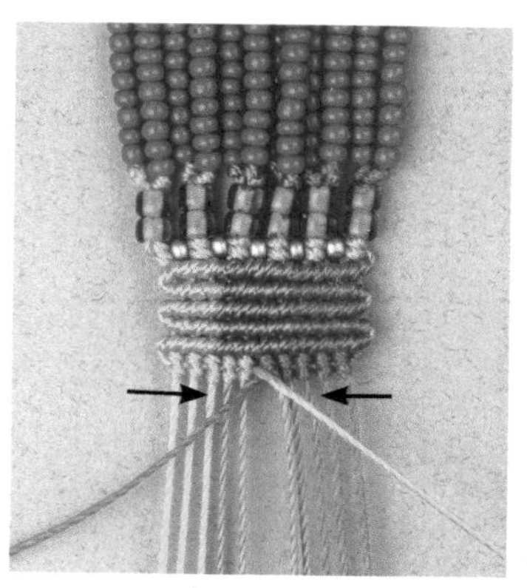
Figure 23

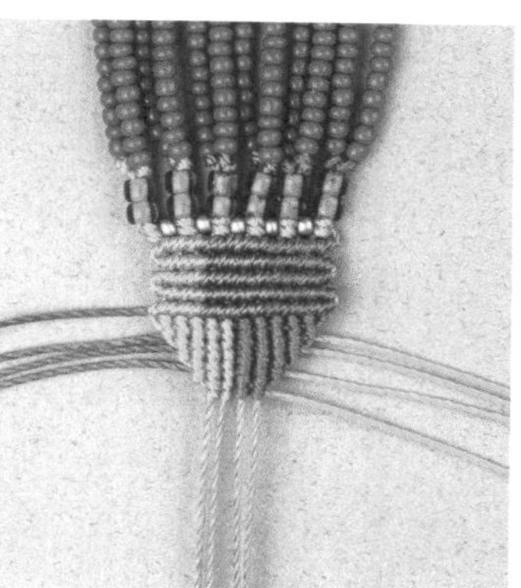
Figure 24

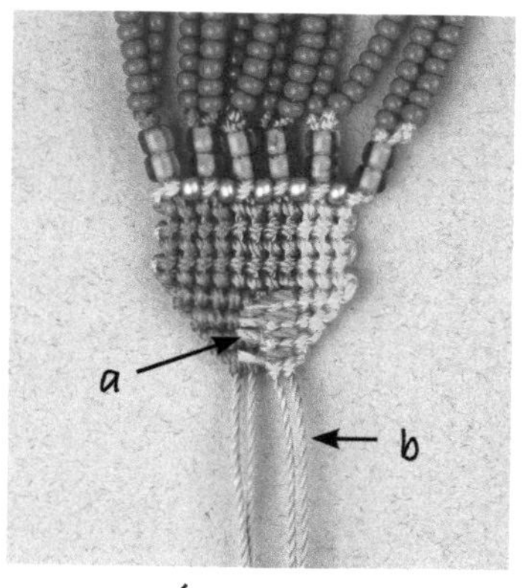

Figure 25

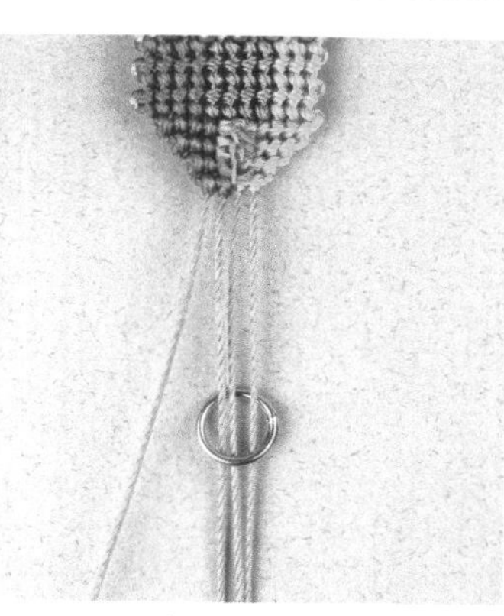
Figure 26

24. There are now 8 warp cords. Bring Cd #1 to the right and make **VDHH**s around Cds #2 - 4. Bring Cd #8 to the left and make **VDHH**s around Cds #7 - 5. Bring the two **KC**s which meet at the middle to the back of the piece.

25. There are now 6 warp cords. Bring Cd #1 to the right and make **VDHH**s around Cds #2 and 3. Bring Cd #6 to the left and make **VDHH**s around Cds #5 and 4. Bring the two **KC**s which meet at the middle to the back of the piece.

26. With a sewing needle and matching thread, backstitch up and down the center "valley" between the two colors. Flip the piece to the back and cut off the 8 horizontal cords about $\frac{1}{8}$" from the center (see Fig. 25a). Do not cut off the 4 downward hanging cords (see Fig. 25b).

27. Pin the piece to the board with the back facing towards you and the four remaining cords hanging downward. Thread a soldered ring onto Cds #2 - 4 (see Fig. 26).

28. Position the ring 1" below the base of the knotwork (the length may be adjusted if you desire a longer neck chain). Fold the 3 ring cords upward (see Fig. 27a). Take a 6" piece of matching color beading thread (or a 1-ply piece of spare nylon cord) and make a knot around the bundled cords just above the ring to hold them all together (see Fig. 27b). Adjust the length if necessary.

29. Wrap the thread tightly around the bundled cords 3 or 4 times and sew the ends under the wrapped threads to keep them from unravelling (see Fig. 28a). Bring the thread ends upwards with the bundled cords. Using Cd #1 as the **KC**, make a **LHK** (Larks Head Knot) around the entire bundle of cords/threads at the base of the knotwork (see Fig. 28b). Place a downward angled pin in the ring to hold it in place (see Fig. 28c).

30. Continue making a chain of **LHK**s around the entire bundle until you get to the ring and there is no more space to make **LHK**s (see Fig. 29).

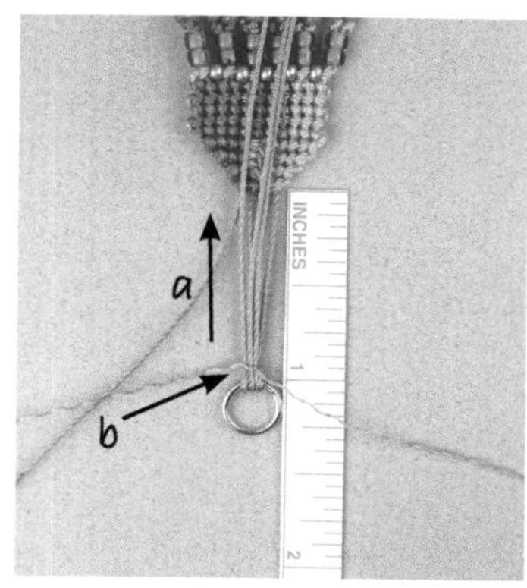

Figure 27

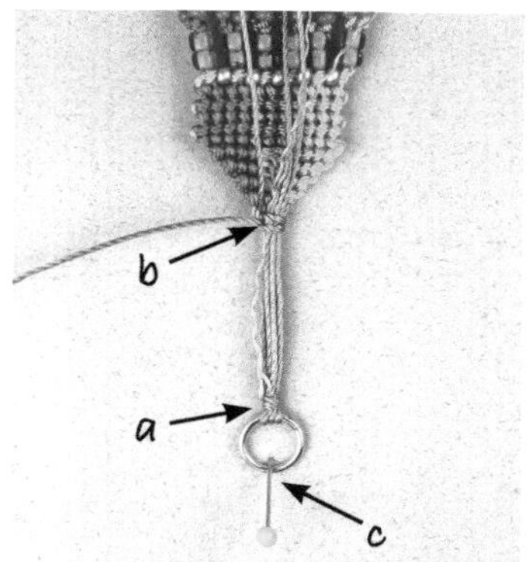

Figure 28

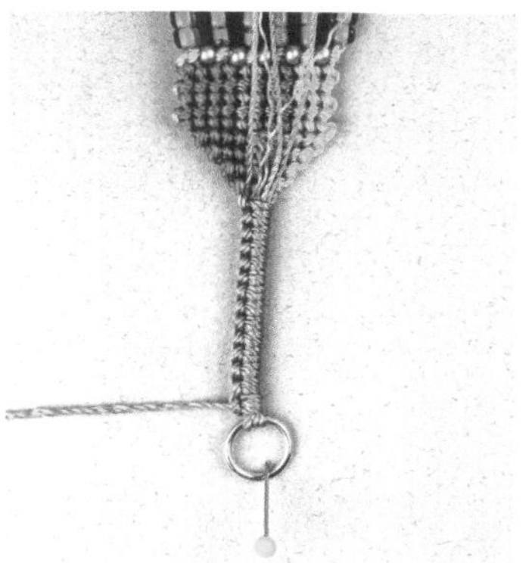
Figure 29

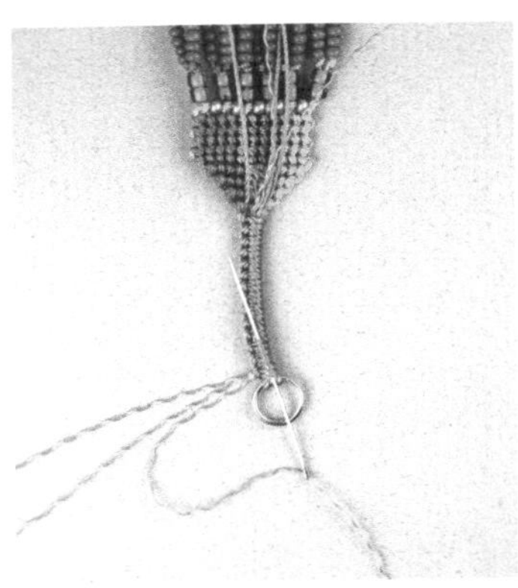
Figure 30

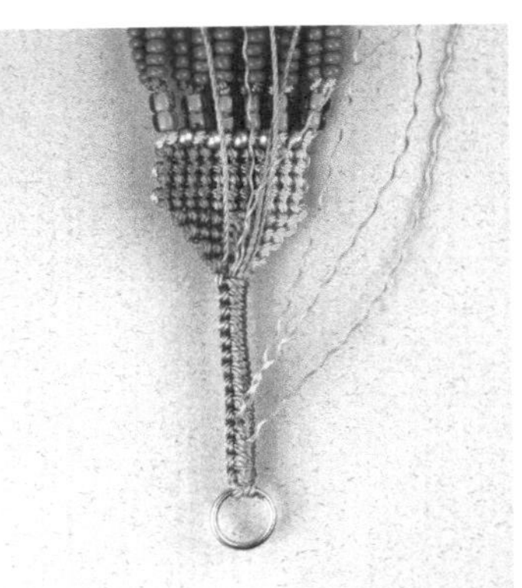
Figure 31

Figure 32

Figure 33

Figure 34

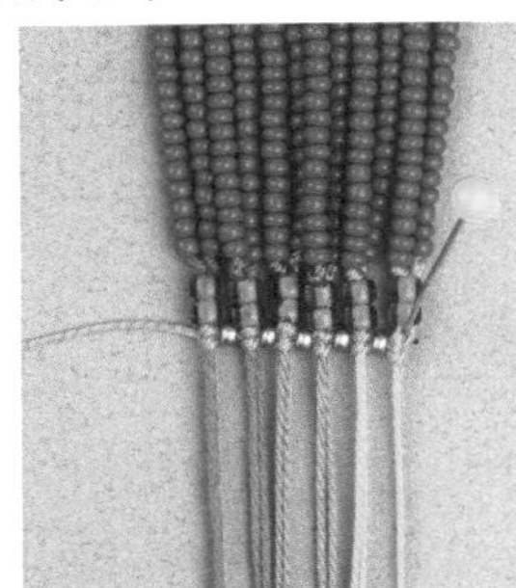
Figure 35

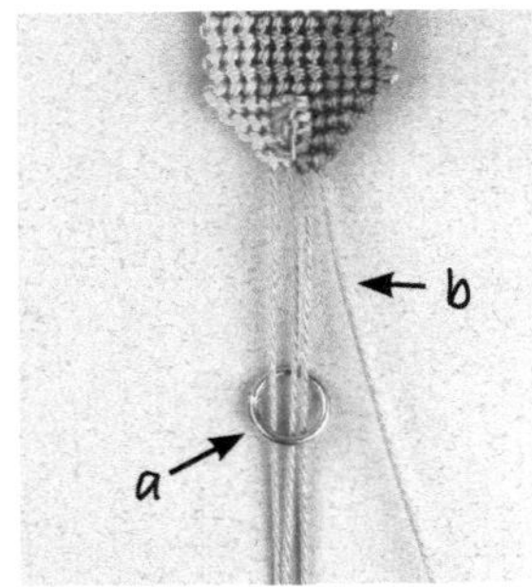

Figure 36

31. Untwist the **KC**, separating the 3 plies of the cord. One at a time, thread a 1-ply threads onto a narrow sewing needle and sew under the final 3 or 4 **LHK**s, exiting between **LHK**s (see Figures 30 and 31). **Note -** depending on how tight your **LHK**s are, it can be difficult to get a needle under them. Use a thimble or chain nose pliers to push the needle under the **LHK**s and pull the needle out the other end with the pliers if necessary.

32. Cut off the 1-ply threads flush with the **LHK** chain. Cut off all of the excess bundled cords at the base of the knotwork (see Fig. 32).

Right Side, Neck Chain:

33. Thread a Tila bead onto each of the 6 pairs of cord. Put an **OVK** in each cord flush with the bottom of the Tila bead (see Fig. 33). This right side of the neck chain is a mirror image of the completed (left) side.

34. Thread 10° seed beads onto each of the 12 cords. The length of Cd #12 should be 4½" and the length of Cd #1 should be 6" (see Fig. 34). The other strands should form an even edge between the two outer cords.

35. Repeat Step 19.

36. Place a pin between Cds #11 and 12, just below the beads. Bring Cd #12 to the left and using it as a **RC**, make a **VDHH** around Cd #11. Thread a 10° bead onto the **RC**. Make one **VDHH** around (joined) Cds #9 and 10. Repeat the pattern across the entire row (see Fig. 35).

37. Bring the **RC** around to the right and make five rows of **DHH**s.

38. Repeat Steps 22 - 26.

39. Pin the piece to the board so that the 4 cords are hanging downward. Thread a soldered ring onto Cds #1 - 3 (see Fig. 36a).
Important - on the right side neck chain the **KC** was Cd #1 and the **LHK**s were made in a left to right direction. On this side the **KC** will be Cd #4 (see Fig. 36b) and the **LHK**s are made in a right to left direction.

40. Repeat Steps 28 - 32.

41. Attach the clasp parts to the soldered rings.

Moonflower Pendant

The Moonflower pendant has a repeating pattern of knotted and beaded chains surrounding a center button. It's suspended by an easy to make chain. This pretty pendant will be a welcome addition to your jewelry collection.

Materials

18g. Nylon Cord - 11 @ 60" (Warp Cords), 1 @ 70" (Anchor Cord) and 1 @ 110" (Neck Chain)
(1) 1" Round button with shank
Beads:
(60) 4mm round
(60) 4mm Magatamas
(24) 3.4mm drop
(26) 8° seed beads
(136) 10° seed beads
(64) 1.5mm cube beads
(1) 8mm rondelle

Project Twelve

Part 1 - The First Half of the Pendant

1. Gather all of the 60" cords together so that the ends are aligned. Fold the cords in half to find the center point. Take a piece of spare cord and group the cords together with a tight **MH** (Mounting Hitch) (see Fig. 1). About an inch to one side of the **MH**, tie all of the cords together with an **OVK** (Overhand Knot). Position the cords vertically on the board with the **OVK** above the **MH**. Pin through the **OVK** to hold the cords in place (see Fig. 2).

2. Thread an 8° seed bead followed by a 4mm Magatama (drop) bead onto the center of the 70" **AC** (Anchor Cord). Pass one end of the cord back up through the 8° bead and pull through. There should be two equal lengths of cord exiting the beads. One will serve as the **AC** for the right half of the pendant and one will serve as the **AC** for the left half.

3. Pin the double **AC** strand to the board even with the level of the **MH** and ½" to the left of the **OVK** (see Fig. 3). Remove the **MH** cord. Working from left to right, attach each of the 11 cords to the top **AC** with **DHH**s (Double Half Hitches), forming a horizontal row (see Fig. 4a). Next, attach each of the 11 cords to the lower **AC** with **DHH**s (see Fig. 4b). Tape the top **AC** out of the way for now.

• There are 11 warp cords to work with in this next segment. I will refer to each as Cd (Cord) #1 - 11 according to it's sequence from left to right•

4. Thread an 8° bead onto Cd #7. Bring the lower **AC** back around to the left. Using the width of the bead as a guide, make a row of **DHH**s with Cds #11 - 7 (see Fig. 5). This row should be at a 90° angle to the first two **DHH** rows.

5. Bring the **AC** back around to the right and make a row of **DHH**s with Cds #7 - 11. This row should be parallel and touching the previous row (see Fig. 6).

6. Thread an 8° bead onto Cd #7. Bring the **AC** back around to the left and make a row of **DHH**s with Cds #11 - 7. This row should be at a 45° angle to the first two (long) **DHH** rows (see Fig. 7).

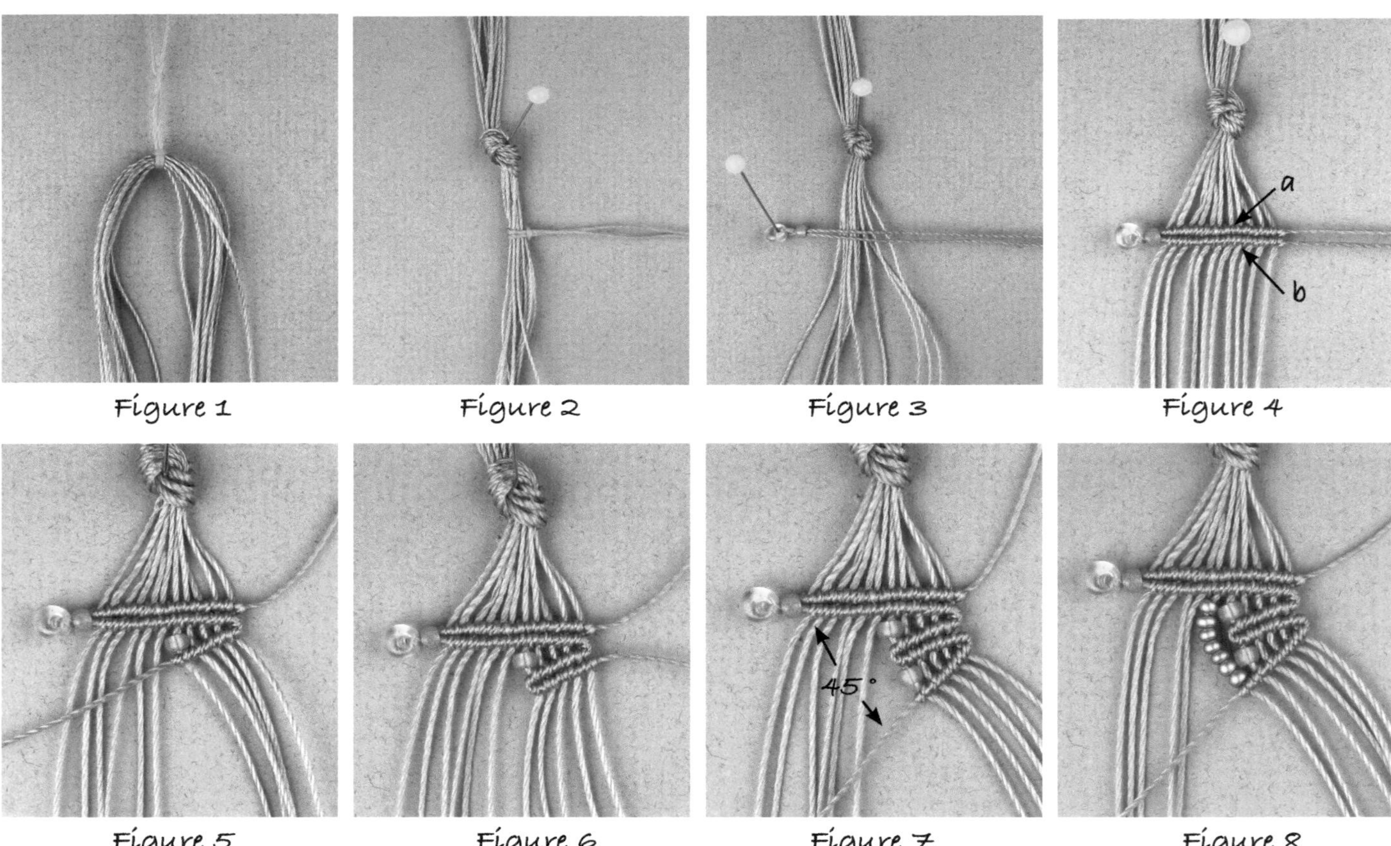

Figure 1 Figure 2 Figure 3 Figure 4
Figure 5 Figure 6 Figure 7 Figure 8

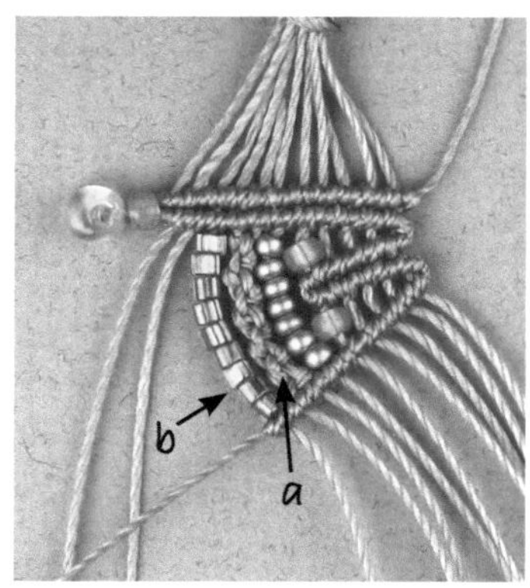

Figure 9

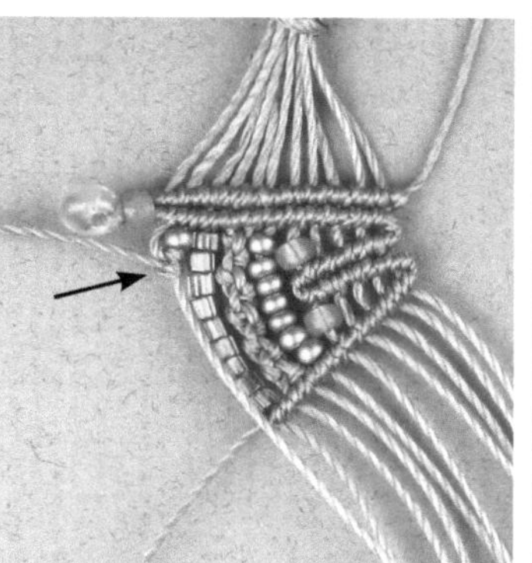
Figure 10

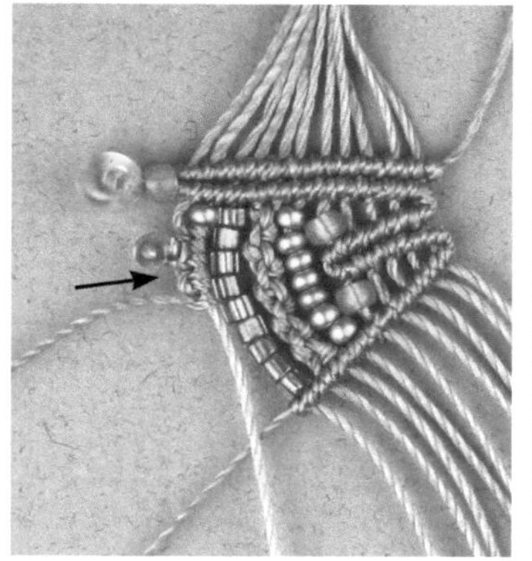
Figure 11

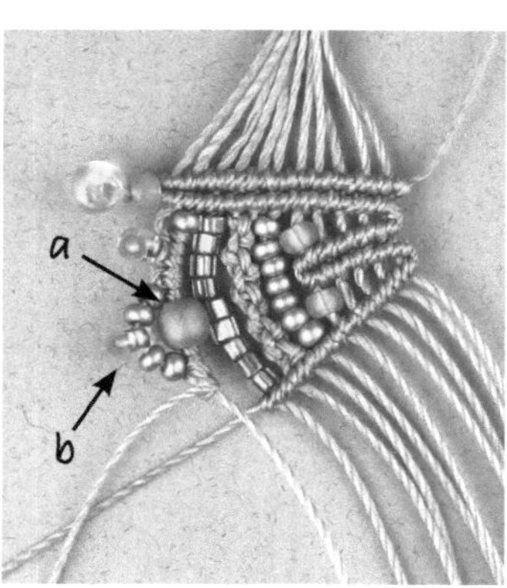

Figure 12

Note - The pendant is made up of eight 45° segments which equal a 360° circle when completed. It may be helpful to draw out a guide and tape it under your knotwork to keep your **DHH** rows at the correct angle (see Fig. 15). Notice that the inside edge of the knotting does not come to the exact center of the circle. There will be a center opening about the size of a dime (about $\frac{3}{4}$" or 18mm across).

7. Thread (7) 11° seed beads onto Cd #6. Attach this cord to the **AC** with a **DHH** (see Fig. 8). **Note -** bead widths can vary, so adjust the bead count if necessary for the correct fit. The row of **DHH**s should continue at the same angle as it began.

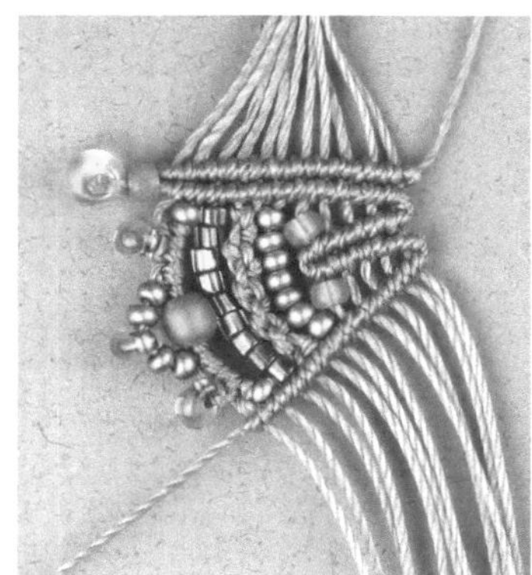
Figure 13

8. Make an **AHHch** (Alternating Half Hitch Chain) with Cds #4 and 5. There should be about 11 **HH**s in the chain (add or subtract a **HH** if necessary for the correct fit). Attach these cords to the **AC** with **DHH**s (see Fig. 9a).

9. Thread (8 - 9) 1.5mm cube seed beads onto Cd #3. Attach this cord to the **AC** with a **DHH** (adjust the bead count if necessary for the correct fit). Attach this cord to the **AC** with a **DHH** (see Fig. 9b).

10. Larks Head Knot Chain - With Cd#1 acting as the **KC** (Knotting Cord) and Cd #2 acting as an **AC**, make a **LHKch** in the following way (pay close attention to whether the beads are threaded onto the **KC** or **AC**!): *1.* Thread an 11° bead onto the **AC**, make a **LHK** below it (see Fig. 10). *2.* Thread a 3.4mm drop bead onto the **KC**, make two **LHK**s (see Fig. 11). *3.* Thread a 4mm round bead onto the **AC** (see Fig. 12a). Thread (2) 11°, (1) 4mm drop, and (2) 11° beads onto the **KC**. Make two **LHK**s (the beads on the **KC** will wrap along the edge of the 4mm bead, see Fig. 12b). *4.* Thread a 3.4mm drop bead onto the **KC**, followed by a **LHK**. *5.* Thread an 11° bead onto the **AC** (see Fig. 13).

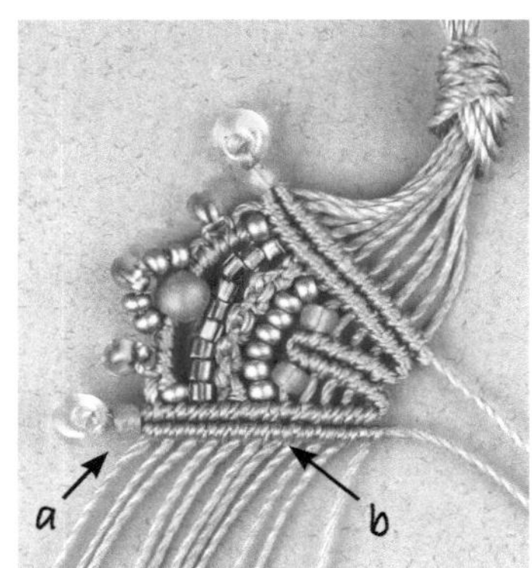

Figure 14

11. Attach the **LHKch** cords (Cds #1 and 2) to the **AC** with **DHH**s (see Fig. 13).

12. Thread an 8° seed bead followed by a 4mm Magatama bead onto the main **AC**. Pass the end of the cord back through the 8° bead and pull through (see Fig. 14a).

13. Make a row of **DHH**s with Cds #1 - 11. This row should be parallel and touching the previous row (see Fig. 14b).

14. Repeat Steps #4 - 13 two times. Repeat Steps #4 - 11 one time (see Fig. 16).

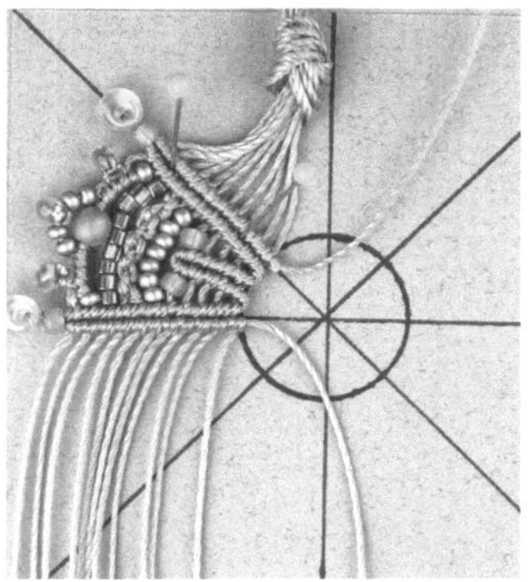
Figure 15

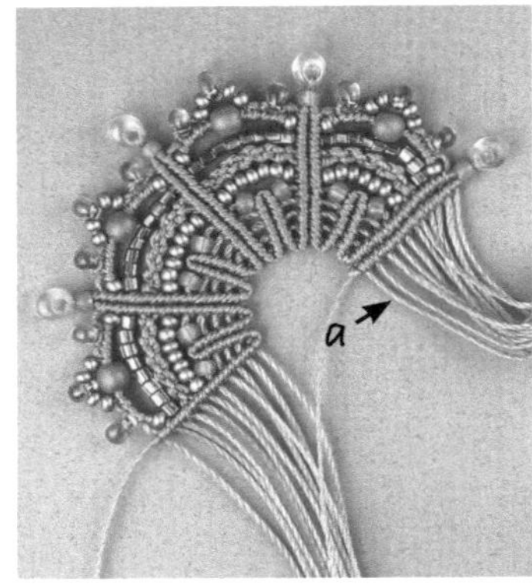

Figure 16

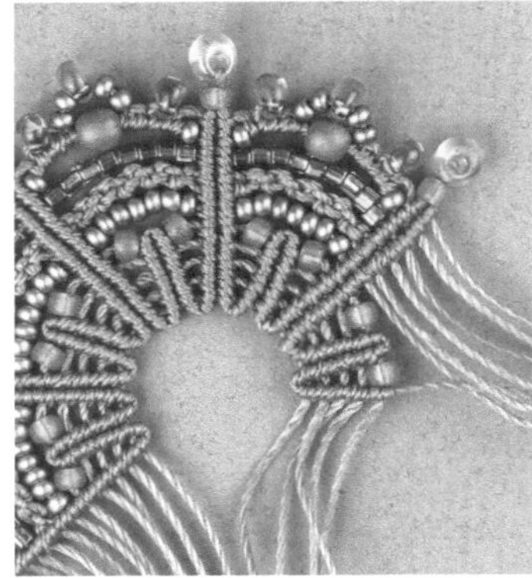
Figure 17

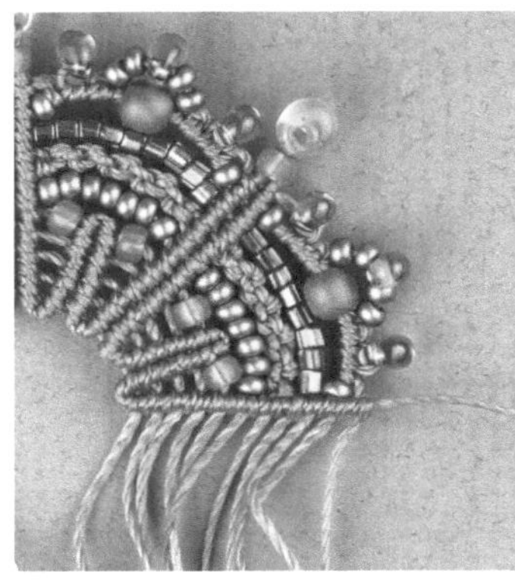
Figure 18

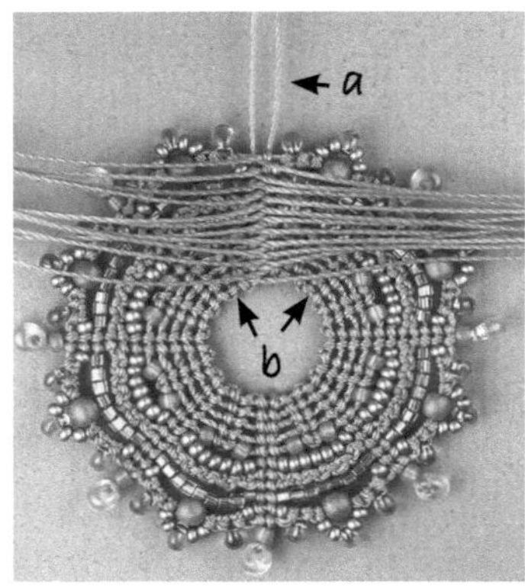

Figure 19

Part 2 - The Second Half of the Pendant

15. The second half of the pendant is a mirror image of the first half (Steps #4 - 14). Undo the **OVK** and position the piece on the board as in Fig. 16. You will now be working with the right-hand cords (see Fig. 16a).

16. Thread an 8° bead onto Cd #5. Bring the **AC** for this half of the pendant to the right. Make a row of **DHH**s with Cds #1 - 5 (see Fig. 17 for Steps 16 - 18).

17. Bring the **AC** back around to the left and make a row of **DHH**s with Cds #5 - 1. This row should be parallel and touching the previous row.

18. Thread an 8° bead onto Cd #5. Bring the **AC** back around to the left. Make a row of **DHH**s with Cds #1 - 5.

19. Thread (7) 11° seed beads onto Cd #6. Attach this cord to the **AC** with a **DHH** (see Fig. 18 for Steps 19 - 23).

20. Make an **AHHch** with Cds #7 and 8. Attach these cords to the **AC** with **DHH**s.

21. Thread (8 - 9) 1.5mm cube seed beads onto Cd #9. Attach this cord to the **AC** with a **DHH**.

22. Larks Head Knot Chain - With Cd#11 acting as the **KC** and Cd #10 acting as an **AC**, make a **LHKch** in the following way (pay close attention to whether the beads are threaded onto the **KC** or **AC**!): *1.* Thread an 11° bead onto the **AC**, make a **LHK**. *2.* Thread a 3.4mm drop bead onto the **KC**, make two **LHK**s. *3.* Thread a 4mm round bead onto the **AC**. Thread (2) 11°, (1) 4mm drop, and (2) 11° beads onto the **KC**. Make two **LHK**s. *4.* Thread a 3.4mm drop bead onto the **KC**, make a **LHK**. *5.* Thread an 11° bead onto the **AC**.

23. Attach the **LHKch** cords (Cds #10 and 11) to the **AC** with **DHH**s.

24. Thread an 8° seed bead followed by a 4mm Magatama bead onto the main **AC**. Pass the end of the cord back through the 8° bead and pull through.

25. Make a row of **DHH**s with Cds #1 - 11. This row should be parallel and touching the previous row.

26. Repeat Steps #16 - 25 two times. Repeat Steps #16 - 23 one time.

27. Reposition the piece so that the back is facing you and the two **AC**s are pointed upwards (see Fig. 19a). Bring the top centermost cord (below the **AC**s) from the right-hand side over to the left, then bring the top centermost cord from the left-hand side over to the right just below it. Continue the same pattern working downward, interlacing the rest of the cords, alternating one right-hand cord to the left then one left-hand cord to the right and so on (see Fig. 19b).

28. Reposition the piece so that the two **AC**s are pointed to the left. Bring Cd #11 (from the downward hanging 11 cords) to the left and using it as an **KC**, make **VDHH**s around Cds #10 - 1 working from right to left (see Fig. 20a).

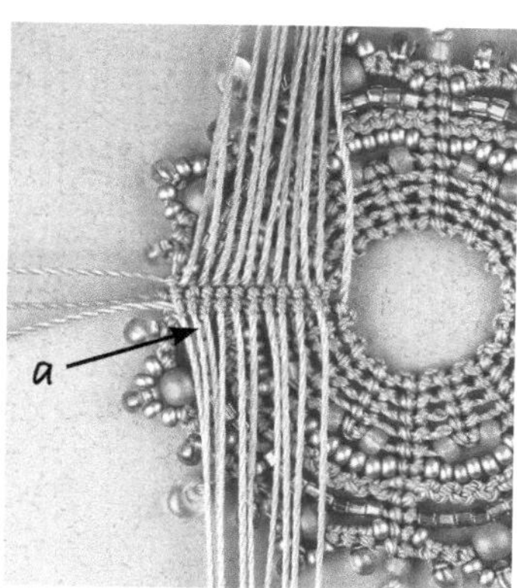

Figure 20

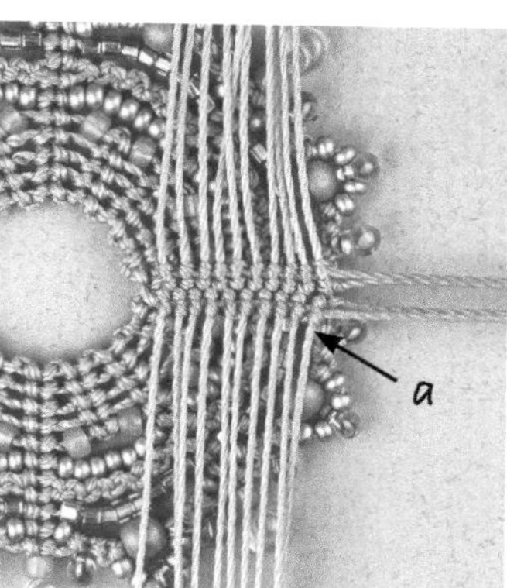

Figure 21

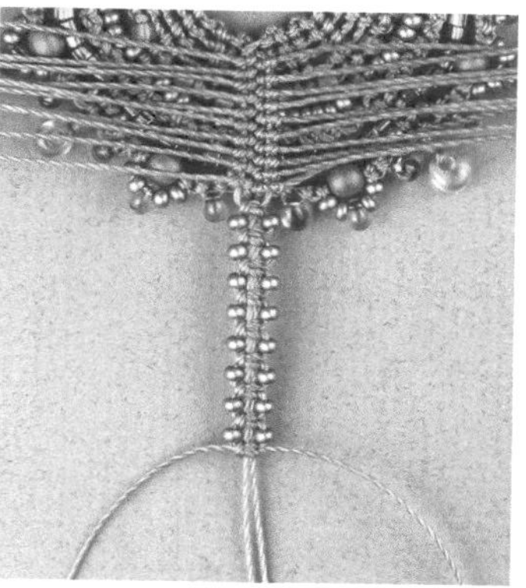
Figure 22

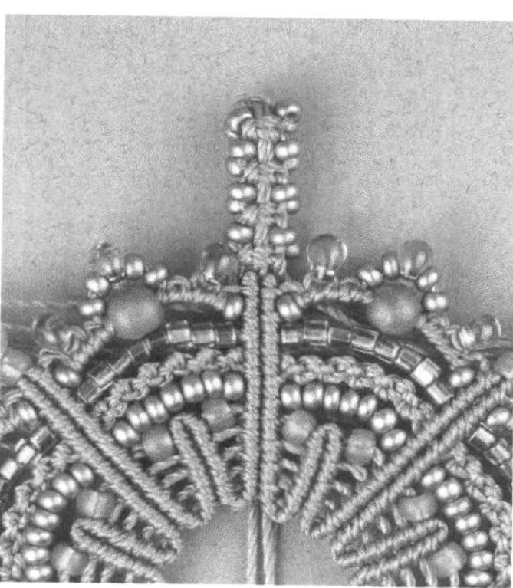
Figure 23

29. Reposition the piece so that the two **AC**s are pointed to the right. Bring Cd #1 (from the downward hanging 11 cords) to the right and using it as an **KC**, make a row of **VDHH**s around Cds #2 - 11 working from left to right (see Fig. 21a). Unpin and pull outwards on the two opposite groups of cords, bringing the pendant sides tightly together at the top center. Check the front view to make sure there isn't a gap between the rows of **DHH**s.

Note -The bail is made with a beaded **SQK** (Square Knot) Chain. If you wish to use a different (thicker) neck chain than the one described in Part 3, you can make the **SQK** chain longer. Make sure that the bail loop is long enough so that the widest part of your neck chain can pass through it.

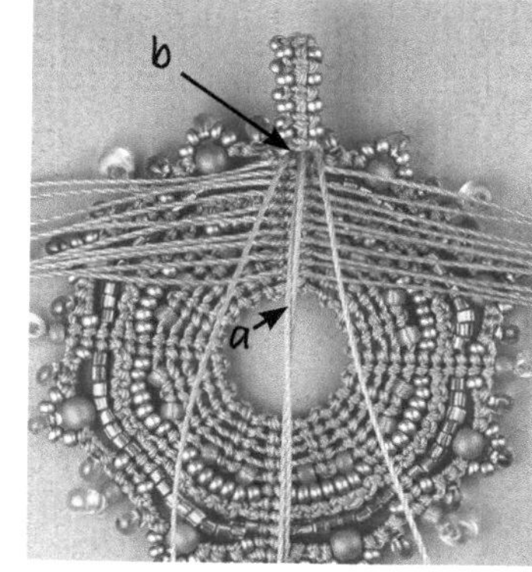

Figure 24

30. Reposition the piece so that the two **AC**s and the two **KC**s from the **VDHH** rows are pointed downward. Make a **SQK** (use the cords from the **VDHH** rows as the **KC**s). Thread a seed bead onto each of the outer **KC**s and push them up. Make a **SQK** below the beads, locking them into position. Repeat the same pattern (**SQK**, beads, **SQK**, beads, **SQK**, etc…) until the bail is the correct size when folded over. To accommodate the beaded neck chain in Part 3, the bail should have (8) **SQK**s with beads between each **SQK** (see Fig. 22).

31. Fold the bail over towards the front. Sew the **AC**s (one at a time) from front to back through the center space between the first **SQK** and the top of the **DHH** rows. Sew the left-hand **KC** through the space to the left and the right-hand **KC** through the space to the right (see Fig. 23 and 24).

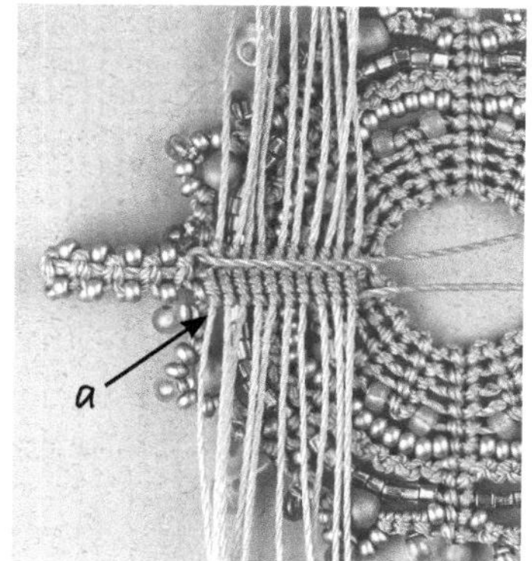

Figure 25

32. Flip the piece to the back. Separate out 1-ply from each of the 2 center cords (see Fig. 24a). Carefully cut off the 2-ply sections of each cord. Make a tight **OVK** with the 1-ply cords at the base of the **SQK** (see Fig. 24b). Apply a dab of clear nail polish and let dry. Cut off the 1-ply cords below the **SQK**.

33. Reposition the piece so that the bail is pointed to the left. Bring the lower **KC** of the bail to the right and using it as an **KC**, make **VDHH**s around Cds #1 - 10 working from left to right (see Fig. 25a). This row of **VDHH**s needs to be very tight with no gap between it and the row above it.

34. Reposition the piece so that the bail is pointed to the right. Bring the lower **KC** of the bail to the left and using it as an **KC**, make **VDHH**s around Cds #10 - 1 working from right to left (see Fig. 26a). This row of **VDHH**s needs to be very tight with no gap between it and the row above it.

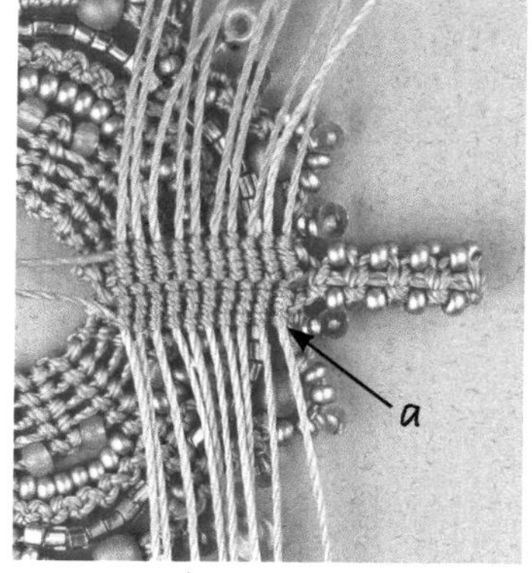

Figure 26

Figure 27

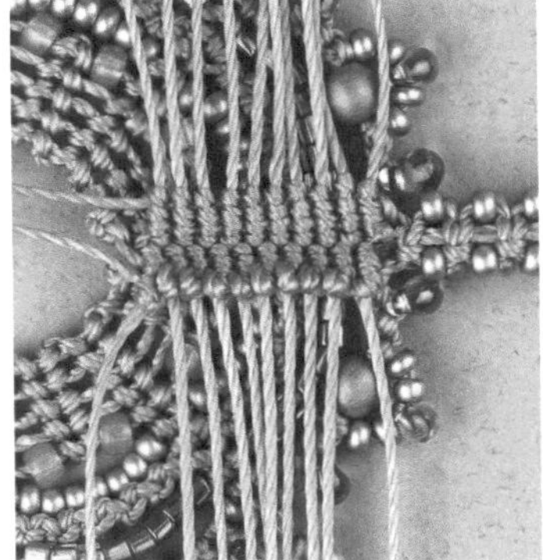
Figure 28

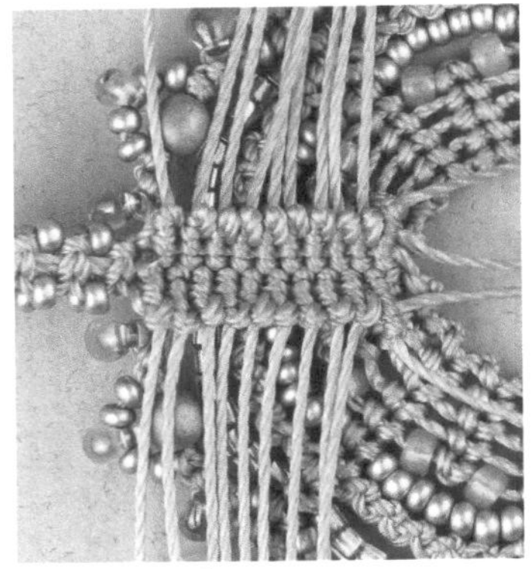
Figure 29

•Steps 35 - 40 show how to finish off the 20 cords that exit from the **VDHH** rows on each side. Another method is to make a tight **OVK** in each individual cord next to where it exits the **VDHH**. Apply nail polish and cut off the excess cord flush with the **OVK**. Although this is an easier method, the **OVK**s will have a rough texture when the nail polish has dried. The following method is a bit more involved, but it creates a smoother edge.•

35. Unpin the piece from the board and hold it in your hand with the bail pointed to the right. Lift the **VDHH** rows slightly up and away from the main pendant to make the next steps easier.

36. Thread Cd #10 (from the downward hanging cords) onto a narrow embroidery needle. Pass the needle down through middle of the "valley" between the **VDHH**s in Cds #9 and 10 and pull through (see Fig. 27). Remove the needle. This is just a simple stitch around the edge (not a knot).

37. Thread the needle onto Cd #9. Pass the needle down through middle of the "valley" between the **VDHH**s in Cds #8 and 9 and pull through. Remove the needle. Repeat the same steps with Cds #7 - 2. Make a tight **OVK** with Cd #1 (since there won't be a space to the left of it). Pull on each cord to make sure the stitches are not loose (see Fig. 28).

38. Hold the piece with the bail to the left. Thread Cd #1 onto the embroidery needle. Pass the needle down through middle of the "valley" between the **VDHH**s in Cds #1 and 2 and pull through. Remove the needle. Repeat the same steps with Cds #2 - 9. Make a tight **OVK** with Cd #10. Pull on each cord to make sure the stitches are not loose (see Fig. 29).

39. Thread 20" of matching color nylon sewing or beading thread onto a sewing needle and make a line of back-stitching along the inside edge of the cord stitches on both sides to secure them and prevent them from pulling out.

40. Apply a generous coating of clear nail polish along the front and back edges on both sides, completely covering the cord edge-stitching and the **OVK**s. Let dry and carefully cut off the excess cords under the **VDHH** rows on both sides close to the back stitching (see Fig. 30a). Do not cut off the two descending cords at the center below the **OVK**s! (see Fig. 30b).

41. Attaching the button: With the back of the piece facing you, position the button so that the shank is at the center of the "donut" hole. Pass the two cords downward through the shank (see Fig. 31a).

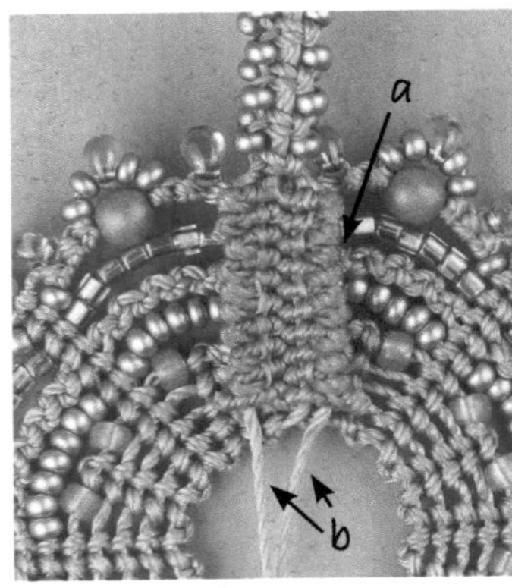

Figure 30

Figure 31

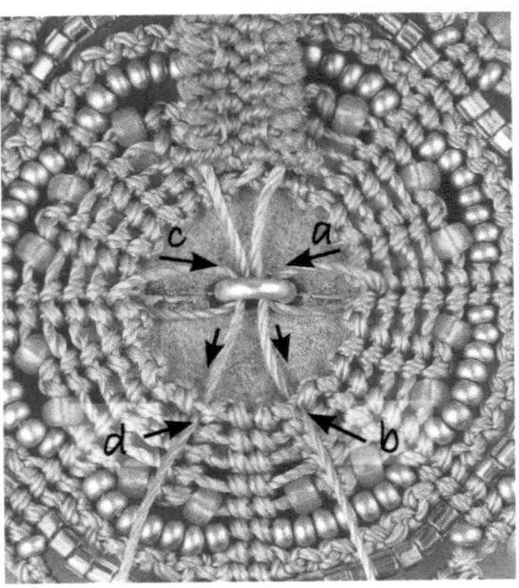

Figure 32

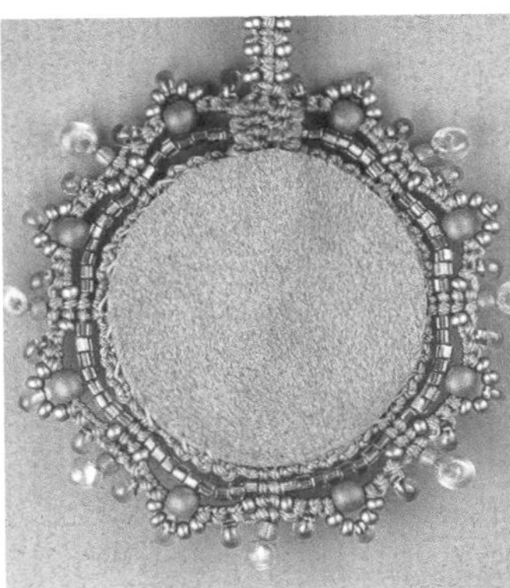
Figure 33

42. Thread the right-hand cord onto an embroidery needle and sew it under and up through the space next to the right inside edge and halfway between the top and bottom of the circle (the space is in between two **DHH** rows when viewed from the front) (see Fig. 31b). Remove the needle. Thread the left-hand cord onto the needle and sew it under and up through the space next to the left inside edge and halfway between the top and bottom of the circle (see Fig. 31c).

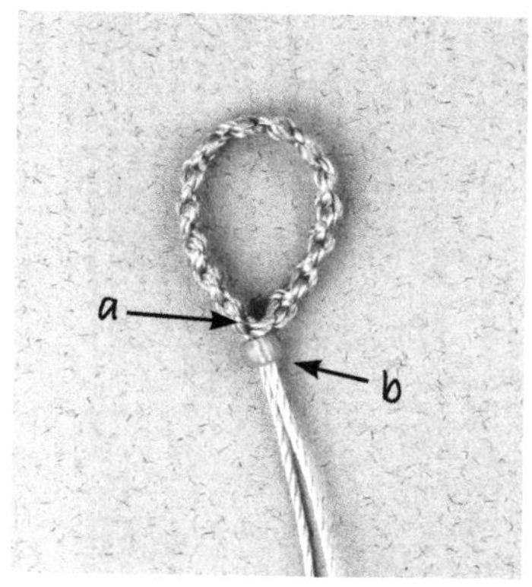

Figure 34

43. Thread the right-hand cord onto the needle and sew it downward through the shank (see Fig. 32a). Then sew under and up through the space in between two **DHH** rows just to the right of the bottom of the circle (see Fig. 32b). Thread the left-hand cord onto an embroidery needle and sew it downward through the shank (see Fig. 32c). Then sew under and up through the space in between two **DHH** rows just to the left of the bottom of the circle (see Fig. 32d).

44. Adjust and tighten the cords until snug so that the button is perfectly centered (check the front view). Make an **OVK** in each cord where it exits at the bottom (see Fig. 32b and d) and apply clear nail polish to the knot. Let dry and cut off the excess cord flush with the **OVK**.

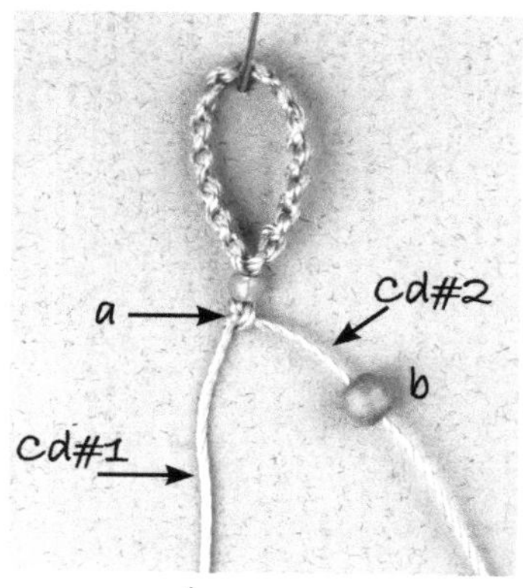

Figure 35

• **Optional** - lift the knotting away from the button and apply a small amount of E-6000 glue around the underside of the button near the edge (not to the cords). Be careful because this can be messy, use the glue sparingly. Adhere the button to the knot work, centering it. Let dry before proceeding. •

45. Ultrasuede lining: Cut out a circle of paper 1.5" in diameter. The outside edge of the paper pattern should lie along the inside edge of the **AHH** chains when laid on the knotwork, adjust the pattern if necessary. Trace the pattern onto ultra suede and cut it out. On the underside of the suede, apply a thin layer of E-6000 glue (caution - too much glue will seep through the knot work!). Adhere the lining to the back of the piece, centering it. Whip stitch around the edge, making your stitches on the backside of the **AHH** chains so they don't show at the front (see Fig. 33).

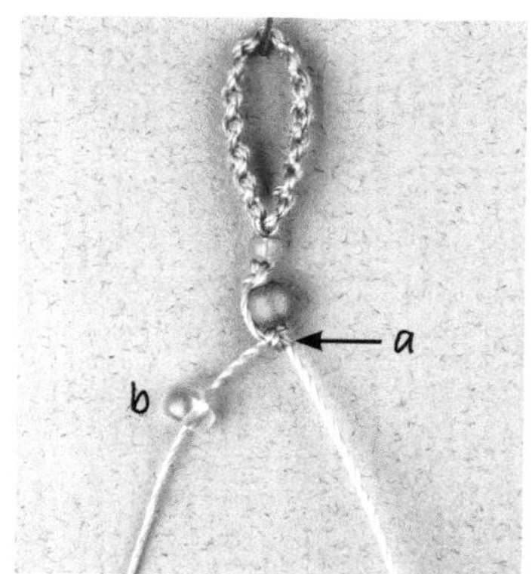

Figure 36

Part 3 - Beaded Neck Chain

46. Fold the 110" cord in half and drape it over a pin. Make an **AHH** chain approximately 1.5" long. Unpin it from the board and thread one of the cord ends through the small loop at the top of the **AHHch** and pull through (see Fig. 34a). Check that it fits snugly around the rondelle bead. Thread an 8° bead onto the two cords (Cds #1 and 2) and push it up below the loop (see Fig. 34b).

47. With Cd #2, make a **LHK** around Cd #1 (see Fig. 35a). Thread a 4mm round bead onto Cd #2 (see Fig. 35b). With Cd #1, make a **LHK** around Cd #2 (see Fig. 36a). Thread a 4mm Magatama bead onto Cd #1 (see Fig. 36b).

48. Repeat Step #47 until your neck chain is the desired length.

49. End the chain with a 8° bead followed by the rondelle bead and another 8° bead. Make a tight **OVK** below the final bead. Apply a dab of clear nail polish, let dry, and cut off the excess cord flush with the **OVK** (see Fig. 37).

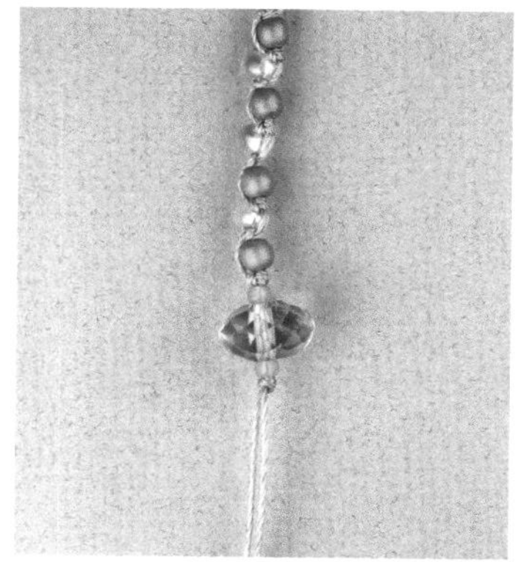
Figure 37

Joan Reeder Babcock

is an internationally recognized fiber artist, jewelry designer, teacher, and author who has been creating one-of-a-kind jewelry and fiber art since 1988.

She is known for her unique style of blending cords, beads, and metal elements together, and specializes in the technique of "Cavandoli" or tapestry knotting. Her work has been featured in numerous fiber art and bead related books and magazines.

She is the author of "Micro-Macramé Jewelry: Tips and Techniques for Knotting with Beads", "Wired Micro-Macramé Jewelry: Enhancing Fiber Designs with Wire" and a DVD, "Micro-Macramé & Cavandoli Knotting, Level One".

Joan lives in Santa Fe, New Mexico with her husband and business partner Jeff and their two cats.

You can see her jewelry and fiber art at www.joanbabcock.com.

You can find more of her classes, ePatterns and micro-macramé supplies at www.micro-macramejewelry.com.